Working Class Without Work

Critical Social Thought

Series editor: Michael W. Apple
Professor of Curriculum and Instruction and Educational Policy
Studies, University of Wisconsin-Madison

Already published

Working Class Without Work

High School Students in a De-industrializing Economy

L O I S   W E I S

Routledge

New York   London

For my husband, Tereffe Asrat

First published in 1990 by

Routledge
An imprint of Routledge, Chapman and Hall, Inc.
29 West 35 Street
New York, NY 10001

Published in Great Britain by

Routledge
11 New Fetter Lane
London EC4P 4EE

Printed in the United States of America

Library of Congress cataloging in publication data

Weis, Lois.
    Working class without work : high-school students in a de-
industrializing economy / Lois Weis.
        p.   cm. — (Critical social thought)
        ISBN 0-415-90048-4; 0-415-90234-7 (pb)
        1. Working class—Education (Secondary)—United States. 2. High
school students—United States—Economic conditions. 3. High school
students—United States—Attitudes. 4. United States—Economic
conditions—1981- 5. Unemployment—United States. I. Title.
II. Series.
LC5051.W4   1990
370.19′341—dc20   89-10896

British Library cataloging in publication data also available.

Contents

Series Editor's Introduction

The "American Century" has been cut short. No longer can the United States assume its continued economic, political, or even cultural dominance throughout the world. Part of this is the result of a significant restructuring of the American economy. In the context of the internationalization of markets and corporations, of capital flight and attacks on labor, major changes have occurred that have altered the *accord* or compromise that structured class relations in the United States since World War II. And, in the continuing conflicts between person rights and property rights that lie at the heart of capitalism, property rights have again taken the upper hand.[1]

Allen Hunter provides an excellent picture of the post-World War II accord:

> From the end of World War II until the early 1970s world capitalism experienced the longest period of sustained economic growth in its history. In the United States a new "social structure of accumulation"—"the specific institutional environment within which the capitalist accumulation process is organized"—was articulated around several predominant features: the broadly shared goal of sustained economic growth, Keynesianism, elite pluralist democracy, an imperial America prosecuting a cold war, anticommunism at home and abroad, stability or incremental change in race relations and a stable home life in a buoyant, commodity-driven consumer culture. Together these crystallized a basic consensus and a set of social and political institutions which was hegemonic for two decades.[2]

At the very center of this accord was a compromise reached between capital and labor in which labor accepted what might be called "the logic of profitability and markets as the guiding principles of resource allocation." In return they received "an assurance that minimal living standards, trade union rights and liberal democratic rights would be protected."[3] In essence, a bargain is struck in which decent wages and rights are given in exchange for control.

This accord has come under concerted attack as the crisis in capitalist economies has had to be dealt with. Labor has had to be "disciplined"; the gains made by women, people of color, and workers (these categories are obviously not mutually exclusive) have had to be rescinded because they are "too expensive." Rates of profit and accumulation have had to be raised in order to "protect investment" and one's share of a market. One of the effects of this complicated situation has been the *de-industrialization* of entire sections of the United States. Closed plants, lost jobs, lives in disarray, all this and more have characterized the failure of the American dream for many people.

The long-term effects of such economic decisions will be felt not only in the economy but also at the level of one's very being, at the very core of what it means to be a person. Our sense of self and others, our hopes and fears, and our daily interactions in local communities are often largely structured by these decisions. It is here where Lois Weis enters.

Becoming a person is exactly that—a social production. Who one is, how one's identity is formed as a classed, gendered, and raced subject, occurs in specific economic, political, and cultural circumstances. Schools play a major part in this process of identity formation. Yet, schools, and the students, teachers, and parents involved in them, are situated in a larger constellation of institutions. *Working Class Without Work* tells the story of what happens to the identities of white working-class young men and women, and their teachers and parents, in a situation in which the community in which they live has been "de-industrialized." The industrial plants of the city are dark, its future far from rosy. What does this mean to the school experiences of its students?

In his justly well-known book, *Learning to Labor,* Paul Willis demonstrates that many working-class students will use the school as a site for the development of an oppositional culture.[4] They will often subvert the overt and hidden curricula of the school, challenging its focus on individual achievement and mobility. This is, of course, something of a Pyrrhic victory since in the process, as Willis also shows, important elements of capitalist ideology, as well as patriarchal and racist forms of interaction, are produced as well. Thus, Willis's "lads" glorify manual labor and think of book learning as only being suited for "girls" and for "ear'oles" (earholes—those students who sit still and listen). In the process, while they partly subvert some of the dominant meanings of a society, they manage to produce in their daily lives sexist norms and the separation of conception from execution that lies at the heart of the control process in capitalist production.

All this is provocative. But the lads are able to do this in part *because* there are manual jobs waiting for them in the heavy-industrial sectors of the economy. Yet, what would happen if there were no such jobs? Just as importantly, since Willis largely focuses on the relationship between schooling and paid work and on the male experience, what happens to young women's, as well as young men's, processes of identity formation in schools in such a context? *Working Class Without Work* answers these questions in new and insightful ways.

Conceptually, Weis's analysis takes us well beyond the theories of reproduction and resistance that dominated most of the critical educational literature during the past ten to fifteen years.[5] She has been influenced—and correctly so—by those who claim that we must focus on the ways social movements organize and reorganize society.[6] In her words, "society is best understood as a dynamic set of social movements—as the material accomplishment of conflicting groups struggling for control of the field of historical cultural action." It is this focus on a social-movement perspective and the integration into it of issues of identity formation among working-class youth that sets this book apart from so many others. In so doing, the author is able as well to help us think about questions that go beyond class dynamics.

While *Working Class Without Work* uncovers aspects of working-class identity that are similar to other studies, its picture of how youth create themselves by defining "the other," and the class, race, and gender dynamics involved in this, is striking and goes beyond any previous investigation. Its analysis of the growth of contradictory attitudes toward education that are emerging in working-class youth—ones similar to those often found in the African-American "underclass"—adds particular power to its portrayal.

Most studies of working-class students focus on exactly that—class. Weis brings center stage the gender and racial dynamics involved here, thereby avoiding the class reductionism prevalent in all too many explanations of the relationship between schools and society.[7]

For the white males portrayed here, blacks are "others." African-American young men are a threat. African-American young women are hardly thought about at all. For these same white-male youth, young white women aren't "other"; they are "less than." They are inferior and should be subjected to male control. In essence, white girls are property.

The white young women reject this. Their identity has a "critical moment of critique," in Weis's words, built into it. These girls believe that men cannot be counted upon for a whole array of reasons. The promise of their own wage labor takes on a primacy in these girls' lives, not necessarily the life of a wife who keeps the "home fires burning bright" while the man goes out to earn the family wage. The girls are attempting to control the conditions of their own lives in important ways. These attempts go partly beyond those found in previous well-known studies of female student culture.[8]

While there are major differences among the students, there are very real similarities, especially in their general reactions to schooling. Many of the students react in ways that are reminiscent of those found in Linda McNeil's interesting discussion of the reality of students' and teachers' lives in secondary schools.[9] It is almost as if there were a cynical bargain between students and teachers. Students basically do what they are told, but they don't actually *do* it. They are disengaged at best. They participate in the "appearance of order." They turn work in; but the work is unimportant and largely meaningless.

Many of these same students avowedly wish to leave the working class, to go on to college. After all, in a declining economy they know what may await them. Yet, even given this, large numbers of these young women and men will not even apply to college, much less attend. The contradictory sense of self here and the actions that arise from it are again reminiscent of what Weis uncovered in her earlier book on inner-city African-American students in a community college.[10]

Working Class Without Work directs our attention not only to the lives and identities of students in a context of de-industrialization. It also focuses on teachers and parents. What happens to teachers in these schools? How do the race, gender, and class conflicts and pressures that pervade the lives of students work their ways out in the reality of teachers' lives? What happens to the relationships between parents and teachers in this situation? By examining these aspects as well, Weis is able to give us a much clearer look at the totality of experiences that make working-class high schools look the way they do in a de-industrializing economy.

What does the future hold in terms of identity for these students? Weis provocatively argues that—given the attitudes and beliefs that have become part of the students' identities—it is the New Right that will be able to articulate themes that resonate with white-male (and to a lesser extent, white-female) experiences here. Rightist social movements and a conservative restoration—what has been called the politics of authoritarian populism—may be the winners here.[11] In a paradoxical way, schools of this type, even though they seem overtly neutral politically, may be supporting a New Right political agenda both because of the very ways in which they are organized and because of the ways in which the students' emerging identities are formed in this environment.

Yet, as Weis also shows, there are contradictory tendencies at work here. For example, women's experiences in the school and their emerging identities could lead to more progressive social tendencies. We cannot, of course, know this in advance. What we can do is listen carefully to the story Lois Weis tells if we wish to understand and act on the tendencies she illuminates so well. She concludes her book with the following words: "I encourage others to look carefully at the identities of the working class and others as we move into post-industrial society. It is, after all, our future and that of our children that is at stake." She is exactly correct here, and *Working Class Without Work* expressly shows us how important these stakes are and how they are constructed in the lives of our children.

Michael W. Apple
The University of Wisconsin, Madison

Acknowledgments

In many ways there is no way that I can truly acknowledge all those who, in one way or another, influenced my thinking when I was writing this book. The book took me into the field for a year—into the lives of those male and female faculty, staff, and students who live and work in Freeway. Although they must remain nameless, I express my deep appreciation for their time, energy, and patience. The volume should not in any way be construed as criticism of those people. They are part of the movement of history, just as we all are, and my attempt here is to understand this movement in human terms. Craig Centrie, Ava Shillin and Sally Ruth acted as research assistants in the field, and the work could not have been completed without them. Mariajosé Romero and Helen Kress provided additional assistance and I thank them as well.

Numerous individuals contributed to this endeavor once I left the field. Sheila Slaughter, Philip Wexler, Michelle Fine, Catherine Cornbleth, Allen Hunter, and Michael Apple read and commented upon a draft of the manuscript, and all offered important criticisms which I considered carefully in preparing the final copy. Michael Apple, as series editor, must be thanked, in particular, for his support and long-term influence on my thinking. Gail Kelly, Philip Altbach, and Hugh Petrie must also be thanked for contributing to my general thinking about schooling and society over the years. All have acted as sources of personal support in addition to being people with whom I could exchange ideas. Pat Glinski typed the manuscript and I thank her for her patience, perseverance, and exceptional skill, all of which enable my work to go forward.

I would also like to acknowledge the contributions of my family. Tereffe Asrat, my husband, always encourages me to look at things in a slightly different way from that which has become comfortable, and consistently raises insightful points about the workings of society. It is for this insight and the love which surrounds it that I dedicate this volume to him.

Sara Asrat, Jessica Asrat, Welela Tereffe, and Woinam Tereffe all make my day-to-day life enormously special. I feel so fortunate and, indeed, blessed to have all these poeple in my life that there is very little else to say. I am truly grateful for all that I have been given. I hope that this volume in some small measure begins to give back all that I receive from those outside myself.

Note to the Text

The following keys are provided to aid in reading the transcripts in the text. An * indicates the material is from field notes, not transcription. Brackets ([ ]) enclose background information. Ellipses (. . .) indicate a pause. Finally, ellipses enclosed within parenthesis [(. . .)] indicate that material has been edited out.

While the tides of suburbanization and secularism swept over America in the post—World War II years, the citizens of the steel community carried on undisturbed, in the shadow of the mill smokestacks and the skyway's sweeping arc. Little noticed by outsiders, they preserved their blue-collar world, with its commitment to family, to hard work, to God, to one's own people, and to labor solidarity. Their local schools taught children to value the ways of their parents. Their ward organizations provided jobs and services. And their labor unions helped workers share in the prosperity of the American steel industry in all its glory.—*Rusted Dreams: Hard Times in a Steel Community*, p. 37.

Office of the Mayor
City of Freeway

In the late 1800s, the township of East Holland included an approximate twenty-seven-square-mile area known as Chestnut Hill, a ridge composed of limestone that was higher in elevation than Large City [the large city ten miles from Chestnut Hill]. Eventual dissatisfaction of the taxpayers caused, in part, the withdrawal of this area from East Holland.

The Freeway Iron and Steel Company located in Freeway Hill and the community grew rapidly. In 1909, this area, once a part of East Holland, became the City of Freeway.

The history of Freeway is rich in tradition. It contained one of the most diverse ethnic compositions in the entire nation; a true melting pot. This blending of ethnic groups created distinct neighborhoods, cultures, and religions, and wove a fabric truly unique.

The Freeway Iron and Steel Company became Freeway Steel, and the Freeway plant become one of the most modern, largest, and productive in the world. In the 1960s, employment reached more than 20,000.

During World War II, Freeway sent more men, per capita, into the armed forces than any other city in the country. Many made the supreme sacrifice, dying on foreign soil in defense of this great nation.

Freeway has, perhaps, experienced more than its share of prosperity and disappointments. It was a city with one taxpayer paying nearly 65 percent of its taxes [the steel plant]; a city with an average income that reflected the wages of those employed in heavy industry. It also bore the scars of smoke and dirt that accompanied industry. No one seemed to mind.

The fortunes of the steel industry declined rapidly, as did production and employment during the 1970s and early 1980s. In December of 1982, Freeway Steel announced the end of steelmaking in Freeway. The tremors were heard throughout the nation, receiving nationwide media attention.

Many predicted the demise of this tough little town; they were wrong. With help from county, state, and federal levels of government, and the sacrifices at the city level, default was avoided.

The City of Freeway will someday be known as the city that refused to die. In darkest of hours, Freeway displayed the courage, tenacity, and spirit to survive. Anyone who underestimated Freeway underestimated the people of Freeway. Our spirit is rekindled, our goals redefined, our vision is for a new Freeway that will give our children, and their children, a great city to live in, to raise their families, to worship, to educate their children. They will say with pride, as we have, "We live in Freeway."

Statement by the mayor on the occasion
of the Freeway Diamond Jubilee
Commemorating Seventy-Five Years of Progress.
July 31, 1984

1
Introduction

This book is an examination of the identity-formation process among white working-class youth in the context of the de-industrialization of the American economy. For present purposes, "identity" can be defined as a sense of self in relation to others. Identity formation refers, therefore, to the processes through which people, either individually or collectively, come to see themselves in relation to others in particular ways.[1] In this volume I explore these processes among white working-class male and female high school students in Freeway—a city located in the northeastern "rust belt" of the United States.

In the 1970s I was greatly influenced by the literature on education and social and economic reproduction.[2] The question here is how does the institution of schooling, which was once hailed as the great engine of democracy, in fact act to reproduce the relations of domination and subordination necessary to the maintenance of a capitalist economy? Whether one approaches this question from a largely structuralist point of view, such as that of Samuel Bowles and Herbert Gintis, or a largely culturalist one, such as that of Paul Willis, the basic premise is that schools serve largely to reproduce the existing social order—a social order marked by great disparities of wealth, power, and privilege.[3] The question is, how?

Since the late 1970s, however, there have been radical changes in the economy which have rendered some of the assumptions and claims of the reproduction theorists (even those "revisionist" reproductionists such as Paul Willis) naive. The period from the end of World War II to the late 1970s represented the longest period of sustained economic growth in the history of world capitalism.[4] Central to this period of relative stability and growth was what Allen Hunter and others have called the "capital-labor accord," which "represented, on the part of labor, the de facto acceptance of the logic of profitability and markets as the guiding

3

principle of resource allocation . . . in return for an assurance that minimal living standards, trade union rights, and liberal democratic rights would be protected."[5] It was logical, then, that scholars critical of the notion that schools were the great engine of democracy and distributor of opportunity would focus their attention on the role of schooling in the perpetuation of the class structure. Things did, after all, appear as if they were being reproduced. Given this apparent reproduction, it was deemed important to understand how it is that working-class youth, for example, obtain jobs similar to those of their parents despite the official ideology associated with schooling.

With the demise of the "capital-labor accord" and the accompanying de-industrialization of the economy, it is important for scholars to reexamine the notion that schools prepare students to occupy positions in the industrial order similar to those of their parents.[6] Although it is understandable how the reproduction framework took hold among academics in a period of relative stability, it is becoming increasingly clear that this framework will be unable to illuminate complex social processes currently unfolding. It is important, then, for scholars to break out of the reproduction framework and begin to explore alternative conceptions of society and the ways in which schools are linked to this society.[7]

In this book I use ethnographic data generated within one high school in a de-industrializing area to shed light on one such alternative understanding; that being that society is the material accomplishment of conflicting groups struggling for control of the field of historical cultural action.[8] Specifically, I focus on the current struggle of white working-class youth as they produce themselves in a society vastly different from that of their parents and grandparents. I interpret the experiences and cultural praxis of youth in light of two general types of collective action that have occurred in the United States, that being the continuation of struggles related to social class and gender since the 1960s and 1970s. I also tie these struggles and the identity formation of white working-class youth to the emergence of the New Right in the United States and speculate as to the meaning of male and female identity formation in relation to this movement. As I will suggest later in this chapter, this perspective differs radically from that embedded in a social and economic reproduction framework.

The focus on social movements in this volume is important. Philip Wexler has argued persuasively that "liberal and critical work in American education [specifically work on social and economic reproduction] that was made possible by historical, collective social action now devel-

4

ops a mode of analysis that does not place collective action at its center."[9] Wexler points to the irony of the lack of a movement or social-action perspective in the work which owes its very existence to the social action of the 1960s, in particular. The civil rights and women's movements encouraged academics to question the extent to which schools are the great engine of democracy. It is truly ironic, then, that social action was forgotten as the social-reproduction framework took hold in the academy.

In this volume I take the notion of social action seriously both in terms of my definition of society as *constitutive* of such action, as well as in the fact that I explore youth identity formation in light of broader social movements. This is the first full-scale ethnography, to my knowledge, in which this task is attempted.[10] Ethnographies generally rest at the level of description or, when theorized, are couched in terms of some variant of reproduction theory.[11] Here I bring in a social-action perspective by viewing student identity in relation to larger movements. I argue that youth exist in a dialectical relationship with such movements—they are both "created" by them and "create" them at one and the same time. I do not use the term "create" in a deterministic fashion, however. Youth are not passive recipients of social movements any more than they are passive recipients of any aspect of culture, whether dominant or otherwise.[12] All of us exist in relation to social action, but not in any mechanistic sense.

This book does more than detail the formation of working-class youth identity in relation to social movements. I also focus on the way in which the school itself is related to the construction of identity. Specifically, I argue that youth identities form in relation to aspects of both school and teacher culture and that there is a dialectical quality to these relationships. Each is formed by, and at the same time forms, aspects of the other. The relational aspects of identity formation, both in terms of the school and larger social movements are, then, a key focus of this volume.

Philip Wexler has suggested that the school acts as a blockage to the path of collective identity formation.[13] While this certainly may be the case, especially in terms of *collective* identity, he potentially simplifies what does go on within the site of the school. To assume that the school acts necessarily as a repressive apparatus and that it, therefore, blocks the path of collective identity formation ignores the fact that the school itself is the site of the very struggles that Wexler discusses. It also leads us back into the "black box" notion of schooling which the work of "new sociologists" of education has helped us move well beyond.

This is not to say that the school may *not* serve this function, but that the role of the school is itself a question for research. It is also possible that the school may serve to both block *and* further the identity-formation process, whether collective or not, at one and the same time, and that these contradictory pressures may reflect contradictory self-production processes in evidence among youth. My point here is that one has to look carefully at the site of the school to see what is, in fact, happening on a day-to-day basis rather than conclude, as Wexler does, that the school acts necessarily to block the path of identity formation.

My intent, then, is to capture the identity-formation process of white working-class youth in a de-industralizing economy and theorize this process in relation to both the school and broader social movements. I will also, at a later point, touch briefly on the role of parents in this process.[14] These social movements, which lie at the heart of my analysis, must be seen in light of current economic trends. It is to the broader economic context that I now turn.

De-industrialization and the post-industrial society

At the end of World War II, American corporations dominated world markets. The American steel industry, for example, was virtually the only major producer in the world. By the 1960s, Germany, Japan, France, Italy, and Britain had rebuilt their steel industries, using the most advanced technology, and they became highly competitive with American industry. By the 1970s the American steel industry was in decline relative to that of other nations. For whatever reasons (and many have been offered), the industry continues in a decline and its effects are widely felt in the United States.

Factory closings are not restricted to the steel industry, and while more common to the northeastern United States, are not confined to this area. Gone are many of the jobs in heavy industry, automobiles, and manufacturing. The largest growth sector in the economy is now service, not production. Jobs in the service sector demand retraining, pay less, provide less security and fewer benefits, and often demand relocation. De-industrialization means a less secure, generally lower, standard of living for working-class Americans.

Barry Bluestone and Bennett Harrison, labor economists, note that "when the employment lost as a direct result of plant, store, and office shutdowns during the 1970s is added to the job loss associated with runaway shops, it appears that more than 32 million jobs were destroyed. Together, runaways, shutdowns, and permanent physical cutbacks short of complete closure may have cost the country as many as 38 million jobs."[15]

Pursuing Bluestone and Harrison's argument, Katherine Newman asks, "Why should American manufacturing sound its own death knell?" As she states,

> Manufacturers have been pinched by a profit squeeze, whose origins lie both in increased foreign competition and in the victories of organized labor. Unionized workers have been able to bargain for higher wages, thus limiting the flexibility of management just as the competitive environment has become tough. From management's perspective, the most effective way to respond was to cut and run. And from a logistical standpoint, it had become much easier to run. Labor and transportation costs are low enough to make it more profitable to produce cars in Korea and ship them to the United States than to manufacture them in America's heartland.[16]

Many displaced workers remain unemployed today; others obtained jobs in the much lower paying service sector.[17] De-industrialization, it must be stressed, is not a temporary phenomenon. It represents a radical shift in the nature of the American economy and the way in which American workers intersect with this economy. It is also the case that de-industrialization is now reaching beyond the "rust belt" industries. Newer industries (which represent the "high-tech solution"), such as microelectronics, are also exporting assembly jobs to Asian subsidiaries, thus eroding even further the employment base of the American working class.[18]

Capital is, in fact, more mobile than ever before. Investment is still taking place but in ways that signal a radical departure from previous decades. Basic production is, in fact, still occurring with the help of American finance, but American labor is being used less and less in this capacity. Jobs available in the United States are simply different from those available even a decade ago. Bluestone and Harrison are worth quoting in full here:

> U.S. Steel has billions to spend, but instead of rebuilding steel capacity, it paid $6 million to acquire Marathon Oil of Ohio.

General Electric is expanding its capital stock, but not in the United States. During the 1970s, GE expanded its worldwide payroll by 5,000 but did so by adding 30,000 foreign jobs and reducing its U.S. employment by 25,000. RCA Corporation followed the same strategy, cutting its U.S. employment by 14,000 and increasing its foreign work force by 19,000. It is the same in the depressed automobile industry. Ford Motor Company reports that more than 40 percent of its capital budget will be spent outside the United States, while General Motors has given up its plans to build a new multibillion-dollar plant in Kansas City, Missouri, and instead has shifted its capital spending to one of its facilities in Spain.[19]

The nature of the American economy has changed drastically within recent years, and the jobs upon which the white working class built their existence have been severely eroded. What is important for current purposes is that the landscape of the American economy has changed and that this represents a permanent shift which affects not only the Traditional Proletariat but all Americans.

Alain Touraine's points regarding the new social order—what he calls post-industrial society—must be taken seriously here. As Touraine suggests,

The characteristic feature of post-industrial society—which I have described more exactly as programmed society—is that the central investments are now made at the level of production management and not at that of work organization, as is the case in industrial society. Like all historical societies, industrial society, which should be defined rather in terms of production relations than of techniques, is based on the hold exerted by the masters of industry over salaried labor; this is why the place where class awareness and class conflict is situated is the factory, even the workshop or workplace, all of these being situations in which the boss-organizer imposes production rates and methods on workers. Whether the regime be capitalist or socialist, class domination in industrial society is always of the Taylorian type. By contrast, in programmed society class domination consists less in organizing work than in managing the production and data-processing apparatus; i.e., ensuring the often monopolistic control of the supply and processing of a certain type of data and hence of a way of organizing social life. This is the definition of the technocracy controlling the running of management apparatus. Resistance to this domination cannot be limited to a particular sphere, any more than can the domination itself. What is crucial now is no longer the struggle between capital and labor in the factory but that between the different kinds of apparatus and user-consumers or more simply the public—defined less by their specific attributes than by their resistance to domination by the apparatus.[20]

Touraine's points are important. The social structure is being re-aligned. We are no longer an industrial society characterized by the primary struggle between capital and labor. Rather, we are moving into a post-industrial era, one that is, by necessity, characterized by struggle over the symbolic realm of information and the production of culture more generally. This is not to say that industrial conflict has disappeared totally. As Touraine reminds us, "The new social categories still fall under the domination of work organization and inhuman work norms. New regions are becoming industrialized; women and immigrant workers are being subjected to new assembly lines; office workers' jobs are becoming more mechanical; and the working conditions of many workers are deteriorating, particularly due to the rapid incursions of shift work; proletarianization is forging ahead. Industrial class relations do not disappear with the emergence of the class relations of programmed society."[21]

It must be pointed out here that the reorganization of society about which Touraine speaks is linked fundamentally to social movements. Under this framework, macro-economic change of the sort represented by de-industrialization is best understood as a part of a movement strategy of certain dominant factions of capital to relocate primary industry outside of the United States, leaving much of the identity struggle within the United States centered more broadly on the organization of social life and the supply and processing of a certain type of data. The reorganization of society, then, is both accomplished through movements as well as transforming the context within which such movements operate.[22] Taking this point of view seriously necessitates a clearer understanding of what these social movements are—not just the social movements of elites whereby production is moved outside of the United States, but also the "naive" as well as organized responses of class fractions, women and so forth. Thus, from this perspective, society is best understood as a dynamic set of social movements—as the material accomplishment of conflicting groups struggling for control of the field of historical cultural action. This is a fundamentally different way of viewing society than that embedded in any variant of reproduction theory.

This, then, sets the context for my study of white working-class youth. Such youth are "victims," in one sense, of a reorganization of society over which they had no control. Like all today's youth, they are the recipients of a move to post-industrial society. It must be stressed, however, that post-industrial society represents the *outcome* of the struggle between capital and labor (which represent social movements in and of themselves, of course), whereby certain dominant factions of capital chose consciously to relocate due to the historic movement of labor— a movement that rendered labor relatively expensive and cut into the profit margin of the owners to a considerable extent. Under these historic circumstances, the social identity of white working-class youth is, therefore, a very interesting question. The identity formation of today's youth will both lay the groundwork for the struggles of the future as well as incorporate the struggles of the past and present. My task in this book, then, is to describe the identity that white working-class youth are creating for themselves and link this identity to both the school and current social movements.

Struggles over the symbolic realm of information and the production of culture have been discussed on a theoretical level by Touraine, Alberto Melucci, and others as the "new social movements."[23] These movements must be seen as a struggle over "self-production," or having control over the production of collective and individual identity in increasingly programmed society. Melucci suggests that the production of the human species itself is at stake here—the possibility for people, individually and collectively, to control not only their "products," but also human existence and its quality more generally.

The struggles in post-industrial or programmed society are, then, very different from those that are characteristic of industrial society—and it is not yet clear how the traditional working class relates to these struggles. Given the radical shift from industrial society to post-industrial society which is fueled, in the United States in particular, by conscious decisions to de-industrialize, a set of questions can be raised about the identity-formation process among people who have defined themselves historically vis-à-vis the social organization in particular ways. How does the working class define itself currently, given the emergence of the post-industrial order? How can a group define itself in terms of capital-labor conflicts when such conflicts are no longer at the heart of the social formation? What is the emerging identity of this group? To what extent is the identity *collectively* held, as was certainly the case under industrial society?

Melucci, Touraine, and others note that the new social movements which are, in important ways, constitutive of the emerging society, place strong emphasis upon the control of the symbolic realm of information and culture which, as these authors note, is increasingly contested. The right to define basic categories of experience such as time and space as well as the right to name publicly the situation and one's opponent in a social struggle become hotly disputed. How, then, does the traditional white working class relate to this new social formation, and how does this group connect with these new struggles? Or does it?[24]

As noted above, the school provides the site for this investigation. I am also interested in the day-to-day workings of the school and in the way in which the school encourages and/or blocks the identity-formation process upon which I concentrate. There has been, within recent years, an attempt on the part of scholars working within the "new" sociology of education tradition to take the insides of schools seriously. Thus, scholars such as Jean Anyon and Michael Apple, who focus on knowledge, and Linda McNeil and Charles Payne, who focus on aspects of teacher culture, have looked carefully both at the construction of culture as both a commodity and as a lived form in schools and at the way in which such culture is related to the reproduction of the social order.[25] We have come a long way toward understanding some of these relationships. My task here is different, however, since I see society as constitutive of dynamic social movements rather than an entity that is reproduced. While I certainly gather extensive data on what happens within schools, it is my task to unravel the way in which elements of school culture are related to identity formation and speculate as to the relational aspects of identity in terms of larger social movements—past, present, and future. Thus, I take seriously the notion that these students are constructing an identity and that this identity may be encouraged and/or blocked by a variety of interactions within the school itself. Certainly there are numerous factors outside the school that may impact upon identity formation as well, but it is not my task to consider these here. I will, however, focus carefully on the school and look at the way in which this one state institution, with all its internal contradictions, may be linked to the self-production of youth identity.[26]

Freeway

Data were gathered as part of an ethnographic investigation of Freeway High. I spent the academic year 1985–86 in the high school, acting as a participant-observer for three days a week for the entire year. Data were gathered in classrooms, study halls, the cafeteria, extracurricular activities, and through in-depth interviews with over sixty juniors, virtually all teachers of juniors, the vice-principals, social workers, guidance counselors, and others.[27] Data collection centered on the junior class since this is a key point of decision when PSATs, SATs and so forth must be considered.[28] In addition, this is, in the state where Freeway is located, the time when the bulk of a series of state tests must be taken if entrance to a four-year college is being considered.[29]

Freeway is an ideal site in which to conduct an investigation of identity formation among white working-class youth. The focus on youth is important here. It is, after all, youth who will have to live out during their entire work lives the reorganization of society noted above. While they certainly bring with them the collective identity of the "old" working class, they must forge a new identity as the old industrial order is eroded.

Examination of data gathered for the Standard Metropolitan Statistical Area of which Freeway is a part (data for Freeway per se are not available) confirms a number of trends that are reflective of Bluestone and Harrison's argument noted earlier. Occupational data for 1960–80 (see table 1.1) suggest that the most striking decreases in the area are found in the categories of "Precision, Craft and Repair" and "Operators, Fabricators and Laborers." These two categories constitute virtually all the so-called "blue-collar jobs." When combined, data suggest a relative decline of 22.3 percent in the "blue-collar" category from 1960 to 1980. A look at some of the more detailed subcategories reveals more striking decline. Manufacturers, for example, have experienced an overall decline in the area of 35 percent between 1958 and 1982.

Data also suggest an increase in the "Technical, Sales and Administrative Support" category. These occupations constituted 22.8 percent of the total in 1960 as compared with close to 31 percent in 1980, representing an increase of over one-third. Increases in "Service" and "Managerial and Professional Specialty" categories also reflect a shift away from industry and toward the availability of service occupations.[30]

The change in the distribution of occupations by gender needs to be clarified here as well. During this same time period, female employment

Table 1.1 Occupations by year for Freeway area SMSA,*
all persons

Occupation	% Of All Occupations			Absolute Change	Net % Change
	1960	1970	1980		
Managerial and Professional					
Specialty Occupations	19.2%	21.9%	21.7%	+2.5	+13.0%
Technical, Sales, and Adm.					
Support Occupations	22.8%	25.4%	30.7%	+7.9	+34.6%
Service Occupations	10.1%	12.9%	13.9%	+2.8	+37.6%
Farming, Forestry and Fishing					
Occupations	1.0%	.6%	.9%	−0.1	−10.0%
Precision Production, Craft and					
Repair Occupations	16.8%	15.4%	12.5%	−4.3	−25.6%
Operators, Fabricators, and					
Laborers	25.3%	23.6%	20.2%	−5.1	−20.2%
Occupations Not Reported	5.1%				

*Standard Metropolitan Statistical Area

increased 55 percent, while employment for men decreased 6 percent. For most occupations in the area, a net increase in employment during this period may be attributed mainly to the increase in employed women and a net decrease to a decrease in employed men.[31]

Although the emerging economy has absorbed women at a faster rate than men, it must be noted that the proportion of full-time female workers is still lower than that of full-time male workers. Thus, 67 percent of male workers are full-time in 1980 as compared with only 43 percent of females. In addition, full-time female workers earned 56 percent of what full-time male workers earned in 1980, and women in Sales have average incomes that are only 46 percent of the average income for men. This is particularly important given that a growing number of positions in the Standard Metropolitan Statistical Area are in Sales and that these are filled disproportionately by women. Such trends are reflective of trends nationwide. Thus, the move toward post-industrial society has meant that a higher proportion of females is employed in the labor force relative to earlier years, but that females increasingly earn relatively lower wages than males.

In the Freeway area, de-industrialization and the move toward a post-industrial economy is particularly acute due to the closing of Freeway Steel. The plant payroll in 1969 was at a record high of 168 million, topping 1968 by 14 million. The average daily employment was 18,500.

Production of basic oxygen furnace and open hearth was at a near record of 6,580,000 tons.[32]

In the first seven months of 1971, layoffs at the Freeway Plant numbered 4,000 and decline continued into the 1980s. From 18,500 jobs in 1979, there were only 3,700 production and 600 supervisory workers left in 1983 and 3,600 on layoff.[33] At the end of 1983, the plant closed. All that remains of close to 20,000 workers are 370 bar mill workers.

It should be clear here that the broader social structural configuration in the United States is being reorganized and that Freeway provides an excellent case in point. What, then, does the social identity formation process look like for white youth embedded within the historic working class? How are youth, both male and female, producing both "self" and, taking Touraine's perspective seriously, society?

This book will explore these questions. It is a book about the creation of the "new identity" of the traditional white working class. It is a study of social action, not reproduction. As I have suggested above, there is no white working class to be reproduced. As Touraine argues,

> Nothing can be further removed from this self-production of society than the image of reproduction—a society has neither nature nor foundations; it is neither a machine nor an organization; it is action and social relations. This idea sets a sociology of action against all the variants of functionalism and structuralism.[34]

He further notes:

> Social movements are not a marginal rejection of order, they are central forces fighting one against the other to control the production of society by itself and the action of classes for the shaping of historicity.[35]

Since this is a book about social action, I do not assume stability as to the forms outlined here. My analysis is that of one point in time. It is a key point, however, since it is a time of substantial reorganization. It is my task to capture aspects of this societal reorganization and give written testimony to portions of the change process.

The framework of the book is as follows: Chapter 2 explores the identity of male students; chapter 3 examines the identity of female students, chapters 4 and 5 examine within-school processes and the way in which such processes may serve to block and/or encourage the formations noted in chapters 2 and 3; chapter 6 turns attention to parents; chapter 7 considers the students' identity in relation to broader movements, specifically the women's movement and the American labor movement, as well as the conservative New Right backlash; and chapter 8 offers speculations as to the possible future of the white working class. Chapters 2 through 6 represent more traditional ethnographic work; chapters 7 and 8 delve more deeply into theoretical considerations.

The social-action perspective discussed here will not be sustained in each chapter. Rather, I will return to these issues in chapters 7 and 8, after the more traditional ethnographic material is presented. The social-action perspective thus provides a way of interpreting the identities described in the earlier chapters, as well as suggesting, on a theoretical level, that such identities and the struggles associated with their formation and relatedness to other groups are constitutive of society itself.

2
Freeway Males

This chapter explores the emerging identity among white males at Freeway High. As noted earlier, I do not link these data with a social-action perspective per se in this chapter. Rather, I will return to this perspective in chapter 7.

Several aspects of the identity detailed here are similar to those uncovered in previous investigations of the white working class. Specifically, opposition to authority which suggests an emerging "them-us" orientation reminiscent of the relations of the factory; racism; and sexism have been noted in past studies. These orientations emerge in the Freeway study as well, and, in the case of racism and sexism, in a particularly virulent form. There is, however, also an emerging contradictory set of attitudes toward education and schooling more in line with the orientation of the black underclass in America than the white working class.[1]

I will detail the emerging identity of white working-class males and compare this identity with that observed by previous investigators. Although the framework used to interpret identity is different in previous studies from that employed here, it is nevertheless useful to compare data generated by Paul Willis and others with those reported in this volume. It is in the meaning of such data for the nature of the social formation that investigators would part ways. Thus, data reported in Paul Willis's study, for example, need not be interpreted necessarily within the reproduction framework in which they were generated. They can potentially be used to enlighten a different understanding of society.

I will argue here that white male identity emerges in relation to that of female identity and that of blacks. Thus white males elaborate an identity that is "other than" female and "other than" black. It is this relational aspect of identity that is key here. Identity does not take its shape and form in any linear fashion. It is forged in a dialectical relation with that of constructed others and its shape and form will change as

16

that of the "other" changes, and vice versa. All of this, it must be remembered, takes place within a particular economy and social configuration.

Attitude toward institutional authority and school meanings

Previous studies of white working-class boys suggest that opposition to authority and school meanings is deeply embedded within the cultural formation. Ultimately, it has been argued, this leads to an elaboration of an "us versus them" ideology which is appropriate to the historic struggle between capital and labor. The most obvious dimension of the lads' culture in *Learning to Labour,* for example, is generalized opposition toward authority and school meanings. The lads engage in behavior designed to show resentment while stopping just short of outright confrontation. They also exhibit extensive absenteeism, signaling their generally oppositional stance; their "struggle to win symbolic and physical space from the institution and its rules, and to defeat its main perceived purpose: to make you 'work.' "[2] The core skill here is being able to get out of any given class, thus preserving personal mobility within the school. Personal mobility encourages the preservation of the collective (cutting class means meeting friends elsewhere) and thus can be seen as a partial defeat of individualism.[3]

While it is tempting to relate these behaviors to adolescence, it is important to note that white working-class males in the community college in the United States exhibit similar attitudes toward authority and engage in comparable behavior and that students from a different background do not.[4] About a month or so after school opened, students in Howard London's study of a community college began injecting *sotto-voce* taunts into classroom lectures and discussions. This opposition took a distinctively class form in that, for the most part, it was done by students in manual-training programs and aimed at liberal-arts teachers or vocational-training teachers who were considered too abstract. Law-enforcement students did not harass teachers who were ex-detectives, for example, but they did harass the lawyer who taught legal aspects of police work. Students reacted negatively only in those classes that were "too intellectual," that is, too centered on mental labor.[5]

A third example of white working-class male identity comes from Robert Everhart's ethnography of a junior high school, also in the United

17

States.[6] Unlike Willis, Everhart does not focus on those students who create *overtly* oppositional forms in the school, but the disengagement from mental labor is nevertheless clear. He focuses on those who more or less strike a compromise with school culture, giving the bare minimum, taking care to complete necessary assignments without causing undue trouble.

That Everhart's students complete assignments and do not engage in the overt and calculated rejection of school content or form does not mean that they are involved in the process of schooling, nor that their valuation of achievement qua achievement is any different from that of the lads. All it means is that they do not value the specific and overt negation of school meanings in the same way the lads do. Students view school as a place to meet friends, "goof off," smoke a joint, and pursue other activities that are not related to the official learning process. To students at Harold Spencer Junior High School, it was important that one should conform to the requirements of the school in sufficient detail so as to "get by," all the while creating a separate culture that permitted the maximum element of self-determination.

A common thread runs through these studies: the often overt and sometimes covert rejection of school meanings and culture. There is an attempt on the part of working-class youth to carve out their own space within the institution—space that can then be filled with their own meanings which are fundamentally antischool. As noted earlier, this has been interpreted for working-class students as an elaboration of a "them versus us" ideology which typifies the struggle between capital and labor.

The same resentment toward authority characterizes the Freeway boys as boys in earlier studies. Basically, resentment is linked to perceived institutional control over student dress and the use of time and space. Time and space are, after all, what students in school live as being most out of their control. Thus, it is logical that both are targeted arenas of struggle. As with Willis's lads, resentment tends to be caged in practice, and stops just short, on most occasions, of outright confrontation. It is noteworthy that this is largely unique to male identity, although females in Freeway exhibit some of the same sort of resentment. It must be pointed out that ideas expressed here were in response to probe questions regarding what they like and do not like about school. Many statements reflect attitudes toward control over space—where students should be and when, and what they should be doing there. Students particularly resent the lack of a place to smoke. This must be seen as largely symbolic, however. Students resent the control institutional authorities have over their lives, in general, and it is expressed most forcefully in the case of smoking.

Tom: I don't like the principals. Most of the teachers are assholes.

LW: Why?

Tom: They have a controlling power over the kids, or at least they try to. Me, I won't take shit from no one. That's the way I am.

(. . .) Whatever they do, they can't bother me, 'cause when I get my diploma I can say what I want to them.

(. . .) The kids should have some rights. Like, let me say for one example, I know there's smokers in this school. A lot of kids smoke. (. . .) To solve all smoking problems with kids going outside and skipping classes, give the kids at least once a day a place to go to—a room—and have one cigarette or something. Five minutes a day.

(. . .) They [school authorities] play head games with kids . . . They think they can push you any which way they want.

LW: If they're pushing you around, why stay for your diploma?

Tom: 'Cause it helps for, like, a job or whatever. It's like a reference for this, this, this.-It's like a key that opens many doors.

. . .

Bob: I think _____ is an asshole. He's an assistant principal. I know he's in an authority position, but he just seems to think he has control over anything that happens in this school at any time.

(. . .) The way the control is handled [is what I resent]. Mr. _____, that man has no sense of humor. He's like, blah, and he just starts acting like God or something.

(. . .) They have to have control somehow. It's

their job. It's just the way they're going about it [that is bad]. The way _____ is going about it bothers me.

. . .

Rob: It's like a dictatorship here [school].

LW: Who dictates?

Rob: Mr. _____, Mr. _____, Mr. _____ is the worst (. . .) He'd take me out of school for being late to class. You woke up late or something, and he comes and kicks you out. He suspended us for two days for skipping class.

(. . .) That just makes you more mad and you wait to get even with him. (. . .) Next time you come in, you come in late again. Put a stink bomb in his office. Walk by and throw it in.

LW: So, who wins in the end?

Rob: Probably he will. Or we do, when we graduate.

. . .

Jim: I'd like to see the teachers give the students a chance to become a mature adult. I'll give you an example. The smoking. About fifty/sixty kids get caught a year and get butt duty. You got to pick up paper. Do you think that is going to stop the kids? No way; that doesn't make any sense.

I'd like to see them give the kids a chance . . . The seniors . . . What they should do is just try it—a lounge, seniors only. Have it supervised every period by the teachers, like a hall duty, but only seniors would go in there.

(. . .) I'd like to see the students pick what they want to wear. (. . .) In the summer it gets extremely hot. You got to wear jeans; you can't wear shorts.

And I think that administration is a little too harsh on students. (. . .) A kid skips a class. Three days' detention. School policy. They're going out of their way to look for what's wrong. They're going out of their way. Like they [the principals] go to [the local doughnut shop] to find the kids.

. . .

Joe: There should be a smoking lounge. Because why should kids get in trouble for smoking? Other schools have smoking lounges. It sounds reasonable.
(. . .) [Also] the detention. The reasons why kids get detention are stupid.

LW: Like, give me an example.

Joe: Like being late a certain amount of times. You get a detention. That should be changed.

LW: Why?

Joe: Because why should somebody get detention for something that might not have been their fault? A locker that won't open. Reasons like that. Go to the lavatory. If you have to go to the lavatory, you're gonna be late. Teachers don't let you go during the period.

Generally speaking, students adhere to school rules, and anyone walking into the high school would gain the impression of "order." Students, when overtly challenging the institution, do such things as skip class and go to the local doughnut shop; smoke cigarettes or drink alcohol in the parking lot; or, on occasion, throw stink bombs into the vice-principal's office. It is significant that students generally *leave* the school building when they challenge authority rather than confront it directly within the confines of the institution itself. In addition, although they may go to the parking lot (which is directly behind the school) or the doughnut shop, they inevitably return before the day is over. These are short-term "visits" rather than reflective of large-scale absenteeism so characteristic of large urban centers. There is, therefore, a continual grumbling about school authority and the way in which it plays itself out regarding control over time and space, but there are few direct challenges to this authority that result in a true breakdown of order within the school.

Students also express a noticeably more positive attitude toward schooling and accompanying mental labor, at least in the abstract, than is the case in earlier studies. As will be seen below, students in what is called the advanced curriculum tend to desire to pursue college more than other students, but virtually *all* students articulate *some* value for education, albeit in highly utilitarian terms.[7] The wholesale rejection expressed by Willis's students, for example, is not in evidence in Freeway, and it is significant that a comparable group of "lads" does not exist. It is also the case that students tend to tie their more positive attitude toward education directly to factory closings.

John: College prep [is my major]. It's the only thing to do.

LW: What do you mean?

John: Well, around here, 'cause there's nothing else. Everything's going down south. Like any kind of good jobs, a better education's what you're gonna hafta need. Unless you plan to sweep the floors someplace the rest of your life. And that ain't really gonna be my style.

(. . .) Like, I work at the Aud Club [private club] now, and he'll [dad] pick me up and I'll be complaining and he'll say, "See, get a good education, get a good job."

I'm a busboy. I wait on people. Serve 'em shrimp cocktail. Pick up their dirty dishes, things like that (. . .) You're there and you do nothin' but runnin' around. Do this and do that for this person. Get their dishes and bring these people soup. It's a bitch.

He [dad] says, "Wouldn't you rather have these people waiting on you? Go to school and get an education." My father never got a high school education. He got a GED [high school equivalency diploma]. He wants me to keep going.

. . .

Bob: Well, I want to go to college. I don't know what for yet. I was thinking of something like biology, something like that. Probably [City Community College] or [Suburban Community College]. Probably transfer [to a four-year school].

(. . .) My mother wants me to [go to college]. So does my father. My mother has post-education [at a local hospital]. She was a worker there. But my father quit school in the middle of twelfth grade. (an advanced student)

. . .

LW: What do you think you want to do when you graduate?

Sam: I want to go to college for two years. And, then, hopefully, get into computers. If not that, the business field.

. . .

LW: What do you hope to do when you leave high school?

Jerry: College, but I'm still not certain which one. I'm looking around here, but if I get a scholarship, I'll go away. Right now it looks pretty good, whether it be sports or educational. (an advanced student)

. . .

Jim: I've got a couple of colleges I've been looking at. University of Maryland or University of Seattle. And I was thinking of pursuing the commercial art field and becoming, eventually, a comic book artist or an illustrator (. . .) I'll probably take out student loans. [I'm] working part-time. I'm a stock boy. I have a bit of money put aside. I've been doing it six months.

. . .

Seth: I'm going to go to college; hopefully an aeronautical school in Chicago. I been thinking to myself, I'm really going to do well in college.

LW: What made you decide to do that?

Seth: The greediness. The money. I want a well-paying job.

. . .

LW: What do you plan to do when you graduate?

Steve: Go to college.   -

LW   For what?

Steve: I haven't decided (. . .) I just wanna go. Can't get a job without going to college. You got to be educated to get a job, a good job: you don't want to live off burgers when you're old.

. . .

LW: What do you plan to do when you leave school?

Larry: Go straight to college.

LW: Where do you want to go? What do you want to do?

Larry: You know, I can't tell you specifically, but I want to

23

make money (. . .) I don't want to end up like my parents. Nothing against them.

LW: What do you mean?

Larry: Well, I want to own a house. I don't want to use the term "make ends meet." I don't ever want to have that in my vocabulary. (an advanced student)

. . .

Bill: My dad is a machinist. He needs one more day in the plant to get his twenty years. He's fighting now to get one more day.
(. . .) [I want to get to college] 'cause I see what happened to him. He's working for like seven/eight dollars an hour. Like [what] he used to get in the plant, compared to that, it's nothing. To get a better chance, you got to go to college.

I do not mean to imply here that all white working-class youth intend to go to college, or that they discredit manual-laboring jobs totally. Indeed, that is not the case. It is noteworthy, however, that of the boys interviewed, 40 percent express a desire to go to a two- or four-year college, and there is *far* less celebration of manual-laboring jobs than earlier studies suggest. If students celebrate traditionally working-class jobs, they are skilled or craft jobs, such as motorcycle mechanic, machinist, tool and dye maker, and so forth. Such jobs require further training as well. Not one boy interviewed discussed the possibility of being a generalized wage laborer.

Freeway boys tend to look at schooling in highly utilitarian terms. The school will allow them to make a lot of money, get a "good" job, and so forth. They are explicit about the fact that they expect the school to keep them "off burgers"; enable them not to use the phrase "make ends meet"; and buy a house. They may resent institutional authority and school meanings as boys in previous studies have, but many intend to pursue schooling simply because they feel they "have to." It is not the flavor of Willis's lads at all; indeed, even those most negative about school concede the importance of the "credential." As Rob puts it when discussing the warfare between students and school officials: "I guess we [win] when we graduate," suggesting the utility of the diploma.

The point here is that students express some affirmation of school culture and knowledge. They do not necessarily act on this affirmation in any meaningful fashion, however. In previous studies of the white working class, behavior within the institution follows more or less logically from perceptions of the institution. Thus, in the case of Willis's lads, absenteeism signals their generally oppositional stance; their "struggle to win symbolic and physical space from the institution and its rules and to defeat its main perceived purpose: to make you 'work.' "[8] Students are adept at winning space for themselves and place a high priority on this. These actions do not contradict their negative perceptions of school and school authority. London also concludes that high absenteeism at the community college follows more or less logically from perceptions of the institution.[9]

My own study of black students at an urban community college, as well as studies by John Ogbu and others who have studied black students in the United States, suggest a different pattern. There is, among poor black students, in particular, a tendency to affirm and reject school-based meanings and culture at one and the same time. Ogbu refers to this as a "paradox"; I refer to it as a "lived contradiction."[10] The point is that poor black students tend *not* to reject totally school meanings and culture, and, at the same time, act as if they do. In the community college, for example, students actively affirm knowledge and the idea of teachers. Criticism of faculty centers on beliefs that they are not trying hard enough, are not meeting their contractual obligations (showing up to class), or are too impersonal. Yet, there is a strong sense on the part of students that faculty possess knowledge that is worthwhile. Despite this, the absentee rate is exceptionally high; there is a high withdrawal rate; students often walk in late to class; engage in extensive drug use on campus; and exert little effort. Thus, unlike the case of previous studies of white working-class males, black students (both males and females) exhibit a contradictory set of cultural elements. They embrace and reject schooling at one and the same time.[11] Ogbu argues similarly based on his studies of black secondary-school youth.

Freeway males, in particular, appear to be moving toward this same contradictory relationship with official school knowledge and culture, fueled, as I will argue in chapter 4, by the institution itself. Although their expressed valuation of education is higher than would be expected on the basis of previous studies, there are other lived elements of their emerging identity that suggest contradiction.

Freeway youths tend to attend school. The rampant dropout rates so characteristic of urban black and Hispanic students, in particular, are not in evidence in Freeway.[12] Students may skip classes here and there but, for the most part, are in class. Attendance figures for the academic year 1985–86 indicate that, on average, almost 94 percent of the second-ary-school student body is in attendance on any given day.[13] Given that cities such as Boston bemoan the fact that only 50 percent of their students are in attendance on any given day, this is high, indeed. This suggests a desire on the part of the students at least to comply with school rules and, as noted above, reflects the sentiment that schooling has *some* value.

Along these same lines, the school is strikingly "well run." In all the time I spent at Freeway, I saw only one class "out of control." There were occasional fights in the hallways, but very occasional. There is nothing that even remotely resembles a breakdown of order.

On the other hand, in spite of the fact that the majority of students express a desire to continue their education, only 33 percent of juniors took the Preliminary Scholastic Aptitude Test (PSAT) and 27 percent of juniors and seniors took the Scholastic Aptitude Test (SAT). This is striking in light of expressed desires to attend college since the SAT is mandatory for entrance into most four-year schools. In addition, even given the relatively low proportion of students, both male and female, who took the PSAT and SAT, results for these students are barely average. Out of a possible 800 on the math and verbal sections of the SAT, the average scores for Freeway youth during the academic year 1985–86 were as follows: white male verbal, 432; white male quantitative; 493; black male verbal, 395; black male quantitative, 375; white female verbal, 410; white female quantitative, 450; black female verbal, 316; black female quantitative, 374. Although I provide data for all students, only 3 percent of students who took the SAT were black. Forty-three percent were female.

While these are not, overall, poor scores, such scores would probably not enable entrance to the university sector, including State University, where a combined score of 1150 is necessary. They might, however, enable entrance to a number of comprehensive colleges, including State College.

In addition, as table 2.1 suggests, grades do not tend to be high at Freeway. Grades were gathered for all juniors during the academic year 1985–86 in English, social studies, math, and science. They were obtained from official transcripts for ninth and tenth grade.

Freeway students do not, generally, achieve high marks. The grades for whites are higher than those for blacks, and white females tend to obtain slightly higher marks than white males. What is striking, however,

Table 2.1 Mean grades for Freeway juniors, 1985–86

	9th Grade	10th Grade
English		
White Male	76.6	80.0
Black Male	68.0	71.4
White Female	83.7	85.2
Black Female	81.6	78.2
Social Studies		
White Male	79.1	78.1
Black Male	66.2	69.9
White Female	79.5	80.2
Black Female	73.5	71.5
Math		
White Male	77.1	79.9
Black Male	55.6	63.5
White Female	76.0	80.9
Black Female	60.2	76.4
Science		
White Male	74.6	78.3
Black Male	64.6	69.3
White Female	77.3	81.0
Black Female	66.9	73.2

is the extraordinarily "average" nature of grades. While grades must be seen as "constructed" in some sense, it is nevertheless noteworthy that they are so low. Grades for whites tend to be in the mid to high 70's, which can be translated into a letter grade of C. Such grades, in combination with low SAT scores, will not enable students to obtain entrance into even the comprehensive college sector in the United States.

Indeed, most students are concerned only with "passing," not with "excelling" or even "doing well." The language of "passing" a test, or "passing" a course dominates student discourse, as the excerpts below suggest.

Office Procedures Class, Nov. 24, 1985[*]

Sam: We're getting our social test back today.

Jennifer: Do you think you passed?

Sam: Yeah, I copied a couple of answers from you.

Jennifer: You better not have. I didn't study.

Social Studies, January 30, 1986[*]

Jerome: [comes in all smiles.] "This is my last day in this class."

Paul: "Did you pass?"

Jerome: "I passed . . . I got a 68. [65 is passing] I passed!" [He is *very* excited.]

. . .

Social Studies, April 5, 1986[*]

[Ed gets his test back. He got a 78 [a C].]

Ed: [Smiling] "I like to see those passing marks."

. . .

Social Studies, April 5, 1986[*]

Paul: Teacher passes the test back. Paul turns the paper over fearfully: "I *passed!*" [with *great* happiness; he got a 66; 65 is passing].

The point here is that the vast majority of students, at least in their discourse, are not overly concerned about anything more than passing. It is the expressed "getting through" school that counts, not doing even minimally well. In the final analysis, however, most end up with C's and D's. While this is true for both males and females, it stands out more for males since males take a stronger stand on the lack of available jobs to begin with. Indeed, as we will see in the next chapter, female aspirations and behavior tend to be a bit more congruent than that of males.

The desire to "get through" is further apparent regarding the issue of homework. It is not that it is done well (pride in craft), that one learns something, or even that it will help one get something which is desired later on (a good grade on a test, for example) that is important. As the following excerpts make clear, it is *simply* something to be done and students copy from one another constantly so that they can hand something in:

Social Studies, September 17, 1985[*]

One student to another: "Did you do this [homework]?"

Another student: "No, I missed it."

[Several others are saying they didn't do their homework.]

Second male: "Fuck. I remember in school and
then forget at home." [He grabs the
paper of another student and copies
it.]

. . .

Social Studies, January 26, 1986*

Mr. _____ walks around checking to see whether the
worksheet is completed. They all show him the sheet. As I
[LW] walked into the class, Charles was copying from
someone. He had the two sheets on his desk. Ed shows
Mr. _____ and I said, "Who'd you copy from?" He said,
"Sam," and pointed across the room.

. . .

Study Hall, February 3, 1986*

Nine A.M. Several students in the back of the room were either
discussing homework, exchanging homework, or returning it
after copying it. Technically, there is supposed to be no talking
in study hall but almost everyone does.

. . .

English, January 24, 1986*

During the video [of *Macbeth*] everyone was very quiet until
the end of the tape when Mr. _____ requested that everyone
who was going to take the exam on Monday was to come up to
the desk to get instructions and to get their corrected homework.
When Vern and Chris returned, Chris was disgruntled because
Vern had copied her work but got a better grade.

. . .

Study Hall, January 24, 1986*

Vern was required to do a writing assignment in English class.
He acquired another student's homework, and copied it
verbatim and signed his name [the assignment was to write a
letter to an admissions counselor at a university].

. . .

Social Studies, September 11, 1985*

At the start of class, kids are switching homework and copying
from one another.

October 29, English[*]

Mr. James: "Okay, pass in your homework." I asked Vern and Chris whether different people did the homework at different times and then they share. They said "No, one guy always does it [in here] and six of us copy. In chemistry, one guy does it and the whole class copies." I asked if the teachers notice. They said, "Most don't." Chris said, "I don't care if they do."

form
vs
Substance

The point here is that, again, students are not involved in the process of learning. They are involved in the *form* of schooling, but not its substance. These working-class students value schooling more highly than previous studies suggest but, at the same time, are not engaged in its substance at all. This holds true for both males and females, although it is more exaggerated for males. They tend to work less and copy from other students more.

An adherence to form but not substance is apparent in classroom observations below. Students rarely cause trouble in school; in other words, as noted earlier, they rarely act on their own expressed negativity and resentment of institutional authority. Nevertheless, while they dutifully attend class most of the time, hand in their homework, and so forth, the fact is that most copy homework, and the appearance of order in the classroom masks complete nonengagement. Students just sit in class and do what they are told. Rarely can students articulate what the class discussion or lecture had even been about.

English, February 12, 1986[*]

In Mr. _____'s class, students alternated with Mr. _____ reading from a verse. Everyone in the class was exceptionally quiet and followed instructions closely, or at least enough so as to give the impression they were following instructions. When Mr. _____ called on specific students to read, they were [often] unable to pick up at the appropriate place.

. . .

Social Studies, November 26, 1985

Teacher passes out a worksheet on women. He says, "Okay, this is to be done in class today. If you don't complete it here, do it for homework. I'll check tomorrow." [some chatter]

Teacher: "There are additional questions on page 193. If you don't have enough to do now, I can add them."

The room is completely quiet.

. . .

Math, March 7, 1986*

Today's class is on processing equations—solving for X. A major portion of the class was spent on isolating X.

The entire class is almost completely engaged in looking down at their desks or writing. Few people are actually watching the chalkboard where the teacher is going through various steps. [The algebra is the equivalent of eighth-grade work].

Mr. _____ frequently reminded the students to study hard because there was going to be a test on Monday.

As noted above, I saw only one class "out of control" during the entire year. By this I mean that the teacher could not keep order; students were running around the room, and so forth. Significantly, this was when a substitute was present, as below:

Social Studies, October 29, 1985*

A sub is here; an older black male.

On the board was the following: "If you have not finished yesterday's assignment, finish it today and read and answer question number 2 on p. 87."

The word was out on the sub. Three black females and one Hispanic male were there who normally are not. Two black males walked in and then walked out. Four white males were called out, sequentially, to "go to Mr. _____'s or Mr. _____'s office [the vice-principals]." They were called out by their friends.

The place was disorderly, and this is the first time I've seen this at this school.

Eddie [a Hispanic male] called out, "Hey, black girls, what did Martin Luther King say before he died?"

Martha: "I had a dream!" [laughter]

Eddie: "Seven black girls in one class, Whoo—ee!"

31

The girls started rapping [singing phrases to the rhythm of a current song]. The sub just smiled.

This was the first and last time I witnessed such a scene at Freeway. Normally students pay attention by not paying attention, but they do not collectively disrupt the class. In fact, of course, this is not ironic at all since order can perhaps be best maintained insofar as education is distanced from the lived, and thereby excitable, experiences of adolescents.[14] At Freeway High, however, this takes on a particularly vacuous form. If students are told to answer questions 1 thru 21, they do so, even though they make no effort to understand the questions, and written answers tend to take the form of several students copying largely inappropriate written paragraphs from the text to serve as responses to the questions and then sharing these paragraphs with others. Even on that contested terrain everywhere—that is, when a substitute is present— Freeway students are generally docile, as the following suggests:

Social Studies, October 23, 1985[*]

A sub is here. Eddie says, "Teacher looks preppie today [he has on tan slacks, a white shirt, red tie, and dark blue jacket with gold buttons]. I like to see the young teachers preppie. [To me] Isn't he handsome?"

[Assignment on Board]

1. Pg. 63–64, #'s 1–24. *Write Out* each question and what you consider to be the correct answer.

2. Pg. 65, #4.

These kids are remarkably quiet. Some chatter. The substitute says, "Quiet down"; they do so.

The point here is that students do not directly challenge either the pace *or* direction of classroom activities even, with one exception noted above, when a substitute is present. They respond passively, doing what they are told but not consciously doing anything at all. They are quiet, but not engaged. They do homework, but don't *really* do homework. This disengagement coexists with a more positive valuation of education than previous studies have uncovered among white working-class youth, particularly males. The more positive valuation plays itself out, however, largely in terms of student participation in the maintenance of the appearance of order and a willingness to "hand something in" in order to pass courses and be, ultimately, "average" at best.

Although most students note that they wish to go on to college in order to pay bills, live a better life than their parents, stay "off burgers," and so forth, the evidence for this based on their actual applications to post-secondary institutions is somewhat less clear. Although I have no way of tracking who went to which post-secondary school (the school does not have such information), an analysis of where transcripts were sent over the past five years is instructive. Table 2.2 presents the number of colleges applied to; data are broken down by race and sex, except for 1980 when data by race were not available.[15] These data include applications to the community college, but do not include files sent to the local two-year business institute.

A substantial proportion of students did not apply to any college, including the community college. In 1983, 35 percent of white males did not apply to any school and 41 percent did not apply to college in 1985. The figures for minorities and females are even higher.

In point of fact, the overall proportion of students who did not apply to *any* college has gone up in the five-year period under consideration. In 1980, 38.9 percent and 47.1 percent of males and females, respectively, did not apply to college. By 1983 the comparable proportions were 40.7 and 34.7 percent. By 1985, 51.4 and 49.2 percent of males and females, respectively, did not apply to college.

One must be careful here, however, since data coded by race were not available for 1980. Thus, the slight downward trend may be attributable to black students rather than white students applying in lower relative numbers. In the absence of such data for 1980, however, I have no way of testing this proposition.

All this is not to suggest that the number who do apply to tertiary-level institutions is inconsequential. It is, indeed, *very* significant that over 50 percent of white males in 1985 applied to at least one college. This reflects a marked change from previous generations of white working-class students and represents a shift in the college-going population generally. Nevertheless, there is a sense among students that "college" is so important that one *must* attend if one is to have any kind of life at all. Given this, it is important to note that large numbers of students do not even apply, much less actually attend.

Table 2.3 reports the rating of the "best" school applied to by employing Carnegie categories, a standard way of assessing institutional prestige.[16] Only 6 percent of white males in 1983 and 2 percent in 1985

Table 2.2 Freeway students, number of colleges applied to: 1980, 1983, and 1985*

	None	1	2	3	More than 3	Total
1980						
Male	38.9 (70)	28.9 (52)	15.0 (27)	10.0 (18)	7.2 (13)	100.0 (180)
Female	47.1 (73)	29.0 (45)	12.3 (19)	5.8 (9)	5.8 (9)	100.0 (155)
Total	42.7 (143)	29.0 (97)	13.7 (46)	8.1 (27)	6.0 (20)	100.0 (335)
1983						
White						
Male	35.2 (38)	25.0 (27)	17.6 (19)	13.0 (14)	9.3 (10)	100.0 (108)
Female	39.4 (43)	34.0 (37)	14.0 (15)	7.3 (8)	14.7 (6)	100.0 (109)
Total	37.3 (81)	29.5 (64)	15.7 (34)	10.1 (22)	7.4 (16)	100.0 (217)
Black						
Male	46.2 (6)	23.1 (3)	0.0 (0)	23.1 (3)	7.7 (1)	100.0 (13)
Female	30.0 (6)	35.0 (7)	10.0 (2)	10.0 (2)	15.0 (3)	100.0 (20)
Total	38.7 (12)	32.2 (10)	6.5 (2)	16.1 (5)	6.5 (2)	100.0 (31)
1985						
White						
Male	41.2 (42)	25.5 (26)	18.6 (19)	10.8 (11)	3.9 (4)	100.0 (102)
Female	51.8 (59)	21.9 (25)	17.6 (20)	4.4 (5)	4.4 (5)	100.0 (114)
Total	46.8 (101)	23.3 (51)	18.0 (39)	7.4 (16)	4.2 (9)	100.0 (216)
Black						
Male	61.5 (8)	15.4 (2)	15.4 (2)	0 (0)	7.7 (1)	100.0 (13)
Female	46.7 (7)	26.7 (4)	6.7 (1)	13.3 (2)	6.7 (1)	100.0 (15)
Total	53.6 (15)	21.4 (6)	10.7 (3)	7.1 (2)	7.1 (2)	100.0 (28)

*Not including the local two-year business institute.

34

Table 2.3 Freeway students, rating of best school applied to, 1980, 1983 and 1985*

	No School Applied To	Professional & Other	Two Year	Other Liberal	Liberal Arts I	Comprehensive Universities and Colleges	Other Doctoral Granting Institutions	Doctoral Granting Institutions I	Total
1980									
Male	39.4 (71)	1.7 (3)	21.1 (38)	0.6 (1)	0.0 (0)	13.9 (25)	18.9 (34)	4.4 (8)	100.0 (180)
Female	46.2 (72)	0.0 (0)	29.5 (46)	1.3 (2)	1.3 (2)	11.5 (18)	8.9 (14)	1.3 (2)	100.0 (156)
Total	42.6 (143)	0.9 (3)	25.0 (84)	0.9 (3)	0.6 (2)	12.8 (43)	14.3 (48)	3.0 (10)	100.0 (336)
1983									
White									
Male	33.3 (36)	1.9 (2)	17.6 (19)	0.9 (1)	0.0 (0)	15.7 (17)	25.0 (27)	5.6 (6)	100.0 (108)
Female	40.3 (44)	0.0 (0)	25.7 (28)	0.0 (0)	1.8 (2)	11.0 (12)	19.3 (21)	1.8 (2)	100.0 (109)
Total	36.9 (80)	0.9 (2)	21.7 (47)	0.5 (1)	0.9 (2)	13.4 (29)	22.1 (48)	3.7 (9)	100.0 (217)
Black									
Male	46.2 (6)	0.0 (0)	30.8 (4)	0.0 (0)	0.0 (0)	7.7 (1)	15.4 (2)	0.0 (0)	100.0 (13)
Female	30.0 (6)	5.0 (1)	20.0 (4)	0.0 (0)	0.0 (0)	5.0 (5)	20.0 (4)	0.0 (0)	100.0 (20)
Total	36.4 (12)	3.0 (1)	24.2 (8)	0.0 (0)	0.0 (0)	18.2 (6)	18.2 (6)	0.0 (0)	100.0 (33)
1985									
White									
Male	43.1 (44)	2.0 (2)	10.8 (11)	1.0 (1)	0.0 (0)	17.6 (18)	23.5 (24)	2.0 (2)	100.0 (102)
Female	49.1 (56)	1.0 (1)	17.0 (19)	0.0 (0)	1.8 (2)	14.9 (17)	15.8 (18)	0.9 (1)	100.0 (114)
Total	46.3 (100)	1.4 (3)	13.9 (30)	.46 (1)	.93 (2)	16.2 (35)	19.4 (42)	1.4 (3)	100.0 (216)
Black									
Male	61.5 (8)	0.0 (0)	7.7 (1)	0.0 (0)	0.0 (0)	15.4 (2)	15.4 (2)	0.0 (0)	100.0 (13)
Female	46.7 (7)	0.0 (0)	20.0 (3)	0.0 (0)	0.0 (0)	6.7 (1)	20.0 (3)	6.7 (1)	100.0 (15)
Total	53.6 (15)	0.0 (0)	14.3 (4)	0.0 (0)	0.0 (0)	10.7 (3)	17.9 (5)	3.6 (1)	100.0 (28)

*These are calculations based on the Carnegie categories. *The Carnegie Commission on Higher Education. A Classification of Institutions of Higher Education* (Berkeley: The Carnegie Foundation, 1973). Numbers reported here may differ slightly from those reported in table 1.1.

applied to the top schools—those in the Doctoral Granting I category. White males tend to apply more often to college relative to white females and minority males and females, and they tend to do so at better schools. Thus, 25 percent of white male students in 1983 applied to "Other Doctoral Granting Institutions," compared with 19 percent of white females and 18 percent of minorities. In 1985, 24 percent of white males applied to "Other Doctoral Granting Institutions," compared with 16 percent of white females and 18 percent of minorities. Generally speaking, white females and minorities of both sexes tend to apply more frequently to the two-year sector than white males. Again, this does not tell us where the students actually go to school, or even if they go to school, but it does suggest what they consider to be future possibilities.

Given the above, it might be hypothesized that a high proportion of students enter the two-year business institute or the military. Again, transcripts sent to these institutions suggest that this is only partially correct (see table 2.4). In 1985, only 2 percent of white males had transcripts sent to the business institute and 6 percent to the military. Seven percent of white females had transcripts sent to the business institute and less than 1 percent to the military. Again, this does not mean that this proportion of students actually went to these places, only that they availed themselves of the opportunity to do so.

The picture that is emerging here is that approximately one-third of high school students have not had their transcripts sent anywhere, but that, on the other hand, two-thirds have at least thought about some form of further education, whether it be the business institute, the community college, or a four-year institution.

In this light, the emerging contradictory relationship with education can be clarified somewhat. White working-class males resent institutional authority as in previous studies. However, the Freeway students attend school and adhere to the *form* of schooling to a seemingly greater degree than others have suggested. They do not, however, embrace its substance. They copy homework, elaborate the language of "passing," reject the competitive and individualistic ethos of schooling by a willingness to be simply "average," and do not really pay attention in class, even though their expressed valuation of school meanings and culture is more positive than previous studies would have led one to expect. They want to go to college and see some value in education. They also act on this desire to go to college to a certain extent, in that many students at least apply to go on to school. On the other hand, many do not take college entrance examinations which would enable a range of tertiary-

Table 2.4 Percentage of juniors who had transcripts sent to the
military or the two-year business institute—1980, 1983, and 1985

	Two-Year Business Institute	Military
1980		
Male	11.1 (20)	7.2 (13)
Female	23.7 (37)	1.3 (2)
Total	17.0 (57)	4.5 (15)
1983		
White		
Male	3.7 (4)	5.6 (6)
Female	8.3 (9)	1.8 (2)
Total	5.8 (13)	3.7 (8)
Black		
Male	15.4 (2)	7.7 (1)
Female	25.0 (5)	5.0 (1)
Total	21.2 (7)	6.1 (2)
1985		
White		
Male	2.0 (2)	5.9 (6)
Female	7.0 (18)	0.9 (1)
Total	9.3 (20)	3.2 (7)
Black		
Male	7.7 (1)	7.7 (1)
Female	0.0 (0)	20.0 (3)
Total	3.6 (1)	14.2 (4)

level choices, and many do not apply to college, even the two-year
sector, for which one does not need to take the entrance examinations.
They are not, then, necessarily behaving in terms of their own positive
expression; there is some apparent conflict operating within the emerging
collective identity regarding the value of schooling. The fact is that an
adherence to the form will *not* enable these students to pursue the type
of college education that will be necessary for them to scale the class
structure.

This emerging contradictory relationship with schooling is more reminiscent of the black underclass than the white working class in the United
States, although the contradiction is far more exaggerated among poor
blacks at the moment and takes a very different form from that outlined
here. Poor blacks, for example, do not adhere to the form of schooling
as is the case in Freeway. The pattern detailed here characterizes both

males and females (I have provided data for both white females and minority students so as to enable comparisons), but it is in the emerging white-male identity where these contradictions are beginning to be most apparent. It is also the case that it is males who have been consistently and overtly negative in terms of both attitude and behavior regarding schooling in the past, thus rendering these current tensions more striking.

In some ways, the contradictory attitude toward schooling is reminiscent of Richard Sennett and Jonathan Cobb's observation a number of years ago that the white working class harbors a contradictory code of respect toward education to begin with.[17] On the one hand, an educated person commands respect from anyone and is, therefore, to be emulated. On the other hand, there is a sense that the educated do not do *real* work; they push papers and, as many of Sennett and Cobb's respondents note, even cheat. There is a revulsion against the work of educated people at the same time that there is a respect for the educated because they seem more internally developed than the "working man." Sennett and Cobb note,

A workingman looks at the privileges high culture bestows in much the same light as does Ortega y Gasset or William Pfaff—that high culture permits a life in which material need can be transcended by a higher form of self-control; he looks at the claims of intellectual privilege, however, with the same jaundiced eyes as does Sartre.[18]

The students' emerging contradictory attitude regarding education does, to some extent, reflect Sennett and Cobb's observation about the class in general. However, it must be pointed out that Sennett and Cobb interviewed adults, not youth, and that the contradictory code of respect toward schooling noted by Sennett and Cobb emerged, according to the respondents, in working-class adults *after* they entered the work force and experienced the brutality and alienation of their jobs at first hand. Willis notes the same change when he suggests that schooling paradoxically comes to be perceived as a means of liberation *after* the lads enter the work force; what had been considered total oppression came to be seen as the means to salvation. What is interesting in the Freeway study is that this contradictory code of respect is emerging *while the students are still in school,* not, as in previous studies, after they enter the work force. Again, the early adoption of this contradictory code, albeit in a different form, is more reminiscent of the black underclass in America than the white working class.

Patriarchal relations

A second element of identity noted by previous investigators of the white working class is that of sexism. The most articulate on this point is Willis, but other investigators have noted this theme as well. Willis argues that male white working-class youth identity is formed at least partially in reaction to that of the ideologically constructed identity of females. For example, mental labor is not only less valued than manual labor, but it is less valued *because* it is seen as feminine. This encourages patriarchal relations in the sense of separate spheres for males and females, the male sphere being superior. The lads also impose upon girlfriends an ideology of domesticity, "the patterns of homely and subcultural capacity and incapacity," all of which stress the restricted role of women.[19] The very cultural affirmation of the male self, and the particular form of the constructed female "other," therefore, affirms patriarchal relations.

In terms of affirmation of male supremacy, Freeway males exhibit the same virulent sexism uncovered in previous studies. This is particularly striking, as I will suggest in the next chapter, in light of the emerging identity of females in Freeway. One or two boys seem to exist slightly outside of these boundaries, but basically white working-class males affirm a rather virulent form of assumed male superiority which involves the constructed identity of female not only as "other," but also as "less than" and, therefore, subject to male control. Discussions with males indicate that the vast majority speak of future wives and families in highly controlling and patriarchal terms. This, as I note above, contrasts sharply with the current sentiments of females.

LW: You say you want more kids than your parents have. How many kids do you want?

Bob: Five.

LW: Who's going to take care of these kids?

Bob: My wife, hopefully. Unless she's working, too (. . .) If she wants to work, we'd figure something out.

	Day-care center, something like that. I'd prefer if she didn't want to. I'd like to have her at home.
LW:	Why?
Bob:	I think it's up to the mother to do it [raise children; take care of the home]. I wouldn't want to have a baby-sitter raising my kids. Like, I think the principles should be taught by the parents, not by some baby-sitter.

. . .

LW:	How about your life ten years from now; what do you think you'll be doing?
Rob:	Probably be married. Couple of kids.
LW:	(. . .) Do you think your wife will work?
Rob:	Hopefully she won't have to, 'cause I'll make enough money.
LW:	Would you rather she didn't work?
Rob:	Naw [Yes, I'd rather she didn't work].
LW:	Women shouldn't work?
Rob:	Housework.

. . .

Jim:	Yes, I'd like to get married, like to get myself a nice house, with kids.
LW:	(. . .) Who is going to be taking care of those kids?
Jim:	Depends how rich I am. If I'm making a good salary, I assume that the wife, if she wanted to, would stay home and tend to the kids. If there was ever a chance when she wanted to go someplace, fine, I'd watch the kids. Nothing wrong with that. Equal responsibility because when you were consummating the marriage it was equal responsibility.
LW:	So, you're willing to assume it?
Jim:	Up to a certain point . . . Like if she says I'm going to go out and get a job and you take care of the kids, "You draw all day" [he wants to be a commercial artist]. "So, I draw; that's what's been supporting us for so many years." I mean, if she starts dictating to

me (. . .), there has to be a good discussion about the responsibilities.

(. . .) When both parents work, it's been proven that the amount of education they learn, it goes down the tubes, or they get involved in drugs. Half the kids who have drug problems, both of their parents work. If they are doing terribly in school, their parents work.

. . .

LW: When you get married, what will your wife be doing?

Lanny: Well, before we had any kids, she'd be working; but if we had kids, she wouldn't work; she'd be staying home, taking care of the kids.

. . .

Seth: I wouldn't mind my wife working as far as secretarial work or something like that. Whatever she wanted to do and she pursued as a career. If there was children around, I'd like her to be at home, so I'd like my job to compensate for just me working and my wife being at home.

. . .

LW: Do you think your wife would want to work?

Sam: I wouldn't want her to work.

. . .

LW: Let's say you did get married and have children, and your wife wanted to work.

Bill: It all depends on if I had a good job. If the financial situation is bad and she had to go to work, [then] she had to go to work.

LW: And if you got a good job?

Bill: She'd probably be a regular woman.

LW: Staying at home? Why is that a good thing?

Bill: I don't know if it's a good thing, but it'd probably be the normal thing.

Without question, most of the boys are envisioning family life in highly male-dominant terms. They see the possibility that their wives

41

might work, but only out of "necessity," or, more likely, before children are born. They wish to see their own income sufficient to "support" a family; they expect to earn the "family wage," thus enabling their wives to assume the "normal" role of taking care of the home and children. Male students state that they would "help when they could," but they see children as basically the woman's responsibility and they intend for their wives to be at home in a "regular" womanly fashion.

Only a handful of boys constructed a future other than that above. Significantly, only one boy constructed a future in which his wife *should* work, although he does not talk about children. A few boys reflect the sentiment that marriage is a "ball and chain," and one boy said the high divorce rate makes marriage less than attractive. Both these latter themes are elaborated by the girls, as I will argue in chapter 3.

LW: What kind of person do you want to marry?

Vern: Someone who is fairly good-looking, but not too good-looking so she'd be out, with other people screwing her up. Someone who don't mind what I'm doing, let me go out with the guys. I won't mind if she goes out with the girls either. I want her to have a job so she ain't home all the time. 'Cause a woman goes bonkers if she's at home all day. Give her a job and let her get out of the house.

(. . .) People tended to get married as soon as they got out of school, not as soon as, but a couple of years after. I think people nowadays don't want to get married until twenty, thirty.

LW: And that's because of what?

Vern: They've seen too many divorces.

It is noteworthy that Vern is the only boy to discuss divorce as an impediment to marriage. Almost every girl interviewed discusses divorce, and it is a topic of conversation within all female groupings. Despite Vern's relatively more open-minded attitude toward females, it is significant that he still envisions himself "allowing" his wife to work, and sees his role as one of controlling her time and space. He does not, for example, want her to be "too good-looking" because then she would be out, with "other people screwing her up." He also notes that he "does not mind" her going "out with the girls," and that he wants "her to have a job so she ain't home all the time."

The boy below expresses the sentiment that marriage is a "ball and chain," and that he, therefore, wants no part of it. Only a couple of boys expressed a similar sentiment or elaborated the theme of "freedom" associated with being single. Again, this is unlike the girls.

Tom: I don't want to get married; I don't want to have children. I want to be pretty much free. If I settle down with someone, it won't be through marriage.

LW: Why not?

Tom: Marriage is a ball and chain. Then marital problems come up, financial problems, whatever. I don't really want to get involved in the intense kind of problems between you and a spouse.
(. . .) To me it's a joke.

LW: Tell me why you think that.

Tom: Well, I see a lot of people. I look at my father and mother. They don't get along, really.[20]

The vast majority of boys at Freeway High intend to set up homes in which they exert control over their wives—in which they go out to work and their wives stay at home. Only a few question the institution of marriage, and only one begins to question a fundamental premise of patriarchy—that women's place is in the home and men's place is in the public sphere. As noted above, however, even this one boy sees himself largely controlling the actions of his wife. Central to the boys' identity, then, is the establishment of male dominance in the home/family sphere as well as in the paid labor force.

Male supremacy as a key element of identity is borne out by classroom observations where boys stated similar positions as those above. Girls, although they challenge this position rather seriously on one level (see chapter 3), do *not* tend to speak out against the boys in class, leaving the male-envisioned future largely unchallenged, at least verbally in the public arena. When the male vision is challenged, it is done so by male teachers, although not always for the most progressive of reasons. I will explore more fully the role of the school in encouraging male and female identities in chapter 4.

Social Studies, December 3, 1985*

Mr. _____: "Why should women be educated?" A lot of

chatter; many males saying they shouldn't be, or perhaps that they should be for secretarial science.

Mr. _____: "Look, you [the women] are better equipped to teach the children; you are better able to communicate with your husband if you are an educated woman. Also, today not everybody gets married. The better the education, the better the opportunity for a good job for *both* men and women."

Mr. _____: "Women today probably need education more, because today in broken marriages and divorces, the women normally have the children."

Ben: "But men have to pay child support—a hundred dollars a week . . ."

Mr. _____: "Hey, you talk to many women, they don't get a penny from their former husbands. What about the guy who just got laid off from the steel plant—how are you going to pay a hundred dollars a week?"

Ben talked to Mr. _____ after class and said his dad sends one hundred and twenty dollars a week for child support. Mr. _____ says, "Great, but isn't it true that your mom has to wait for checks; sometimes some bounce; so isn't it better that she has her own job?" Ben says [rather sheepishly], "She works, too."

. . .

*Social Studies, December 4, 1985**

Mr. _____: We were talking yesterday about whether it was a waste of time to educate women and we con-cluded that it wasn't. I concluded that it wasn't, and you agree if you want to get the right mark.

Jim: Who asked you?

. . .

*Social Studies, December 12, 1985**

[P. 103. of the text] Mr. _____ goes over the multiple-choice questions and asks students to answer.

Mr. _____:	"Question: Women are basically unwilling to assume positions in the business world. Agree or disagree?"
Sam:	"Agree."
Mr. _____:	"Why?"
Sam:	"Because women want to raise children and get married."
Mr. _____:	"All women?"
Sam:	"No, but most.
Mr. _____:	"Anyone disagree?"

No disagreement

. . .

No doubt the "correct" answer to the question was "disagree," but there was no further discussion.

The point, again, is that males envision a future in which they inhabit the public sphere, and women the private. Men also expect to exert control over their wives in the private sphere. They intend to earn the "family wage," in return to which women will take care of the home and children. Although females, as I will show in the next chapter, challenge this in their own envisioned future, they tend *not* to challenge it directly in the classroom. This follows logically from the individualistic nature of the challenge to begin with, as I will argue in later chapters. The affirmation of male superiority and envisioned control over women within white male working-class youth identity remains, therefore, largely intact in the public arena of the school.

Racism

Among boys, there is also evidence of racism within the school, as was the case in earlier studies of white working-class youth.[21] Freeway is a divided town, even though it is small, and blacks and a small number of Arabs and Hispanics live largely on one side of the "tracks," and whites on the other, although there are whites living in a certain section of the predominantly minority side. Virtually no minorities live in the white area, which is not true of larger American cities where one finds areas of considerable mix. Most of the blacks live in a large public housing project, located near the old steel plant. Most project residents receive welfare and have done so for a number of years. Much of the expressed racism plays itself out around "access" to females, and, to some extent drug use, as the examples below suggest.

> *Jim:*   The minorities are really bad into drugs. You're talking everything. Anything you want, you get from them. A prime example, the _____ ward of Freeway; about twenty years ago the _____ ward was predominantly white, my grandfather used to live there. Then Italians, Polish, the Irish people, everything was fine. The houses were maintained; there was a good standard of living (. . .).
>
>   (. . .) The blacks brought drugs. I'm not saying white people didn't have drugs; they had drugs, but to a certain extent. But drugs were like a social thing. But now you go down to the _____ ward; it's amazing; it's a ghetto. Some of the houses are okay. They try to keep them up. Most of the homes are really, really terrible. They throw garbage on the front lawn; it's sickening. You talk to people [surrounding suburbs]. Anywhere you talk to people, they tend to think the majority of our school is black. They think you hang with black people, listen to black music.
>
>   (. . .) A few of them [blacks] are starting to go into the _____ ward now [the white side], so they're moving around. My parents will be around there when that happens, but I'd like to be out of there.
>
>   . . .
>
> *LW:*   There's no fighting and stuff here [school], is there?
>
> *Clint:*   Yeah, a lot between blacks and whites.
>
> *LW:*   Who starts them?
>
> *Clint:*   Blacks.
>
> *LW:*   Do blacks and whites hang out in the same place?
>
> *Clint:*   Some do; [the blacks] live on the other side of town.
>
>   (. . .) A lot of it [fights] starts with blacks messing with white girls. That's how a lot of them start. Even

if they [white guys] don't know the white girl, they don't like to see . . .

LW: How do you feel about that yourself?

Clint: I don't like it. If I catch them [blacks] near my sister, they'll get it. I don't like to see it like that. Most of them [my friends] see it that way [the same way he does].

LW: Do you think the girls encourage the attentions of these black guys?

Clint: Naw. I think the blacks just make themselves at home. They welcome themselves in.

LW: How about the other way around? White guys and black girls?

Clint: There's a few that do. There's people that I know of, but no one I hang around with. I don't know many white kids that date black girls.

. . .

Bill: Like my brother, he's in ninth grade. He's in trouble all the time. Last year he got jumped in school . . . About his girlfriend. He don't like blacks. They come up to her and go, "Nice ass," and all that shit. My brother don't like that when they call her "nice ass" and stuff like that. He got suspended for saying "fucking nigger"; but it's all right for a black guy to go up to whites and say stuff like that ["nice ass"].

(. . .) Sometimes the principals aren't doing their job. Like when my brother told [the assistant principal] that something is going to happen, Mr. _____ just said, "Leave it alone, just turn your head."

(. . .) Like they [administrators] don't know when fights start in this school. Like there's this one guy's kid sister, a nigger [correction]—a black guy—grabbed her ass. He hit him a couple of times. Did the principal know about it? No!

LW: What if a white guy did that [grabbed the girl's ass]?

Bill: He'd probably have punched him. But a lot of it's 'cause they're black.

Racial tension does exist within the school, and it reflects tension within the community and the society as a whole. It is clear that white boys attribute much of it to blacks hustling white girls. This is the male perception, but I heard no such comment from any female in the school. White males view white females as *their* property and resent black males speaking to them in, at times, crude terms. However, it must be noted that white boys themselves might say "nice ass" to white girls, and so forth. It is the fact that *black males* do it, and not that males do it, that is *most* offensive to white males. I never saw a white male go to the defense of a white female if she were being harassed by another white male. It is only when the male is black that their apparently protectionist tendencies surface, indicating a deep racism which comes out over girls, in particular. White girls are considered "property" by white boys, as the above section on sexism suggests, and they resent black intrusion onto *their* property. White males are intending to earn the "family wage," thus enabling them to establish male-dominant homes. This gives them, in their estimation, certain *rights* to white females, rights that black males do not have. Not one girl voiced a complaint in this area. This is not to say that females are not racist, but that it is not a central element of their identity in the same way as it is for boys at this age. It is possible that such racism emerges among females later in life when they feel they must "protect" their children. Although there have been no studies to suggest this, one might speculate that this is the case.

Observational data support the notion of racism among white youth. This is mainly directed toward blacks, although, as the excerpts below indicate, racism surfaces with respect to Arabs as well. There is a small population of Yemenites who emigrated to Freeway to work in the steel mills, and it is this group that is targeted to some extent also.[22]

Social Studies, November 26, 1986[*]

Sam: Hey, Abdul, did you come from Arabia?

Abdul: Yeah.

Sam: How did you get here?

Abdul: I walked.

Sam: No, seriously, how'd you get here?

Abdul: Boat.

Sam: Where'd you come from?

Abdul: Saudi Arabia.

Sam: We don't want you. Why don't you go back.

[no comment]

Terry: What city did you come from?

Abdul: Yemen, if *you* ever heard of it.

. . .

Social Studies, December 11, 1986*

Ed: Do you party, Nabil?

Nabil: Yeah.

Paul: Nabil, the only thing you know how to play is polo on camels.

[Nabil ignores]

. . .

English, October 2*

LW: [To Terry, who was hit by a car two days ago]. How are you?

Terry: Look at me [sic] face. Ain't it cool? [He was all scraped up].

LW: What happened?

Terry: Some stupid camel jockey ran me over in a big white car. Arabian dude.

Most of the virulent racism is directed toward blacks, however. The word "nigger" flows freely from the lips of white males and they treat black females in the same way, if not worse, than they say black males treat white females.

At the lunch table, February 21, 1986*
[discussion with Craig Centrie, research assistant]

Pete: Why is it [your leather bag] so big?

Mike: So he can carry lots of stuff.

CC: Yes, I bought it because my passport would fit in it.

Pete: Passport! Wow—where are you from?

CC: Well, I'm American now, but you need one to travel.

Pete: Can I see? [He pulls out his passport; everyone looks].

Mike: This is my first time to ever see one. What are all these stamps?

CC: Those are admissions stamps so [you] can get in and out of countries.

Mike: Look, Pete, N-I-G-E-R-I-A [pronounced Niggeria]. Yolanda [a black female] should go there. [everyone laughs]

Pete: (. . .) [Did you see any] crocodile-eating niggers? [laughter]

. . .

In the lunchroom, January 21, 1986*

Students [all white males at the table] joke about cafeteria food. They then begin to talk about Martin Luther King Day.

Dave: "I have a wet dream—about little white boys and little black girls." [laughter]

. . .

In the lunchroom, March 7, 1986*

Once again, in lunch, everyone complains about the food. Vern asked about a party he heard about. Everyone knew about it, but it wasn't clear where it would be. A kid walked past the table [of white boys].

Clint: "That's the motherfucker. I'll whop his ass." The entire table goes "ou' ou' ou'."

CC: "What happened with those tickets, Pete?" [some dance tickets had been stolen].

Pete: "Nothing, but I'm pissed off at that nigger that blamed me."

Pete forgot how loud he was speaking and looked toward Yolanda [a black female] to see if she reacted. But she hadn't heard the remark.

. . .

At the lunch table, February 12, 1986*

Mike: That nigger makes me sick.

Pete: Who?

Mike: You know, Yolanda.

Pete: She's just right for you, man.

Mike: Not me, maybe Clint.

. . .

At the lunch table, February 12, 1986*

About two minutes later, Darcy [a black female] calls me [CC] over. "What's your name?"

CC: Craig; what's yours?

Darcy: It's Darcy. Clint told me a lie. He said your name was Joe. Why don't you come to a party at Yolanda's house tonight?

Yolanda: Why don't you just tell him you want him to come. [everyone laughs]

Clint: Well, *all right,* they want you!

Pete: What do you think of Yolanda?

CC: She's a nice girl. What do you think?

Pete: She's a stuck-up nigger. Be sure to write that down.

. . .

[A group of males talk about themselves.] "We like to party all the time and get high!" [They call themselves "freaks" and "heads."] [about blacks] "They are a group unto themselves. They are all bullshitters."

. . .

At the lunch table, February 12, 1986*

Much of the time, students discussed the food. Vern talked about the Valentine's Day dance and began discussing getting stoned before the dance.

CC: "Do you guys drink at the dance, too?"

Pete: "No, I don't know what they would do to us [everyone laughs]. There probably wouldn't be any more dances.

Yolanda and friends walk in. Yolanda and a friend were wearing exactly the same outfit.

Clint: "What are you two—the fucking Gold Dust Twins?"

Yolanda: "Shut the fuck up, 'boy' " [everyone laughs].
Quietly, Pete says, "Craig, they are nasty."

CC: "What do you mean?"

Pete: "You don't understand black people. They're yeach.
They smell funny and they [got] hair under their
arms."

Clint, Pete, Mike, and Jack all make noises to denote disgust.

The males spend a great deal of time exhibiting disgust for racial minorities, and at the same time, asserting a protective stance over white females vis-à-vis black males. They differentiate themselves from black males and females in different ways, however. Black males are treated with anger for invading *their* property [white girls]. Black females, on the other hand, are treated with simple disgust. Both are seen and interacted with largely in the sexual realm, however, albeit for different reasons and in different ways.

It is also significant that white males elaborated upon sex largely in relation to blacks. Certainly their own identity is bound up with sexuality, but this sexuality comes through most vehemently and consistently in relation to black males and females. They use sexuality as a means of "trashing" black males and females, and setting themselves up as "different from" them in the sexual realm. Thus black sexual behavior, both male and female, is seen as being inappropriate—unlike their own. While sexuality is certainly elaborated upon in relation to white girls (and obviously encoded in discussions about children), such discussions do not exhibit the same ugliness as those involving blacks and the constructed sexuality of blacks. It is significant, for example, that when a group of white males was discussing Martin Luther King Day they said, "I have a wet dream—'bout little white boys and little black girls." It is even more significant that Pete said, "You don't understand black people. They're yeach. They smell funny and they [got] hair under their arms." Blacks are talked about largely in terms of sexuality, and sexuality is talked about to a great extent in terms of blacks. Blacks are used to demonstrate the boundaries of acceptable sexual behavior (in that black behavior is unacceptable) and provide a means of enabling whites to set themselves up as "better than" (more responsible, less dirty, and so forth) in this area. Although white boys do say, as I noted above, "nice ass" to white girls, they do not see this as contradictory to their embedded attitudes toward black sexuality given that they feel that white girls are their property to begin with. Black sexuality is simply negative; their own sexuality is, in turn, seen as positive. *In the final analysis, white males elaborate an identity in relation to the ideologically constructed identity of both blacks and females.* In so doing, they set themselves up as "other than" and "better than" each group.

I have described in this chapter the configuration of emerging white-male identity at Freeway High. Certain elements of this identity are similar to those noted by previous investigators. In another sense, however, Freeway males are different in that they exhibit a more contradictory relationship with schooling and school knowledge and culture than others have suggested. In this sense, they are moving toward a relationship with school knowledge and culture more in congruence with the American black underclass. In the next chapter I will explore the emerging identity of females which, as I will argue, is on a collision course with that of males.

3
Freeway Females

"Marriage was invented by somebody who was lucky if they
lived to be twenty without being bit by a dinosaur."
Suzanne, Grade 11

In chapter 2, I explored male identity at Freeway. In this chapter, I
focus on emerging female identity. I analyze here only those elements
that emerged as exceptionally significant in the ethnography. In other
words, I do not intend to do a point-counterpoint analysis with males.
That would be allowing, and indeed encouraging, the identity terrain of
males to be dominant by asking the question, how do females compare
with males? Since that is not my intention, I focus on elements that may
or may not strictly parallel those for boys.

The data suggest that female identity is moving in a more emancipatory
direction than male identity. Specifically, females exhibit what might
be called a *critical moment of critique* of male dominance and patriarchy.
This incipient critique, however, is not, at the moment, reflective of a
collective struggle around the issue of gender. Rather, these girls tend
to pose individualistic/private solutions to their felt notions that the old
forms of male dominance will both not work for them and are, at the
same time, somewhat unjust.

I will suggest here that female identity emerges in relation to that of
constructed male identity. As in the last chapter, it is this relational
aspect of identity formation that will be highlighted. It is significant that
white-female identity is *not* formed in relation to that of constructed
black identity as is the case for boys. I will pursue this point later.

Previous studies suggest that working-class high-school females elaborate, at the level of their own identity, a private/public dichotomy that
emphasizes the centrality of the private and marginalizes the public.
During adolescence, home/family life assumes a central position for

girls and wage labor a secondary position. As many studies have shown, working-class girls elaborate what Angela McRobbie has called an "ideology of romance," constructing a gender identity that serves, ultimately, to encourage woman's second-class status in both the home and workplace. Studies of McRobbie and Linda Valli, in particular, have been important in terms of our understanding of the way in which these processes work upon and through the identity of young women.[1]

This gender identity has serious implications for the position of women in both the family and the workplace in the sense that it represents parameters within which struggles will take place. By defining domestic labor as primary, women reinforce what can be called the Domestic Code, under which home or family becomes defined as women's place  and a public sphere of power and work as men's place. The reality, of course, is that generations of working-class women have labored in the public sphere, and that labor also takes place in the home, albeit unpaid. Yet, as Karen Brodkin Sacks point out, "The Domestic Code has been a ruling set of concepts in that it did not have to do consistent battle with counterconcepts. It has also been a ruling concept in the sense that it "explained" an unbroken agreement among capitalists, public policymakers, and later, much of organized labor, that adequate pay for women was roughly 60 percent of what was adequate for men and need be nowhere adequate to allow a woman to support a family or herself."[2] It was strongly related, then, to the notion of the "family wage."

The Domestic Code is being challenged on a number of fronts, but it is not my intention to elaborate on these challenges here. What I am concerned with here is the extent to which Freeway females elaborate an identity that is congruent with that noted in earlier studies.[3]

Work outside the home

The most striking point about female identity at Freeway High is that there is, unlike the case in numerous previous studies, little evidence of a marginalized wage labor identity. These girls have, in fact, made the obtaining of wage labor a *primary* rather than a secondary goal. Almost without exception the girls desire to continue their education, and they are clear that they intend to do so in order to get their own life in order. It is worth noting that this is reminiscent of the voices of black females in studies of romance, marriage, and the future.[4]

(handwritten marginal notes:) only one girl mentioned marriage first / *men → respond* / *women*

The girls below exemplify this point. It is noteworthy that only *one* girl interviewed mentioned marriage and a family first when talking about what they wish to do after high school. All the rest of the students stressed jobs or "careers," and college or some form of further education was specifically discussed. Only when I actually inquired about a family did most of the girls mention this at all. I will return to this point in the next section. This is in striking contrast to the boys, where the establishment of an envisioned male-dominant family was foremost on their minds. This reflects an interesting inversion of the past: High-school boys in Freeway now envision family life first, whereas girls focus first on the public sphere.

The first set of interviews below details the responses of girls in the "advanced" curriculum. Students in this group generally want to attend a four-year college and girls talk in terms of actual careers, often nontraditional ones. Girls in the "regular classes" also talk about continuing their education after high school, but generally focus on the two-year college, business institutes, or schools for hairdressing. Both groups of girls, however, stress job or "career" rather than a family, although the form of work desired tends to differ.

Judy, Rhonda, Jennifer, Jessica, and Liz are members of the advanced class. With the exception of Rhonda, who wants to become a medical technician, all intend to pursue careers that demand at least a four-year college degree. Some, like Jennifer, intend to go to graduate school. It must be clear that the excerpts below represent responses to a question about post–high-school plans.

Judy:	I'm thinking of [State University] for electrical engineering. I know I'm going to go into that.
LW:	How did you pick electrical engineering?
Judy:	'Cause my brother is an electrical engineer . . . He works for General Electric. He has a BA.

. . .

Rhonda:	[I'll] probably go into medicine.
LW:	Any particular area?
Rhonda:	Medical technician, maybe.
LW:	Would you consider being a nurse or doctor?
Rhonda:	I considered being a nurse. But with all the strikes and them saying they're underpaid. I read a lot about the job.

. . .

Jennifer: [I want] to go to college but I'm not sure where. And I want to go into psychology, I think. (. . .)I'd love to be a psychiatrist but I don't think I'll ever make it through medical school. So I was talking with a guidance counselor and she said you could get a Ph.D. in psychology and there are a lot of good jobs that go along with that. (. . .)I think I'm forced [to go to college]. I don't think I have a choice.

. . .

Jessica: My mother wants me to be in engineering like my brother 'cause he's so successful (. . .) I have an interest with the behavior of marine animals. Which is kind of stupid 'cause we don't live anywhere near an ocean, so I was thinking of going to Florida State. My parents don't want me to go to any other school but [State University] so I haven't brought this up yet. I figure we can wait awhile.

. . .

LW: What are you going to do when you leave high school?

Liz: College.

LW: Do you know which college?

Liz: I'm thinking of [State University] in physical therapy.

. . .

Aside from Jennifer, whose father is head of the chemistry lab at a local hospital, these girls are not from professional families.[5] They are, on the contrary, largely the daughters of industrial laborers and they are thinking of obtaining a four-year college education and entering some type of career. It is noteworthy that two of these girls are being encouraged by their families to go into engineering, one of the most nontraditional fields for women.[6] It might be hypothesized that as working-class individuals obtain professional positions, they are disproportionately in areas such as engineering, which are seen as having a direct relation to hands-on laboring processes. Such jobs, it might be argued, would enable working-class persons to become educated and still do "real" work, thus bypassing, to some extent, the contradictory code of respect toward education noted in chapter 2. Obviously I cannot prove this, but it is of interest that two girls are being encouraged by their families to pursue this end.[7]

Although it is the case that more than 50 percent of graduating high-school seniors currently go on for advanced study directly from high school, the data presented above cannot be seen as *simply* reflective of overall trends regarding college attendance.[8] Scholars who use national data on college trends very often make the error of combining enrollment in all four-year schools with that of enrollment in the community college and other tertiary-level institutions. In other words, although it has been suggested that 50 percent of students are now in college, we do not necessarily know *which* colleges they are in, nor do we know who goes where. In fact, analyses such as that of Jerome Karabel suggest that the elite sector of the tertiary-level institutions is dominated overwhelmingly by students of the middle class and above, whereas the community college sector is dominated by the working class.[9] Michael Olivas makes a similar argument with respect to people of color and attendance at the community college.[10] It is, therefore, not at all inconsequential that the Freeway girls in the advanced class are planning on having careers and that these careers involve the pursuit of four-year degrees, often in relatively prestigious state institutions. When considered in light of data on home/family identity which I will present in the next section, it becomes even clearer that this cannot be seen as simply an example of education inflation.

Statements of girls in the accelerated class can be contrasted with those of girls in the "regular" classes below. They too, are, without exception, planning to pursue jobs, although most are those associated with two-year colleges or business institutes. It must also be pointed out that the girls below wish to pursue jobs largely in the sex-segregated occupational ghettos.

> *Lorna:* Well, I go to [a cooperative vocational education program] for food service and I think I want to be a caterer. I don't want to be sitting down all the time. I like to be on my feet moving. [She does not wish to go into business even though her shorthand teacher says she has "potential."] I like to cook and

stuff [but] you get to do everything, not just stay in the kitchen.

(. . .)[Suburban Community College] has got a two-year course and then if I want to, I can transfer my credits and stuff and go to a four-year college. My mother's got a friend, she teaches food service in a college, and she was telling me about it. Like what to do and stuff.

. . .

Loretta: [I want to go to] [State University].

LW: (. . .) When you get out of [State University], what do you hope to do?

Loretta: Become a lawyer, have a family, I guess, but not until I graduate from college (. . .) A lot of my friends want to go to college.

. . .

Susan: I'll go to [the community college]. I don't want to go four years to school. I can just go two years and become a registered nurse and get a job. I volunteer at [the local hospital] so I'm hoping to have a foot in the door when it comes time for a job.

. . .

LW: When you leave high school, what do you want to do?

Carol: A lot of things. I do want to go to college for fashion design. I don't know how good I'll do.

LW: Where do you want to go?

Carol: I haven't thought about it. But as soon as I graduate [from high school] I want to get my _____ State license [for hairdressing] and get a job, and then save money so that I have money when I want it. (. . .) I want to have my own salon but first of all, I want to start off in somebody else's salon so I get the experience.

. . .

Valerie: I didn't really think I was going to go to college, unless business courses. I'm going to try for a job

[after high school] and if I can get a good job out of
it, then I won't go to college. If it requires college
training, then I'm going to go.

LW: What kind of job?

Valerie: Something with word processing.

. . .

Avis: I want to [go to] college around here . . . They
[business institute] have medical secretary; they have
a lot of business stuff and that will help out. And
they could get you a job. (. . .)

LW: What do you think you'll be doing five years from
now?

Avis: Hopefully working. A medical secretary or
something.

. . .

Gloria: [I'll probably] go to [State University] or [State Col-
lege]. Become a registered nurse specializing in pediatrics.

With the exception of Loretta and Gloria, all the girls in the nonadvanced curriculum wish to attend two-year colleges, business institutes,
or schools for hairdressing. In addition, most are thinking in terms of
sex-segregated occupations. Avis and Valerie are thinking of being
secretaries; Carol wants to be a hairdresser; Lorna, a food-service
workers; and Susan and Gloria, nurses. This is in contrast with the girls
in the advanced curriculum, where there appears to be some desire to
break out of these ghettos.

Analysis of where transcripts are sent (see chapter 2) suggests somewhat more congruence for girls than boys in terms of expressed desires
and actual school applications. Eight percent and 7 percent of 1983
and 1985 graduates, respectively, had transcripts sent to the business
institute, and the rating of the best school applied to for 26 percent and
17 percent of 1983 and 1985 graduates, respectively, was the community
college.

It still must be emphasized, however, that 32 percent and 42 percent
of girls in 1983 and 1985 did not apply to any institution of higher
education, despite the fact that the primacy of a job/career is emerging
within their identity. Thus, the same contradictory tendencies emerge to

some extent for girls as for boys, although many of the jobs girls are envisioning for themselves do not necessarily require further education. To establish a patriarchal family with one wage earner bringing in the "family wage" such as the boys are envisioning would take a great deal of money—money that, for the most part, could only be obtained with a high level of education and, even then, such an income is hardly assured.[11] This makes the fact that boys tend to adhere to only the bare form of schooling that much more striking, given the current economy.

This does not negate, however, the fact that girls, too, exhibit a somewhat contradictory relationship with schooling. They, too, accept and reject school knowledge and culture at one and the same time, although not to the degree boys do. Girls also copy homework and they, like boys, engage in the form rather than the substance of schooling. Two key points emerge, however, with respect to gender and this contradictory relationship with schooling. As noted above, girls are not envisioning for themselves the support of entire families which would certainly necessitate higher education given that well-paying male laboring jobs are gone. Although such jobs are not guaranteed if higher education is obtained, it is clearly at least a necessary condition for such jobs. Second, girls do not evidence resentment toward institutional authority as boys do. They have not done so in previous studies and they do so only to a small degree in Freeway. The acting on resentment of institutional authority is a distinctly male purview, tied at least theoretically to the historic struggle between capital and labor, and throws into sharp relief the more positive male attitudes toward schooling expressed in Freeway than in previous studies of working-class boys. Since girls do not have this same expressed resentment to begin with, the nature of their own emerging contradictory relationship with school knowledge and culture is not as apparent.

Indeed, in contrast to boys as discussed in chapter 2 where resentment is still deeply embedded within their identity, there were only two instances during the year when girls articulated resentment toward authority, as follows:

Chris: I want to wear shorts [in school]. The guys have to wear pants (. . .) No halters [for girls]. If you have something that shows your shoulders, you have to put a jacket on (. . .) They [institutional authorities] complain about the hair—the spiked hair, they said it was disruptive to the school.

. . .

LW: If you could change anything at Freeway High, what would you change?

Carol: A lot of things (. . .) The principals, I think. I don't think they're fair. Mr. _____ [the assistant principal].` Like, if you're late for school. Me and my sister were late two minutes for school and we have to sit in his office the whole period. You miss a whole class.

(. . .) At lunch, he [the assistant principal] treats us like we're stupid or we don't know what we're doing, or we're just, I don't know how to put it. He doesn't give anybody a fair chance. This one table of boys all has to sit and face the window (. . .)

He comes up every day to our table and calls us pigs. There might be garbage on the floor, not just from us, but he still calls us that name. And we're all sitting there going "oink, oink, oink." One day the whole table was sitting there going like that and he didn't know what to do. He acts like we're in prison.

Lunch is a free period and everyone goes in there to talk to each other. It's like a social hour, (. . .) He split our whole table up. He told us we couldn't sit at that table anymore. We went to a different table and he'd come to our table every day and say there's too many people at our table.

(. . .)Like, if you're standing by a door with your jacket on, he'll say, "Get out of here." Or he'll give you a choice between going home or detention for two days.

The girls do not resent authority in the same way that the boys do. Few express any sort of resentment at all, unlike boys, where such resentment of authority is enmeshed within their very identity and, it can be argued, is reflective of historic struggles in an industrial economy.

The supposedly male pattern of going into the armed forces (although data in chapter 2 suggests that this is less the case for males than one might imagine), has little appeal for girls, despite the fact that the armed forces have opened up for women, at least in terms of access. Chris, below, is the only white female who indicates a desire to go in this direction. She gives lip service to attending college, but it is clear that she is not truly interested in pursuing this option.

> *Chris:* I either want to go to college or go in the Air Force (. . .) The Air Force because they say it's the best education around if you want to go into any of the military services.
>
> (. . .) College is like another school to me. Like, I have to go five years to college or something, and then I have to go out and look for a job. It seems like another high school to me. Like the Air Force, it seems like you're going somewhere. It seems like an adventure, kind of (. . .) See, my cousin, she's in the Air Force, and she's doing really well, and she likes it a lot. It's just that basic training is really hard. She says you have to pick a field, though. You can't just go there for the money.
>
> (. . .) Like, whatever they [Air Force] offer me, I could go for nursing. It's [college] not like a high school; I mean you could leave and do whatever you want to do, but it [college] just seems like another school.

Chris is clearly not interested in just "another school," and the Air Force seems to offer her a way out. However, she, too, has selected a traditionally female field—nursing.

Unlike previous studies in which girls elaborate an "ideology of romance," these students think first of continuing their education and establishing themselves in a career or job. Students in the advanced curriculum tend to think more in terms of four-year colleges and training leading out of a sex-segregated occupational ghetto, whereas students in the nonadvanced class tend to think largely in terms of two-year colleges, business institutes, cosmetology, and so forth, leading ultimately to sex-segregated jobs. This relationship is not perfect, however, and there are students in the advanced class who are intending to prepare themselves for jobs that can be obtained with two-year–college degrees. Not all students in the advanced classes are thinking outside of the sex-segregated labor market and not all within the other classes think within its boundaries. The relationship does exist, however, even though it is far from perfect.

Two important points should be noted here. One is the lack of primacy for a home/family identity. These girls are thinking first and foremost of obtaining jobs and talking about the further education necessary to get these jobs, although there are contradictory elements in their relation to school knowledge and culture. Second, it must be noted that some of these girls are, in fact, thinking of nontraditional jobs: marine biologist, engineer, psychologist, and so forth.

Again, this may be somewhat less surprising in light of the fact that 50 percent of American youth now go on to some form of college. However, ethnographic investigations have uncovered the finding that although girls may think of further education, the construction of a home/family identity is, nonetheless, primary. This is not the case in Freeway as data presented in the next section suggest.

Marriage and family

The fact that students do not marginalize a wage labor identity contrasts sharply with data collected by Valli, McRobbie, Jane Gaskell and others.[12] Ann Marie Wolpe, for example, argues:

> By the time teenage girls reach school-leaving age, they articulate their future in terms of family responsibilities. They reject, often realistically, advice about pursuing school subjects which could open up new avenues; the jobs they anticipate are not only within their scope, but more importantly, are easily accessible to them and in fact in conformity with their future familial responsibilities.[13]

The girls in Valli's study similarly had notions of the primacy of family responsibilities: raising children and possibly working part-time. As Valli notes,

> Experiencing office work as either secondary to or synonymous with a sexual/home/family identity further marginalized these students' work identities. The culture of femininity associated with office work made it easier for them to be less attached to their work and their workplace than men, who stay in paid employment because they must live up to masculine ideology

of male-as-provider. Women's identities tend to be much less intrinsically linked to wage labor than are men's.[14]
(. . .) By denying wage labor primacy over domestic labor they inadvertently consented to and conformed their own subordination preparing themselves for both unskilled, low-paid work and unpaid domestic service.[15]

Angela McRobbie's research on working-class girls in England also examines the role of gender as it intersects with class in the production of identity. In spite of the fact that the girls in McRobbie's study know that marriage and housework are far from glamorous simply by virtue of the lives of female relatives and friends, they construct fantasy futures and elaborate an "ideology of romance." They create a specifically female anti-school culture which consists of interjecting sexuality into the classroom, talking loudly about boyfriends, and wearing makeup. McRobbie casts the identity in social control terms as follows:

Marriage, family life, fashion and beauty all contribute massively to this feminine anti-school culture and, in doing so, nicely illustrate the contradictions inherent in so called oppositional activities. Are the girls in the end not doing exactly what is required of them—and if this *is* the case, then could it not be convincingly argued that it is their own culture which itself is the most effective agent of social control of the girls, pushing them into compliance with that role which a whole range of institutions in capitalist society also, but less effectively, directs them towards? At the same time, they are experiencing a class relation in albeit traditionally feminine terms.[16]

The Freeway youth are markedly different from working-class girls in earlier ethnographies. Although some assert that they wish to have some form of home/family identity, it is never asserted first, and generally only as a possibility "later on," when their own job or career is "settled." Some of the girls reject totally the possibility of marriage and children; many others wish to wait "until I am at least thirty," which is, to teenagers, a lifetime away. The primary point, however, is that they assert strongly that they must settle *themselves* first (go to school, get a job, and so forth) before entering into family responsibilities; in other words, the construction of a home/family identity is secondary, rather than the reverse. Only one of the twenty girls interviewed elaborates a romance ideology, and this girl is severely criticized by others. I never once heard informal discussion directed at the romantic nature of boys or marriage in all the time I spent at Freeway. Significantly, unlike the girls in McRobbie's study, girls do not construct fantasy futures as a means of escaping their current condition.

It is important to point out that few girls discuss the possibility of marriage without considering divorce. The attitude toward marriage and children does not differ between the advanced and nonadvanced students. Although these students tend to differ in terms of type of envisioned relationship to wage labor and future schooling, they do not differ at all with respect to the fact that they assert the primacy of a wage labor identity over that of the home and family. The language of wanting to be "independent" is often used in discussions about home/family and the wage labor force. It must be noted again that the initial probe questions revolved around what they wanted to do after high school; what they wished to do in five years, and in ten years. Unlike the boys, who tended to speak of family first, many times the issue of family never even was mentioned by girls. It is only at that point that I asked the girls *specifically* whether they wished to get married and/or have a family. This specific question led to the responses below. Again, I quote at length in order to give the full flavor of the girls' perspectives. The perspectives of the advanced students are presented first.

LW: Why not just get a man to support you and then you can stay home?

Penny: 'Cause you can't fall back on that.

LW: Why do you say that?

Penny: 'Cause what if I get a divorce and you have nothing to fall back on.

LW: Does your mother encourage you to get a job because, "What if I get a divorce"? [Her father is no longer alive.]

Penny: No.

LW: So, where did you get that?

Penny: Just my own ideas. Just how things are today.

. . .

LW: Do you want to get married?

Jessica: Gee, I don't know. After I see all the problems that go on now, I just don't know. All the divorce. Just how can you live with somebody for forty years? I don't know, possibly (. . .) You see it [divorce] all over. I'm not living to get married.

. . .

Judy: I want to go to college for four years, get my job, work for a few years, and then get married (. . .) I like supporting myself. I don't want my husband supporting me. I like being independent.

LW: You're doing something very different from your mother. Why? [Mother was married at nineteen; went back to work when Judy was in grade three.]

Judy: I think I have to (. . .) What happens if I marry a husband who is not making good money? My dad works at Freeway Steel. He's switching jobs all the time [although the plant is closed, there is still piecework going on and workers are called back according to seniority rules at much lower pay than they formerly earned]. He used to work at the strip mill; now he's not. Now everything is gone, benefits and everything.

. . .

LW: Do you want to get married?

Pam: I want to and I don't. I'd like to have a child but not get married (. . .) I would like to have a child just to say it's mine. Just to be able to raise it (. . .) If you get married, like my mother and father are two different people. I would be afraid that my kids would come out like me and my sister. Like I can't talk to my father . . . And if I did get married I'd want to be sure it would last if I had kids 'cause I wouldn't be able to get a divorce. They say that it's "okay" if you get a divorce and have children, but the kids change. I wouldn't want kids to go through that, 'cause I, like, see the people around me.

. . .

LW: Do you think you'll get married?

Rhonda:	I always thought that if I get married it would be after college.
	. . .
LW:	Do you hope to get married; do you hope to have children?
Liz:	After college and everything's settled.
LW:	What do you mean by "everything's settled"?
Liz:	I know where I'm going to live. I know what I'm going to be doing; my job is secure, the whole thing. Nothing's open. Everything's going to be secure.
	. . .
Carla:	Oh, I'm going to do that later [get married; have children]. I'm going to school to get everything over with. I wouldn't want to get married or have kids before that.
LW:	Why not?
Carla:	It'd be too hard. I just want to get my schoolwork over with, get my life together, get a job (. . .) I want to be independent. I don't want to be dependent on him [my husband] for money. Then what would I do if I got divorced fifteen years, twenty years, you know how people are and marriages. Twenty years down the line you have kids, the husband has an affair or just you have problems, you get divorced, then where is that going to leave me? I want to get my life in order first, with my career and everything (. . .) Maybe it has something to do with the high divorce rates. Or the stories you hear about men losing their jobs and not having any job skills, and you see poverty and I just don't want that. I want to be financially secure on my own.

All the above girls in the advanced class express the desire to get their "own lives in order before marrying." They all say that they will get married eventually, however. Only Suzanne, below, says she will never get married.

LW:	Tell me a little bit about whether you want to get married.

Suzanne: [interrupts me] No. No marriage, no kids!

LW: Why not?

Suzanne: I don't like that.

LW: Why?

Suzanne: I don't think you can stay with somebody your whole life. It's dumb (. . .) Like this one kid says, "Marriage was invented by somebody who was lucky if they lived to twenty without being bit by a dinosaur." It's true. It started so far back and it's, like, people didn't live long. Now people live to be eighty years old. You don't stay with one person for eighty years. It's, like, impossible.

LW: (. . .) What makes you say that?

Suzanne: A lot of divorce. A lot of parents who fight and stuff. I couldn't handle the yelling at somebody constantly 'cause I wanted to get out. I just don't want to be trapped. (. . .) Back when they [parents] were kids, like, girls grew up, got married, worked for a couple of years after graduation, had two or three kids, had a white picket fence, two cars. Things are different now.

LW: How so?

Suzanne: Girls don't grow up just to be married. They grow up to be people, too.

LW: And that means they don't want these other things?

Suzanne: Not that they don't want them. A lot of girls in school, they're like, "Hey, you're [Suzanne] crazy. I want to be married sometime, I want to have kids [but] they all want to wait. They all want to get into a career first; wait until they're thirty. It's [marriage] only "if," though, and it's going to be late.

(. . .) You've got to do it [make a good life] for yourself. I don't want to be Mrs. John Smith. I want to be able to do something.

I mean, just from what I've seen, a lot of people cheat and that. I don't want that (. . .) You can't

rely on them [men]. You just can't rely on them
(. . .) [Also] drinking a lot. It's like, I know a lot
of older guys, they drink all the time.

The girls in the advanced class all suggest that they have to get themselves together first before entering into home/family responsibilities. Only Suzanne says she does *not* want to get married, but the rest of the girls clearly want the economic power to negotiate terms within the marriage. It is very clear from these excerpts that the conditions of their *own* lives mediate their response to family and paid work. Numerous students note the high divorce rate. Penny, for example, says, "What if I get a divorce and you have nothing to fall back on?" Jessica states, "After I see all the problems that go on now, I just don't know. All the divorce." Carla also states, "Then what if I get divorced fifteen years, twenty years, you know how people are and marriages. Twenty years down the line you have kids, the husband has an affair or you just have problems, you get divorced, then where is that going to leave me?" The lack of male jobs is also articulated as a problem by the students. Judy, for example, says, "What happens if I marry a husband who is not making good money? My dad works at Freeway Steel. He used to work at the strip mill, now he's not. Now everything is gone, benefits and everything."

The students assert that men cannot be counted on for a *variety* of reasons—high divorce rate, drinking, lack of jobs, lack of skills, affairs, and so forth. They respond to this aspect of their lived experience by establishing, at least in principle, the primacy of wage labor in their own lives in order to hedge their chances. They are attempting to control the conditions of their *own* lives in a way that previous generations of women did not, and, given fewer opportunities and the inability to control reproduction, could not even if so inclined.

It is important to note here, however, that these girls are developing an identity in relation to males, just as previous generations of women have done. In other words, although past studies have suggested that working-class girls elaborate a home/family identity and that this identity is celebrated over a wage labor identity, the fact is that females elaborated this identity in relation to a constructed identity of the "male." Girls in Freeway are *also* elaborating their identity in relation to a constructed identity of the male. It is simply that this constructed identity of the male "other" is different from that elaborated by girls in previous studies and women of previous generations. The "ideology of romance" noted by

McRobbie, for example, whether a celebration of the home of father or an envisioned escape from the home of father, was constructed in relation to men.

The current stress among Freeway girls on a wage labor identity is also elaborated in relation to males. This relational aspect of identity formation in terms of constructed "other" and the way in which the "other" changes through time due to broader economic and cultural alterations is absolutely critical here. *These identities do not form in any linear fashion and they do not form irrespective of an economic context.* They form in relation to constructed "others" within a particular economy.

The issue of a home/family identity and the degree to which girls in the advanced curriculum embrace an identity as a wage laborer first is highlighted in the following discussions. Amy has decided to drop the advanced curriculum in order to pursue cosmetology. She has done this as an assertion that, for her, a home/family identity *is* primary and she articulates this below. Jennifer, also an advanced student, is very critical of Amy's decision, as are the others. It must be clear here that Amy has decided to go into cosmetology in order to work around envisioned family life in much the same way as girls in previous studies envision their lives. She is the *only* girl interviewed in this study who takes this position, and she sees herself as an outsider. It is the "outsider" nature of her previously "normal" female position that is so interesting here.

Amy: They [my friends] don't want to get married. They just want to go out and get richer.

LW: The kids in the honors class?

Amy: *Everybody* [emphasis hers] I talk to (. . .) They just want to be free. They're all going to college [some form of continued education].

Everybody in my class is (. . .) They have a lower opinion of me [because I don't want to go on to some form of school].

(. . .)They talk about it [marriage] as "maybe someday." But they don't really care whether they do or don't. They won't do it in the near future.

(. . .) They [outside the honors class] want to go to college, too. They say, "Why do you want to get married so young?" [twenty, twenty-one] They don't want to get married until they're thirty.

LW: Why do you think that's the case?

Amy: They don't want to be tied down.

LW: What does that mean? Why not?

Any: They think that if they get married, they're going to have to be told what to do. They won't be able to do what they want to do, and they don't, like, want nobody dictating to them; nothing like that.

(. . .)Like, if my girlfriends want me to come somewhere with them and I say, "I'm coming with him [boyfriend]," they just say, "You can come with us, let him go by himself (. . .) Why do you let him tell you what to do?"

I go with him everywhere. That's how they [my girl-friends] are.

At a later point, Amy says:

Amy: I want to get married and have kids and I want to be at home. It's [cosmetology] a good thing to do at home so I don't have to go out and work and leave my kids with a baby-sitter or nothin'. I just don't like the whole idea.

LW: When are you thinking of getting married?

Amy: Three years. We figure we'll get married as soon as he finishes college.

LW: Is having kids something you want to do right away?

Amy: Yeah.

LW: And you're going to stay home with those kids?

Amy: Yeah, I guess I'm old-fashioned (. . .) When I tell my friends about that they look at me funny. Like, why would I want to do that? They want to go out and work, not get married and not have kids. They think I'm crazy or something. I'd just rather stay home, have kids, and be a beautician on the side, at home. Have a shop in my home.

LW: How long do you think you should stay at home?

Amy: Depends on the money situation. Things like that. If we need extra money, I could go out and work. But if we didn't, whatever I felt like doing.

(. . .) I'm just like her [my mother]. I want to do
exactly what she did. She started working seven years
ago. She's a clerk at a drugstore and she hates it 'cause
she's not making much money at all. A little above
minimum. Seven years and she can't get raises. They
won't give her a raise and she complains. She wishes
she went to college. She can't get any kind of good
jobs.

Amy articulates the Domestic Code and, at the same time, notes the
contradictory nature of that code in the real world. She says she wants
to be "just like her mother," even though she notes that her mother is
currently having difficulty getting a job that pays above minimum wage
or that provides opportunities for advancement. It is exactly this Domestic Code and its attendant contradictions in today's society that is being
challenged to some extent at the identity level by working-class females.

It must be pointed out that Amy is articulating the female position as
defined by the males in the previous chapter. Thus, she agrees that
women should take care of the children and work only if the "family
wage" is not entirely adequate. The vast majority of females, however,
challenge directly both Amy and the articulated male vision of their
appropriate place.

The tension over the Domestic Code is exceptionally well articulated
by Jennifer, below, who refers to Amy in her comments:

LW: Do most of the kids in the advanced curriculum plan
           to go to college?

Jennifer: All except for one who plans to get married and
           have kids [said with some disgust].

LW: What is your perception of that one?

Jennifer: We've all told her on many occasions, "It's crazy."
           She's always been in our group and now she is
           taking cosmetology and she thinks she's just going
           to get a small job somewhere to help support when
           she gets married. She's all planned out. She's going
           to get married when he finishes college. She's been
           with this guy for a while. Her whole life is all
           planned out, and, it's like, "Okay, fine, you get
           married, what happens if you get a divorce?" "My

God [she says], that would never happen." "It might, you know; what if he dies, then what are you going to do?" You have to support yourself some way. Even if you do get married and you're happy now, something could happen tomorrow. You could have an unhappy marriage and get divorced. You can't say I'm gonna have a happy marriage, it might not work.

(. . .) Maybe we think it's such a waste. I mean you have the opportunity, it's such a waste. I mean civil rights have come so far. If it were a hundred years ago, I can see saying that, when you were being a rebellious woman if you wanted to go out and get a job. I mean, now we have that opportunity; to relinquish that and say, I mean, I'm a cautious person and thinking of the future and saying, what if something *does* happen? She isn't even thinking of that.

This same beginning challenge is exhibited by girls who are not in the advanced curriculum. Although they are preparing themselves for jobs in largely sex-segregated ghettos, they nevertheless challenge the Domestic Code as strongly as the others. *None* of the girls place home/family responsibilities before wage labor.

LW: Do you want to get married?

Chris: Yeah, eventually. Once I'm settled down with myself and I know I can handle myself.

. . .

LW: Do you see yourself getting married; do you think you'll have children?

Valerie: Yeah, but not right away. I'll wait until I'm about twenty-four (. . .) I just feel that I want to accomplish my own thing, like getting a job and stuff.

LW: Why not find a guy and let him support you?

Valerie: Feels like I have a purpose in life [if I accomplish my own thing]. Like I can do what I want.

LW: As opposed to?

Valerie: Feeling like *he* [emphasis hers] has to support me, and *he* has to give me money.

. . .

Carol: Well, I know I'm not going to get married until I'm at least thirty, and have kids when I'm around thirty-one, thirty-two.

LW: Why?

Carol: 'Cause I want to have my own freedom to experience life, everything, to travel, to go out places without having to have a baby-sitter or worry about kids. Plus with a beauty salon [her envisioned job], it would be hard to have kids to take care of and do that [the beauty salon] at the same time. [17]

. . .

LW: Do you want to get married?

Susan: Yes.

LW: When do you think you'll get married?

Susan: I want to prove to myself if I can be on my own. I don't want no man to have to take care of me.

LW: Why?

Susan: Because my mother told me that, I don't know what the statistics are anymore, but for every marriage that lasts, every marriage doesn't, so . . .

Women, when they go into a marriage, they have to be thinking "Can I support myself?"

. . .

LW: When you think about your life five years from now, what do you think you'll be doing? Do you think you'll be married?

Lorna: I'm trying to get all my education so I can support myself. Why put effort [in] and then let somebody support you?

(. . .) I saw my friends getting pregnant so young. If you get married young, you're going to get pregnant young, and it's going to ruin the rest of your life. That's the way I see it.

(. . .) Five years from now I'll just be able to go

75

out to a bar. I'll be twenty-one. And I don't want to ruin my life in just five years. 'Cause as soon as you get married, you're going to start having kids; then you're going to have to stay home and raise them and stuff. I don't want to have to do that.

LW: Why not?

Lorna: I like to do things. I don't want to have to sit around all the time (. . .) I just don't want to stay home all the time.

LW: Does marriage mean you're going to have to stay home all the time?

Lorna: Well, that's what I think of. You get married; you got to stay home. You can't just go out with other people (. . .) I like to go out with my friends when I want to. I like to be able to make my own decisions and if you're married, you have to sort of ask the other person, "Can I spend the money here, can I do that?" It's, like, you got to ask permission. Well I been asking permission from my parents all my life, you know. I don't want to just get out of high school and get married, and then have to keep asking permission for the rest of my life.

LW: (. . .) Will you ever get married?

Lorna: I was just talking about that today. Probably when I'm thirty. Then I'll take a couple of years to have kids.

Although girls in the nonadvanced class tend to voice the same themes as the advanced-class girls, there is some tendency on their part to elaborate the theme of "freedom" and, in contrast, the restrictions imposed by marriage. This is true for the earlier set of interviews as well, in that a number of girls stressed "independence." Nonadvanced girls, however, seem a bit more strident about it. Lorna, for example, states that "As soon as you get married, you're going to start having kids; then you're going to *have* [my emphasis] to stay home and raise them and stuff." She states, "You get married; you got to stay home. You can't just go out and go out with other people (. . .) I like to make my own decisions, and if you're married, you have to sort of ask the other person,

'Can I spend the money here; can I do that?' It's like you got to ask permission." Valerie, too, notes that she doesn't want to feel that "*he* [emphasis hers] has to support me, and *he* has to give me money." Carol states that she wants "to have [her] own freedom to experience life," implying that marriage means that she forsakes such freedom. The distinction I am drawing here between advanced and nonadvanced girls cannot be pushed too strongly since both groups stress the importance of their own independence. The nonadvanced students do, however, tend to stress the possibly oppressive conditions of marriage in that you have to "ask permission," whereas the advanced students tend to stress the high divorce rate and the possibility that their husbands may leave them or not be able to obtain a good job. Lorna's point about children is particularly interesting in this respect since she assumes that once you marry, you start having children, suggesting that within the bounds of a working-class marriage one cannot assume even basic control over biological reproduction. This is not a reflection of adherence to strict Catholic teaching about birth control, however. It is simply an assertion that marriage is such that a woman can no longer assert this basic control. Given the statements of the boys in Freeway, the perception of the girls regarding loss of control in marriage is certainly understandable.

It is noteworthy that white-female identity is not produced in relation to constructed black identity. Girls do not elaborate an identity in relation to blacks in the way boys do. They do not, in Freeway, set up blacks as "other" as they form themselves. This is not to say that white working-class females are not racist; they may well be. Rather, it is to suggest that the fundamental white working-class female category does not emerge in self-identity terms in relation to a black "other." It does emerge, as I have suggested throughout this chapter, in relation to a constructed "male" other.

While this may be surprising on one level, it is not so surprising if we consider the economy in which such identities are produced. Black and white males have historically been at odds in the economic sphere in the sense that blacks were kept out of well-paid union laboring jobs by white males and, at the same time, used as strikebreakers by white capitalists. There has been a historically based antagonism between the two groups given that both were, to some extent, potentially available to do the same kinds of jobs and were pitted against each other.

This is not the case for black and white females. There is no comparable set of jobs for which each competed historically. In addition, the notion of a "family wage," whereby men would make enough money to cover the cost of supporting a family, including being able to purchase the unpaid labor of a wife in the home, was part of the notion of being female. Thus a similar type of antagonism rooted in the economic realm would not arise to the same extent for females to begin with. White female lives were not bound up in any direct sense with black females. Although white-female lives were indirectly bound given their relationship with white men, it was not experienced directly and, therefore, not as integral a part of their identity formation historically as it is for working-class white men.

The tension between black and white males is apt to be even more intense now given certain affirmative-action regulations which demand the bypassing of union seniority rules (which would favor white males over all others) in hiring and firing. Thus white males are apt, possibly more than ever, to set blacks up as the negative "other" in a way white females would not set up black females. This may explain why it is that white-female identity is not constructed in relation to black identity and why it is that white-male identity in Freeway is inextricably linked with that of blacks and so virulently racist.

I have argued here that the girls' emerging identity exhibits a beginning challenge to the Domestic Code. They are envisioning their lives very differently from girls in previous studies, and very differently than investigators such as Lillian Breslow Rubin and Glen Elder suggest that their mothers and grandmothers did.[18] For them, the domestic is *not* primary; wage labor is. If patriarchy rests on a fundamental distinction between men's and women's labor, and currently the domination of women in both the home/family sphere and the workplace, these girls exhibit the glimmerings of a critique of that. They understand, to the point of being able to articulate, the fact that too many negative consequences result if you depend on men to the exclusion of depending on yourself, and that this means you must engage in long-term wage labor. They do not suggest the "part-time" work solution and/or flights into fantasy futures offered by girls in previous studies.

In this sense, then, their identity embodies a critical moment of critique of an underlying premise of patriarchy: that being the notion that women's primary place is in the home/family sphere and that men will, in turn, "take care" of them. In so doing they question the basis of the "family wage," which, as I suggest in chapter 2, males affirm.

The potential for such a critical moment needs to be considered carefully, and I will pursue this at some length in chapter 8. I will also tie this glimmer of critique to the women's movement in chapter 7. For the moment, suffice it to say that while the girls' identity suggests a glimmer of critique, informed both by the women's movement and by economic changes which ensure both that women *must* work outside the home and *can* obtain jobs, the critique does not necessarily prefigure collective action. Rather it tends to suggest individualistic private solutions rather than political struggle designed to change the prevailing social order revolving around gender. I will discuss this at length later in the book.

As I have suggested here and in chapter 2, white working-class male and female identities are currently on a collision path: the boys envisioning male-dominant relations in the home and the girls exhibiting a challenge to these relations in some important ways. The question must be asked, in what ways does the school block and/or encourage the formation of these identities? To what extent does the school block and/or encourage an understanding that these identities are shared or collective? In the next two chapters I take up these questions. Chapter 4 focuses on the way in which the routines and rituals of the school are related to the identity formation of working-class youth.

4
Within the School

September 9, 1985*(the second day of school)

4th Period Study Hall

Mr. Paul: Okay. This is a study hall. That's what I expect
           you to do.

Joe: Only a hundred and seventy-eight more days until
           the end of the year [to the guy next to him]

Mr. Paul: You're not the only one counting. How many
           days?

Joe: A hundred and seventy-eight.

Mr. Paul: How many hours?

Joe: Let me see [he figures it out]. One thousand four
           hundred twenty-four more periods.

Mr. Paul: One thousand four hundred twenty-four hours?

Joe: No, periods. We don't want too much specificity
           . . . We are now into the second full day of our
           education [everyone was laughing].

The question arises, what does the school do to encourage and/or block the formation of the identities outlined in chapters 2 and 3? To what extent does the school contribute to and/or inhibit these identity formations? Which aspects are inhibited and which are encouraged? In this chapter, I explore elements of school culture and speculate as to their possible effects on student identities.

I will argue two major points here. First, I will suggest that the school embodies and promotes a contradictory attitude toward schooling and school knowledge, with a stress on the form of schooling rather than the substance of learning. This is accomplished both through the way in which knowledge is distributed by teachers in the classroom, and what I call the ritual of control over teacher labor which is enacted between administrators and teachers. Both the treatment of knowledge and the enacted ritual of control serve to contain any real struggle to the surface, preventing meaningful issues from being discussed, and at the same time serving to give the appearance of order. Both coexist, however, with distributed and received messages suggesting that schooling and learning are important in today's economy.

Second, I will suggest that the school serves to encourage the creation and maintenance of separatist identities along gender and race lines, thus encouraging the construction of "other" discussed in chapters 2 and 3. The school also encourages the notion that white-male identity is superior to all others. This is not without its contradictions, however. The identity of females as outlined in chapter 3 is encouraged to some extent within the school by elements of female teacher identity and the fact that the school is itself the site of larger social struggles. In chapter 5, I will look more carefully at the creation of teacher culture and the way in which such culture is attached to themes elaborated in this chapter.

Contradictions with respect to education

Freeway High classes embody the same contradictory code of respect toward knowledge and schooling as is embedded within the identities of youth. Teachers tend to adhere to the form rather than the substance of education, and knowledge tends to be flat and prepackaged. This is reminiscent of curriculum described by Linda McNeil in her high school study, and Jean Anyon in her study of knowledge as distributed through the working-class elementary school. On the one hand, education in Freeway is articulated in highly instrumental terms as positive by teachers—it leads to a better job and so forth. This, again, is much the same way in which the students themselves see it. On the other hand, knowledge distributed through the classes has nothing to do with either thinking or challenging.[1]

Teachers almost uniformly suggest that education is necessary to obtain what they consider to be reasonable employment. This comes through in their conversations with me alone as well as in their verbal classroom posture. The following examples clarify this point:

January 16, Social Studies[*]

A long explanation of the electoral system; national nominating convention; campaigns; and elections. Mr. Sykes then hands out a work sheet on the topic. "Answer the five questions on the bottom. I'll see if you understand everything. Take about ten minutes."

(. . .) "If the steel plant were still open you guys wouldn't have to worry about this. You could crawl into some coil for an eight-hour shift and fall asleep and still get paid for it. That's probably one of the reasons why the plant closed."

Mr. Sykes walks around. "Do you guys take math? You guys are terrible in math. This is simple addition. You want my calculator?"

. . .

October 30, Social Studies[*]

Mr. Simon: Why does level of education prevent you from getting a job? Okay. If there are a hundred jobs on a page in the want ads, ten percent of these, you need an elementary education; forty percent of these jobs you need a high school education; forty percent you need a college education; ten percent of these jobs you need a college plus [education].

The door system works as follows: If you have an elementary education, you can knock on ten doors. If you have a high school education, you can knock on fifty doors. If you have a college plus, you can knock on one hundred doors. Each time you have a piece of paper, you can knock on more doors. Each time you get more education, you can *try* [emphasis his] for more jobs. If you have college plus, you may not get a job, but your chances are going to be better.

The people who live in the poor parts of town have less education and it is more difficult for them to get jobs.

While teachers let students know that they feel that schooling is useful in instrumental terms, there is, in fact, little importance given to the real substance of schooling. The knowledge form is, indeed, very telling, with virtually all classes taking the form of top-down distribution of knowledge. While this may not be particularly unusual, and several studies have pointed to the same phenomenon in the American school, the situation in Freeway is extreme. Teachers tend to tell students *exactly* what to put in their notebooks, for example, down to the outline format and where to place commas. Thus, it is not only a matter of students outlining information presented in a textbook, for instance, as has been documented in a number of other studies. Teachers actually control the *very form of the outline* and students are not encouraged to make the information their own even at the point of transferring it into their notebooks. This form of knowledge distribution is highly routinized in Freeway High and only one class, the advanced social studies class, broke out of it in all the classes I observed. The following classroom observations clarify my point. It is extremely significant that student question posing took *only* the form of asking for clarification of directions. At only one point during the entire year did I see evidence, outside of the advanced class, of students posing questions about and/or challenges to the knowledge itself. In fairness to the students, however, the form of knowledge distributed through the classroom does not leave much room for interaction with that knowledge. In fairness to the teachers, it may not, as I will suggest later in the volume, make any difference even if it does.

*November 12, English**

Mr. Kindley: "Part of the exam we take in June is the listening exercise. There is no reason why you can't get 8 or 9 on the [state external] exam. There is no way you can really study for this, but we can get used to the questions."

"This is not a reading exercise. Nowhere on the exam are you going to find what I read to you. I'm going to read a passage to you. Then I'll tell you where to look for the questions."

He reads a passage about Bulgaria's Communist Party. We then look at the questions in the book and he rereads the passage. *Mr. Kindley:* "Don't look at the passage in the book;

you won't have a passage to read in June. Now, you have five
minutes to put your answers down."

. . .

"Okay. Let's go through them. Don't be upset if you don't do
well. We'll do this five or six times this year, and hopefully,
you'll do better."

The above simply reflects intense preparation on the part of the teacher
for the state external exam to be taken in June, an exam that all students
in this class must take due to new state regulations. In that sense, the
above description is not striking—many schools might look similar.
What is important, however, is Mr. Kindley's follow-up discussion on
taking a listening test below. The precision with which he instructs
students *how* to place the notes in their notebooks is key here.

Mr. Kindley: Okay. Open up to page 11 [in the textbook] and
get your notebooks out. Skip a line and write "Listening Test—suggestions on how to use your
time." There are four steps involved with this.
Roman Numeral I in your notes. Write down,
"During the first reading." Number 1. "Listen to
the topic, usually stated in the first two
sentences, and for the supporting details. Pay
close attention to the conclusion which often
stresses the main ideas." [This is *directly* from
the book.]
Roman Numeral II. "During your reading of
the questions," and [write down] just what it
has on our page 11 there, "Your primary goal at
this time is to become as aware as possible of
all the questions so you will know the specific
information to listen for." Roman Numeral III,
next page, page 12, "During the second
reading, the two things you are asked to do at
this time are to listen to the passage and to
write the answers. Of the two, the listening is
the most important. You must keep listening."
Underline the last sentence.

The point here is that notes are given in extreme detail, including
what to underline, where to place commas, and so forth. This was not

idiosyncratic but occurred in a number of classes, as the following make clear.

*October 24, Social Studies**

Mr. Sykes:	Put down in your notes, "Unit I, Part 4." Put down "Four disadvantaged" [he spells] groups in the population."
Jim:	For?
Jerry:	What do we got to write after that?
Mr. Sykes:	Page 66 [referring to text]. Just list them. Number 1. The American Indian. Number 2. Hispanic Americans. Number 3. American women, page 87.
Jim:	American broads.
Mr. Sykes:	[He ignores the comment on "broads"]. Number 4. American blacks, page 105.

. . .

*December 12, Social Studies**

Mr. Simon:	Open up your book to the first page (. . .). Take out your notebooks. Put at the top, "The Origins of American People" [subheading right out of text]. Put that down, underline it, skip a line. It's the major title for this section of notes. Skip a line. "Pluralistic Society," underline it.

[put] A: "Pluralistic." This means a diversity of population. This diversity is because we are a nation of immigrants.

Go down to the next line—"B."

B. We are all of immigrant origins.
    1. Migrating people
    2. Immigrants
    3. Involuntary immigrants
    4. Occupants of territories [this is an outline of the first page of the book].

Go down to the next line—"C."

C. We have a heterogeneous [he spells] population.

. . .

*October 30, Social Studies**

Mr. Simon: Page 16. Take out your notebooks.
The title. "The Reasons for the Growth of
Cities." Put that down. It is at the bottom of page
60.
A. Industrial Revolution
(. . .)
Skip a line. Take the next subtitle [from the
text]. "B. Problems Facing Cities and Urban
Populations." Take the next five subtopics under
that. Skip a line between each.

Joe: Just one line between each?

Mr. Simon: Yes.

Sam: Just the five?

Mr. Simon: Yes.
(. . .)

Mr. Simon: The public health department has two main functions: 1) enforcing health codes, and 2) to aid,
assist and help those people who do get sick and
cannot afford it.
(. . .)
Put down the functions [in your notes] and
then put down a "dash"; then put down "money"
and a question mark.

The distribution of knowledge in Freeway High is highly routinized.
Students write down in their notebook prepackaged notes that teachers
deliver to them, and students are tested on these notes at a later time. At
no point in this process is there *any* discussion, much less serious discussion, of the ideas or concepts embedded within the original materials.

Obviously, I could not observe all classes in the high school, and
questions may be raised with respect to the representativeness of what
I found. However, it is striking that in all the classes visited over the year
by myself and two graduate assistants (this would add up to hundreds of
class sessions spread throughout the curriculum), it is only in the advanced class that knowledge took on a form different from that outlined
here. This goes even further than the lamentable situation found by
Michael Apple, Linda McNeil, and Jean Anyon in previous studies.[2]

While there may be individual classes in Freeway High that operate differently and were missed in the ethnography, there is absolutely no question that the form reported here is the norm.

Even in the case of the question raised by Mr. Simon above regarding whether the state is able to support public health, there was *never* any discussion of this issue. It was simply a point in the prepackaged notes suggested by a "dash," the word "money," and a question mark. Students had no idea what was meant by this, or, perhaps even worse, any interest in knowing. When students ask questions, they are almost always for the purpose of clarification. Such questions are not for the purpose of clarifying ideas, however, but the form of the notes themselves. Examples of this follow:

Teacher:	The National Origins Act
Female Student:	Is this in our notes or in the book? [In other words, do we have to write it down?]
Teacher:	Notes

. . .

Teacher:	You have two assignments today. Rewrite the last one to correct your mistakes. Also, start question three. Read the entire question first. Find out what the question asks, then answer the question.
Male Student:	Do we have to write the question? [In other words, when we provide the answer, do we have to write down the question first?]
Teacher:	Yes.

. . .

Teacher:	Page 7. We populated the thirteen colonies.
Male Student:	Should we write that down [in our notebooks?]
Teacher:	No, not until you read it.

. . .

Teacher:	On page 37, there were eleven multiple-choice questions. I want you to do this now. You'll have to write an essay on Friday.

[student chatter]

Teacher:	What is the question?
Student:	[Which do we have to do?] The multiple choice or matching?
Teacher:	Not the matching, just the multiple choice.

The point here is that student questions almost always take the form of asking for clarification of minor points related to directions: whether to add a dash or not in the notes, answer this or that question, skip one or two lines, and so forth. It is not a questioning that revolves around clarification of ideas, much less a challenge to such ideas. In the year I was in Freeway [as I noted in chapter 1, I attended classes three days a week], I witnessed only one challenge to an idea in a nonadvanced class, and many more such challenges in an advanced social studies class. Interestingly enough, the one challenge in the nonadvanced class centered on knowledge about alcoholism as did one of the most well-articulated challenges to teacher knowledge in an advanced class. Since drinking is seen by students as *their* knowledge, it is, therefore, significant that challenges emerge in this area. The first observation comes from a nonadvanced English class; the second, an advanced social studies class.

English, October 23[*]

Mr. Kindley:	"Okay, take out your notebooks. In your notes, just skip a line from where you were. Number 1. *High and Outside*. Author is Linda A. Dove, Setting: A town near San Francisco."
	He proceeds to give them notes from the entire book, including characters, plot, and so forth, even though they read the book. [The form of "reading" the book was orally in class].
	(. . .) "Skip another line and we get into Carl Etchen, Niki's father, who has treated her like an adult from the age of fourteen by including her in his wine tasting and afternoon cocktail hours. He was trying to protect her from the wild party drinking of other teenagers. But he unwittingly *caused* [my emphasis] her alcoholism."
Holly:	"How did he cause her alcoholism?" [with

skepticism; indicating that she understood that alcoholism is a disease and that one person cannot cause it to occur in another].

Mr. Kindley: "I know what you're trying to say. What we're trying to do here is get some notes for the end of the year [state exams]. Maybe I should change the word 'cause.' "

Holly: "No, no."

Mr. Kindley: "No, you're making a good point."

It is interesting that Holly had a difficult time sustaining her challenge to teacher knowledge, even though the subject was not unfamiliar to her. When Mr. Kindley said he should "change the word 'cause,' " her comment was "No, no," suggesting that she didn't really want to enter into such a challenge at all, however minor it was.

The following observation suggests a more sustained challenge on the same subject from an advanced student:

*March 4, Social Studies**

An interesting discussion on drinking. It started out as a discussion about the lawmaking process and it turned into a discussion about the twenty-one-year-old drinking age in the state.

Suzanne: "Why penalize young people? There are plenty of men over forty who get drunk all the time."

Mr. Mouton: "Yeah, but they don't go *out* [emphasis his] to get drunk. They don't say, 'Hey, it's Friday let's go out and get bombed.' Adults don't do that."

Suzanne: "Sure they do. They do it all the time."

Mr. Mouton: "I can name twenty-five kids; you name two adults."

Suzanne: "My dad."

Mr. Mouton: "Does he get drunk?"

Suzanne: "Yeah."

Mr. Mouton: "How often?"

Suzanne:	"Three times a week."
Mr. Mouton:	"Oh, name another."
Suzanne:	"We own a bar. There are plenty of guys who come in night after night and get bombed. I work there. I see the same guys all the time."

It is significant that the minor challenge I witnessed to teacher knowledge in the nonadvanced class had to do with a subject students feel is their own—drinking. The second challenge, noted above, is much more sustained than the first and also revolves around drinking. The main point here is that there are virtually *no* questions and/or challenges raised to school-based knowledge in nonadvanced classes. The form of knowledge itself did not encourage such challenge and/or questions, of course, and the students did not take them up on their own. There were, however, some challenges expressed in the advanced social studies class throughout the year. Here knowledge was more open to begin with, and therefore, more accessible to true discussion. It must be remembered, however, that only twenty-five students take the advanced curriculum out of the entire junior class.

This is not to say that the curricular form in evidence here goes totally unchallenged. It goes largely unchallenged, since both teachers and students obtain something from the implicit bargain, but not completely. Mr. Janson, below, is highly critical of the form knowledge takes in the district:

[When I taught at the middle school in the district] one of the things I found very early was that I had better keep my door closed. A lot of the things I was doing in the classroom were not looked upon as educational material. For example, I read a short story, the title escapes me, it's been so long. It was about two students who were involved in an accidental murder of a fellow playmate, and as an activity in class I staged a trial. I had members of the class play the parts of the characters, the jury, the judge, and it actually developed up into, the following year we actually made an eight-millimeter movie of the story. It was a two-year project. I still have the film and I'm really proud of it and I think back to what I did with those kids in the classroom and some of them would come back ten years later, come back and say to me, "In eighth grade, that was one of the most exciting things I ever did in my high school career!" But that idea—first of all I had to do all the filming outside of school. When I ran that courtroom in class, I was called down to the principal's office. They asked me very specifically what my objectives were . . . One of my objectives was to get the kids to engage in some critical thought. I was criticized for it.

Although Mr. Janson is talking specifically about the middle school in the district, he suggests that this form of control characterized the high school as well, although it is not quite as pervasive.

Although there are some minimal challenges by teachers to curricular form as expressed in the district, knowledge, as distributed through this working-class school, largely fits the model of knowledge described by Jean Anyon. As such, "A large portion of what the children were asked [revolved around carrying] out procedures, the purposes of which were often unexplained, and which were seemingly unconnected to thought processes or decision making of their own." An example, according to Anyon, of this type of instruction

was when one of the fifth-grade teachers led the children through a series of steps to make a one-inch grid on their papers without telling them that they were making a one-inch grid or that it would be used to study scale. She said, "Take your ruler. Put it across the top. Make a mark at every number. Then move your ruler down the bottom. Now, put it across the bottom. Now make a mark on top of every number. Now draw a line from . . ." At this point, one student said she had a faster way to do it and the teacher said, "No, you don't; you don't even know what I'm making yet. Do it this way or it's wrong."[3]

The form of knowledge distributed through Freeway parallels that described in Anyon's working-class schools. In her schools, students did not envision knowledge as "thinking" but spoke in terms of behaviors or skills. Knowledge was something, even in fifth grade, that one "acquired" from authorities. One did not interact with it, much less challenge or create it. The Freeway school exhibits similar characteristics. Teachers simply perfected a further prepackaging of the distribution of knowledge, and students perfected the appearance of the passive "absorption" of it. In many cases, they did not even "absorb" it, however, as test data show. In fact, neither group, teachers or students, was involved in their part of the equation other than at the level of ritual, and both were highly alienated from the process and the product. Teachers engaged in the "packaging" of knowledge to a far greater degree than data from any previous ethnography suggest, and students engaged in the passive "acquiring" of it far more than earlier studies uncover. As noted in chapter 2, students challenge the school virtually not at all, whether in the realm of knowledge or otherwise. They just hope to get *through* it by "passing" and are willing to sit quietly in order to get C's. Herein the contradictory attitude toward knowledge and school culture can be seen. Both teachers and students engage in a highly routinized *form* of knowledge but not in its substance. Indeed, the form *is* the curriculum in a sense, since no other curriculum is really available. Neither teachers nor students move beyond this established ritual in the classroom. At the same time, both groups agree that school is important, in the sense that the *credential* is important, thus bringing the contradictory code of respect toward education into the high school, where it has not previously surfaced.

It is important to note here that it is not knowledge itself that emerges as key, but the diploma. The diploma can be obtained whether one questions and/or challenges knowledge [either teachers or students] or not. In other words, one can be alienated and still obtain the short-term instrumental rewards of participating in high school. What this means in the long run is, of course, debatable and I will explore this issue at greater length in chapter 8. It must be noted, however, that the form of knowledge detailed here will *not* enable students to do well on the SAT [the college entrance examination] since the SAT calls for analysis, synthesis, and evaluation of high-culture material, none of which Freeway students are being trained to do. Thus, Freeway students are simply not receiving an education that will enable them to obtain entrance into good colleges and universities and get the type of jobs that will allow them, in the future, to set up middle-class life-styles.

What is important here is that the *school itself* encourages the emerging contradictory attitude toward school culture and knowledge that is in evidence among youth both by stressing the utility of schooling and by distributing a form of knowledge that maintain order. Knowledge is flat and highly controlled within the school—thus divorced from the true experiences of adolescents—and the school simply demands passivity in its face in order to "pass." In this sense, then, the school acts directly to encourage some aspect of emerging working-class identity. As noted earlier, although a contradictory code of respect toward education exists within the broader class culture, it has surfaced in the past only after workers experience the true brutality of labor. The Freeway case reflects the way in which social identity is changing in this regard.

The ritual of control over teachers

Control does not emerge as a theme in relation to knowledge only. It is also salient with respect to teacher labor, and it is the particular areas in which this control is exerted, as well as its public nature, that are important here. There is an ongoing struggle between faculty and administration over control of teacher labor. It is critical, however, that the struggle emerges in relation to four key areas and that it is largely confined to these areas. These are: 1) plan books; 2) audio-visual materials; 3) photocopying; and 4) classroom door windows. I will deal with each of these areas in this chapter.

What is most important is that the interaction between administrators and teachers parallels, to some extent, that between teachers and students. By this I mean that administrators engage in a ritual form of control over teacher labor that does not necessarily affect the selection, organization, or treatment of knowledge—in other words, its content or substance, except insofar as the ritual may suggest that only the form or appearance is important.[4] There is, then, an assertion of the *appearance of control* over teachers when administrators may, in fact, have very little meaningful control. At the same time, the assertion of control over plan books, audio-visual equipment, photocopying, and door window coverings enables administrators to suggest that they are doing something in terms of teacher labor. This emphasis on control over areas only tangentially linked to the selection, treatment, or organization of knowledge (which is, presumably, what schooling is supposed to be all about) parallels the emphasis on form that emerges in the classroom. *What becomes important, then, in both knowledge distribution and administrator/teacher relations is form rather than substance.* It can be argued that this serves to encourage, once again, the emerging contradictory attitude toward schooling and school knowledge in evidence among youth. If administrators stress form, teachers may well stress form in the classroom (this is, however, dialectically linked). Indeed, Linda McNeil suggests this very point in *Contradictions of Control*. Thus the ritual of control, or the appearance of order, at both the administrator and teacher level may well encourage students to engage in the form of schooling rather than its substance. In other words, students, too, will engage in form. I do not wish to suggest a set of linear relationships here. I am convinced that each of these components exists in a dialectical relationship with each of the others.[5] However, it all adds up in the Freeway case to an emphasis on the form of schooling. This coexists with all the distributed and received messages regarding the importance of schooling in today's economy.

A key area in which control over teacher labor surfaces is plan books. During the day-long orientation prior to the opening of classes held on September 3, 1985, teachers were given a set of materials, many of which related to professional responsibilities. Homework policies, classroom discipline, corridor assignments, and subsidized and free student lunch applications were all covered. Directions to teachers were fairly specific, such as that relating to "Overview of Course":

> It is good practice during the first week of school for faculty members to provide students with an overview of the course including standards of academic content and personal conduct which will be required by the teacher. Such matters as the number and frequency of tests, method of grading and reporting the test results and homework policies are valuable information for the student. Policies established at the outset are superior to those developed as emerging situations arise. Students should be expected to keep such outlines in their notebooks for reference (p. 4).

In this same document, the issue of plan books emerges. Teachers are instructed to

> keep [plan books] in the top drawer of your desk. It saves time and lessens confusion when a substitute teacher has to fill in for you. Plan books will be checked periodically. *They should be submitted to the designated Administrator as outlined in Plan Book Guidelines* [my emphasis]. [Teachers Plan Book Lesson Plans Guidelines 1985–86 were handed out to teachers.]

Teachers were told at this orientation that they had to have their plan books *checked* on a weekly basis initially, then biweekly.

The attachment handed out to teachers is quite specific, and examples are given as to the appropriate way of stating behavioral objectives. Teachers are told, for example, that

> The teacher cannot assume that he [sic] knows the details of a subject matter without going over the content of each day's work. A topic that he assumes can be explained without difficulty may provide a stumbling block. A surgeon would not operate without X rays nor an architect build without plans.
>
> Thorough preparation is the *key to success*. All teachers are to keep up-to-date plans at all times. Plans should be clear and concise [at a later point, teachers are instructed not to 'ramble' or "philosophize"]. Well-developed plans serve several functions:
> 1. They provide the teacher with clearly mapped out directions for instructional purposes.
> 2. They enable a substitute, upon short notice, to professionally carry out the intended lesson without the classroom setting simply becoming a "custodial" situation.
> 3. They enable an observer, such as the principal, to quickly acquire a "feeling" for the lesson (p. 9).

Most important, perhaps, is the fact that each teacher is assigned, in this document, to one of three adminstrators to whom he/she must submit his/her plan books *every week for checking*. In this context, the medical analogy in the document is interesting. No one would deny that surgeons would not operate without a plan of action. The question is, do surgeons have to have their plans checked by an administrator each time they perform an operation?

Unquestionably, professionals need to know what they are doing and plan accordingly. No one would argue with this. The issue here is *who* is responsible for the planning process, administrators or teachers? Teachers maintain that it is *their* responsibility and see administrative encroachment into what they consider to be their arena as negative. Administrators, on the other hand, assume that teachers will shirk their responsibility in this area and must, therefore, be monitored and controlled directly. They justify this move largely in terms of the necessity for substitute teachers to know what to do in case of teacher absence.

There is, however, a larger issue here. What does it mean for administrators to exert control over teachers at the level of checking plan books? This is not in any sense meaningful involvement in the academic process on the part of administrators since it is not clear that plan books, even if done "correctly," have any relationship to actual teaching. It is simply a ritual engaged in by the administration as a way of asserting the appearance of order and control. In fact, focusing on plan books contains any real struggle over the curriculum to the surface, since struggle over curriculum becomes flattened and defined as struggle over plans (whether done "correctly" and so forth).

Teachers resent administrator encroachment in the area of plan books (not curriculum, significantly) and correctly perceive a negative bias toward them. When I initially met the new principal, he informed me that he "knows almost all the teachers here" (he had been in the system, although not principal of the high school, for many years). His comment was, "They are, unfortunately, almost all passive. They just get their paycheck every two weeks and to hell with it! Many of them are afraid to let you [LW] in the classroom because they are afraid you'll report directly to me—like a spy." This is a key statement since he had been interacting with the teachers in this position for less than a week at the time of our discussion.

This general negativity is reflected in increased attempts to control teacher labor (although not in any meaningful way, as noted above), such as in the case of lesson plans. Mr. Sykes, a social studies teacher, made the following comment:

October 3*

I knew Gorski [the principal] before, and he wasn't a bad guy. When he came here, someone must have told him to "get tough with the teachers. Be tough from the beginning." I asked him how he felt about Gorski's comments about not using audio-visual equipment [to be discussed later in the chapter] unless it's classroom related. Mr. Sykes said, "It's terrible. That's what I mean—it's going to blow up." Mr. Teichler said he showed a filmstrip last week and Gorski walked by and told him it wasn't in his plan book. He said, "Yeah, I was supposed to give a test today, but the test was not xeroxed." "There's a backlog of two week's worth of xeroxing. How are we supposed to follow our plan books? Sometimes they don't even give us our books back. I didn't have my book on Monday. They say it's for the substitutes. No substitute is going to follow someone else's plan book."

On September 17, the principal announced at a faculty meeting after school that the "system had changed" because plan books were not being submitted properly. He articulates the change in the system below, still maintaining that plan books are for the convenience of substitutes:

Mr. Gorski: Item 7 on the [faculty meeting] agenda is plan books. Plan books were due to the appropriate administrator last Friday. We've gotten only two or three each. Make sure you get them in. Plan books are due next on September 27. On October 11, the plan books will be checked by department heads. This may be a surprise to department heads here, but from now on plan books go to department heads [he hands out the assessment from reprinted below]. This will give the administrators an opportunity to compliment you on your plans.

               Any reactions to this? [Silence. A few teachers appear to be smirking].

As the Lesson Plan Assessment indicates, the need for plan books is couched partially in terms of substitute teachers. Thus, an "evaluator of plans" would tick off whether "a substitute might encounter a problem with sequence of activities" or not, and whether "a substitute could very likely encounter a problem in knowing the direction in which to proceed as a result of these plans." The plan book assessment, however, must be seen as a nonmeaningful attempt to control teacher labor, thus giving the appearance that administrators are doing something, presumably, to improve instruction. As Bill Sykes, suggests, it was understood by teachers as harassment.

Statements regarding the use of audio-visual equipment reflect this same dynamic. Comments in both the orientation session referred to above and the faculty meeting of September 17 are illustrative here, and demonstrate both a deep lack of respect for teachers and the same ritual of control discussed in relation to plan books:

Lesson Plan Assessment

Teacher's Name —————————————   Date —————————————————

( ) Objectives should be clearer   ( ) Excellent objectives

( ) Difficult to understand objectives   ( ) Good objectives

( ) Might be difficult to difficult to   ( ) Appreciate the fact that objectives
measure attainment of objectives   are expressed in behavioral terms

---

( ) A substitute might encounter a   ( ) Sequence of activities is readily
problem with sequence of activities   evident

( ) A substitute might encounter a   ( ) Procedures are very clear
problem with clarity of procedures
                                          ( ) Procedures are clear

---

( ) Plans appear cluttered   ( ) Plans are quite readable

( ) A substitute could very likely   ( ) A substitute or observer could
encounter a problem in knowing the   proceed with or follow the lessons
direction in which to proceed as a   with ease as a result of these plans
result of these plans

( ) Excellent Plans   ( ) Good Plans   ( ) Acceptable Plans

( ) Plans need some "fine tuning"
( ) Plans need a good deal of work
( ) PLANS NOT AVAILABLE FOR ANALYSIS

Orientation Meeting, September 3, 1985

Mr. Gorski: Item number 3. Audio-visual equipment.
Teachers should only use audio-visual equipment
if it corresponds to lesson objectives. They
should not show a movie because they have
nothing planned for today.

Faculty Meeting, September 17[*]

Mr. Gorski: Audio-Visual. Get your requests in two to three
days ahead of time on an audio-visual request
form. (. . .) Certainly we would hope that the
supplies and materials you are using are related
to your field. Somehow I get the feeling that
teachers are using things that are not even related
to their subject matter. Don't just use a film
when you've had a bad weekend.

Statements like "Don't just use a film when you've had a bad weekend" or "Teachers should only use audio-visual equipment if it corresponds to lesson objectives" are obviously not reflective of any meaningful involvement in the selection, organization, and distribution of
knowledge. It is, once again, the appearance of order and control rather
than any substantive relationship with the learning process that is at issue
here.

A further example of what I am calling the ritual of control is the
careful monitoring of photocopying so that students are not simply given
"busy work." In the year that I was at Freeway, a new policy was
initiated. All photocopying machines were moved from the building and
relocated in a central office. Materials for xeroxing had to be cleared by
an administrator, and the photocopying machine previously located in
the high school was removed. While this may conceivably have been a
simple cost-saving measure, it is highly unlikely given the control rituals
outlined above—and it was not read that way by teachers. As Bonnie,
a secretarial science teacher, put it, "Nothing works in this place. I can't
even ditto anything." It is important to remember that these control
efforts were intensified by a principal who was new in this particular
position. It is not, then, a simple case of administration responding to
faculty who have been recalcitrant in the past. There certainly may be
some of this, but the fact remains that a new administrator began to
engage more intensely in creating the appearance of involvement, order,
and control, during his first few days on the job. The following reflects
the sentiments of teachers:

Teachers' Lunchroom, October 30[*]

Talk revolves around the photocopying machine. Duplicating is
being centralized and everyone is talking. There will be no

photocopying machine in the building. You have to put your requests through Mr. Kazi [in central administration] and it will take two weeks to get duplicating. In addition, teachers are saying that "Mr. Kazi will censor what can and cannot be duplicated." Bill said, "He [Mr. Kazi] was a bad teacher and he is a bad administrator."

Bill:	"That's how things are run around here. Grapevine. We [teachers] heard through the grapevine today that the xerox machine is going. It's bullshit" [he leaves].
Jean:	"Yeah, and they wonder why they have teacher shortages. We have no say over anything. They make it impossible to do our job. The only reason that things are as good as they are is because they've exploited bright women in the past. Just wait—things are going to get *really* bad [emphasis hers]. Salaries are low and the conditions of work are terrible."
[Bill returns]:	"I just heard that a truck backed up and took the xerox machine. Can you believe it? We have no say over anything."

. . .

*October 31, Talk in the Lunchroom with Mr. Seneca, French teacher**

Don:	Teachers are really mad about some stuff.
LW:	Yeah, I heard about the xerox machine.
Don:	That's just the tip of the iceberg. They're pushing people around too much. Like this meeting [in-service] tomorrow. We are ordered to report at eight A.M. Well, that's a change in the working conditions for some of us [who normally come in at nine A.M.]. There's a clause in the contract which says they can't change working conditions unless it's negotiated. Normally we wouldn't care, but with all this other crap we are going to meet about it tomorrow. Like the xerox machine.

We are trying to do our job, and we can't even
get materials to teach.

The point is that tension between teachers and administrators emerges
within the school largely in relation to ritual control over teacher labor.
Teachers feel that decisions over plan books, audio-visual materials, and
so forth ought to be theirs to make, and administrators increasingly
attempt to control and regularize these areas. Although this tends to keep
struggle at the surface rather than over anything more substantive, it
does, nevertheless, lead to a set of antagonisms that result in highly
derogatory statements over the public-address system such as the following:

January 30*

Mr. Gorski: Teachers, there are students in the hall. If you
            release students [from homeroom], you are
            wrong. *You are not in control of that homeroom*
            [emphasis his; implying that *he* is in control of
            the homeroom].

. . .

Okay. I think sufficient time has lapsed to take care of lunch
books [books related to the revision of free and/or reduced cost
lunches]. Teachers, you *may* [emphasis his] release students.
To repeat, you may now release students.

. . .

February 6* [in the teachers' lounge]

Principal is on the PA.

Mr. Gorski: Teachers, please fill out schedule cards when you
            come in tomorrow. We are revising our master
            schedule, so please write down all your
            classrooms, room assignments, when you enjoy
            your lunch, and so forth. We are revising the
            master schedule. So, teachers, *please* [he
            repeats].

Joan: We got it, we got it. He drives me crazy.

Clearly there is resentment on the part of teachers toward these efforts
at ritual control. This issue is further explored in the section below on
the covering of classroom windows.

Covering windows

In November, a memorandum was sent out by the principal instructing teachers not to cover up door windows facing the hall. Subsequently, this became a topic of discussion in the union meetings, lunchroom, and other public and private spaces. Teachers perceived this as yet one more attempt to control their labor—labor that they felt should properly be under their control rather than the administrators'. Two teachers comment on this below:

> *Mr. Lunetta:* Okay. There is a basic problem we have in this system. It was worse, I think, under [the previous superintendent]. There is no communication between the teachers and administration. Basically the teachers run the school. It's like the Army; the sergeants run the Army. And teachers, in order to feel good about themselves, need input into the school. Our problem in this district, and it still exists, is that we don't feel we have that input. Then they come now with a silly thing like "Take the thing off your door." What they don't understand is that we have a lot of traffic in this school. Kids are always moving; they are going here [and there]; the announcements; the chess club report, and they [students] stick their nose in your window and if you are trying to teach, they disrupt the class. All [that] covering the door was [supposed to do was] to stop that.
>
> But, again, the administration should . . .; it seems to me that when guys become principals they forget what it was like to teach. "I'm no longer a teacher; I'm an administrator." So, you've got this communication gap between the teachers and the administration and it's a problem. (. . .) We are not asking for everything because we are not always right. But we are in the pits [trenches] with the kids and we're down there. We know what's happening. Most of these guys have not been in a high

school in twenty-five years. They don't know
what we are dealing with. I had a guy [an
administrator] pound the desk, "I know how to
teach, I taught school." I said, "When did you
teach last?" "Nineteen fifty" [he replied]. I said,
'This is 1985. It's all different now. You don't
have all these nice little kids sitting there with
their hands on the desk. It's a different ball
game.'

A second teacher below echoes the same sentiments:

Mr. Johnson: They [administrators] don't have faith in the
teachers. They won't allow themselves to have
faith in the teachers. They want to know . . . I
think they want to keep their fingers on them.
(. . .) Part of the reason they [administrators]
wanted the windows uncovered [was that] they
wanted the principal to be able to come through
the school and make sure the teaching was
really going on. It was a mistrust of the faculty
(. . .) I don't think that should be a matter of
concern by administration in a good school. If
the teacher is not doing their job, it is going to
come back from the parents and things like
that. I certainly wouldn't feel that I had to
monitor the faculty. Here they do.

The dictum by the principal to uncover door windows facing the
hallway was, in fact, perceived by teachers as yet one more example,
like monitoring requests for audio-visual equipment and insistence on
handing in plan books, of administrators attempting to control areas that
ought to be under teacher's professional discretion. At the same time,
this encouraged teachers to think of plan books, windows, and so forth
as areas that necessitate professional knowledge, which, of course, they
are not. The ritual of control, then, served to reduce everything to a
struggle over form and to contain any real struggle that might emerge
over real curricular issues, for example. The analogue with knowledge
as distributed by teachers in the classroom is that the form of knowledge

in Freeway *also* prevents real involvement and struggle over issues. Both, however, buy the appearance of order and control.

A second memo from the principal in late November instructed teachers that "Doors will be covered using professional discretion." In response to this, even those teachers who had not covered their doors previously began to cover them with clearly nonprofessional or borderline nonprofessional materials, thus setting up an explicit warfare over who controls classroom windows. A tour of the two floors of the school in early January revealed the following window coverings:

- A cartoon depicting Elmer Fudd playing an instrument saying "Stop, Wabbit." (an English teacher)
- NFL and [the city] philharmonic orchestra stickers on white paper. (a sociology teacher)
- A piece of stained glass. (an art teacher)
- The cover of *Sports Illustrated* depicting the Hulkster [Hulk Hogan]. (a social studies teacher)
- Two copies of the principal's memo of November 1985 saying that door windows should be covered using professional discretion. (an English teacher)
- Three Funky Winkerhearn cartoons about math on white paper. (a math teacher)
- A picture of a turkey. (a social studies teacher)
- A poster that says "Adult Education Often Begins with Teenager Marriage." (an English teacher)
- A [local team] football sticker on black paper. (a social studies teacher)
- A picture of famous chemists. (a chemistry teacher)
- A picture of a plant. (biology teacher)
- A political cartoon. (a social studies teacher)
- A picture of a sailboat. (an English teacher)

These coverings were not in evidence to nearly the same extent prior to the series of memos on the subject. In fact, I had not noticed door coverings prior to the memos. The point is that teachers genuinely felt that their professional autonomy was being undermined by the controlling impulses of administration. Teachers responded, in turn, to dictums to "uncover windows" and use "professional discretion when covering windows," by more often covering windows with clearly nonprofessional material or materials that could only be seen loosely as professionally related, such as a picture of a plant in the case of the biology teacher. This, along with teachers' comments noted above, suggests strongly that teachers resent such intrusion into what they consider *their* domain but that their domain became reduced, in these interactions, to window coverings, plan books, and so forth, rather than to substantive issues surrounding teaching and learning. It is also of great significance that I heard nowhere near as much public collective talk about salary struggles as about the photocopy machine. Thus plan books, audio-visual equipment, photocopying and classroom windows became *the* arenas of struggle between administrators and teachers.

There is, as I have suggested throughout the chapter, a ritual of control over teacher labor in Freeway High. Administrators engage in this ritual, and teachers engage in a similar ritual with respect to the form of classroom knowledge. Students, in turn, work to "pass" and participate in the control ritual by being orderly. Since the notion that schooling must be taken seriously is distributed at the same time as these rituals are enacted, the contradictory attitude toward education expressed within the youth identities is encouraged.[6] Knowledge as they receive it cannot possibly, after all, encourage youth to focus on anything other than form.

Separatist spheres

A second set of messages in the school revolves around the appropriateness of separatist gender and race spheres, and the normality of certain types of behaviors and attitudes related to this separation. Such separatism is clearly a part of the identities discussed in chapters 2 and 3. However, the school legitimates such separatism through its own set of routines and rituals. This is true both for gender and race, although there are countervailing tendencies within the school which I will discuss at a later point in the chapter. I will address the issue of gender first.

To begin with, it is important to note that separate gender space exists in the school and that men invade female space, whereas women never invade male space. This parallels within the school the traditional allocation of space whereby men come and go from the domestic scene (women's space) but women are expected to remain in this sphere and are not welcome in public male places.[7] This use of space within the school was apparent to me when I made initial contacts with teachers in the spring of 1985 and was reinforced at the faculty in-service on September 3. Men and women simply occupy different space within the school. The faculty lounges [not simply bathrooms] are physically separate, and the faculty lunchroom is separated by virtue of where people choose to sit.

May 21, 1985 [on entering the field]

Meetings with Ms. Hartle and Ms. Jones, both of the business department. Meeting separately with Ms. Hartle at one-fifteen and Mrs. Jones at two-twenty. The meetings were set up by Mr. Jackson, coordinator of the business department, since they could not attend the general meeting for business faculty.

This is the first time I was in the faculty lounge [located down the hall from the principal's office]. The lounge is separate for men and women. The women have their side and the men theirs. When I inquired about this, Ms. Hartle said, "Yeah, that gives us more privacy. We have a rest room on each side." I asked if people ever go into the other side and she said, "The guys sometimes come here if they want to see someone, but we never go to the other side. They come in and talk." [The men are using the door to the women's side of the lounge even though they have their own door.]

reliable research data?

This same segregated pattern was apparent at the first orientation meeting in the fall.

September 3*

The orientation was scheduled to begin at nine. I arrived at eight forty-five and there was coffee and donuts in the cafeteria. Many people were already there. Personnel tended to be gender segregated. Men were at their own tables, and women theirs. It was immediately apparent that this was the case.

Throughout the school year, these patterns persisted. Although there were separate spaces for women and men, it was seen as acceptable that men invaded women's space. Men constantly walked into the women's side of the lounge and sat and talked, for example. I never saw a woman in the men's lounge, and it would have been seen as highly unacceptable.

I myself was made to feel that the men's lounge was not my space, although the women's lounge was theirs. The lunchroom, although ostensibly shared gender space, once again became divided. This partially corresponded to discipline taught, but not entirely, as I will suggest in chapter 5. Only one female, a math teacher, regularly sat with men, and only one male, a social studies teacher, regularly sat with women. The one black female teacher in the lunch period I joined on a regular basis, sat with the monitors, some of whom are black and some white. The white females always sit at one end of the table, the women of color and all monitors and aides sit at the other end of the "female table." This was a stable seating pattern throughout the entire year, and tended to be reflected in all other lunch periods, although I spent most of my time in one of them.

Interactions within the spaces tended to be stereotypically gender specific. Women, for example, often discussed recipes, food, cosmetics, and so forth. Men discuss, on the other hand, computers, football, and betting pools. Significantly, little of the lunchroom talk revolved around students, although there is talk, as noted earlier, about the administration. The stereotypical nature of female discussion is evident in field notes reproduced below:

February 6, 1986[*] [in the lunchroom]

I just realized how much of the time women teachers discuss recipes. One woman had the school lunch of chili.

Ms. Fletcher: There is too much meat in it.

Ms. Butcher: Everyone makes chili differently, I put a lot of celery and beans in it. Some people don't.

Ms. Fletcher: I do, too. This chili has too much meat in it.

Ms. Butcher: My husband likes chili soup. He likes it so thin it's like soup. My kids call it hamburger soup. "When are you going to make hamburger soup, Mom?"

Ms. Sanford: You know, _____ [a restaurant in town] has something like a chili soup with cheese on top of it. It's good. I don't make a good chili; my daughter-in-law does. She adds a can of tomato soup at the end to thicken it. It's really good. No water, just tomato soup.

Ms. Butler: I use a can of tomatoes in mine.

At another point during the year, Ms. Snapple, the cosmetology teacher, handed out a clipping to the women in the lunchroom entitled, "Your Refrigerator Holds Worlds of Cosmetics." In this article were recipes for Avocado Dry Skin Mask, Cucumber Refresher Mask, Banana Mask, Herbal Sauna, Tomato Compress, and so forth. A great deal of time was spent by the women teachers discussing these homemade cosmetics, including what to do if you are allergic to certain fruits. Ms. Snapple pointed out that you should use the cosmetics "within a relatively short period of time, before rancidity or spoilage sets in."

In addition to recipes and related elements of traditional female culture, there are elements within this separate sphere that are directly critical of men. These range from a discussion of how sloppy men are to the fact that women still do not experience equality with males. The issue of unequal pay received quite a bit of attention from a certain group.

Lunch, October 23*

Nancy [a business teacher] was talking about the salaries of secretaries. "Starting salaries in business are four thousand, nine thousand, or ten thousand dollars. You just can't live on that. Men come in as management trainees at seventeen thousand dollars. Secretaries, just because they are women, don't make seventeen thousand dollars after fifteen years. It used to make me so mad [she was a secretary]. These men in the department at [State University, where she used to work] used to make so much money. I was eighteen [years old] and making three thousand nine hundred dollars. Men couldn't survive if it weren't for female secretaries."

Many other times throughout the year this conversation surfaced among female teachers. Jan earlier said, with respect to talk about the photocopy machines, "Yeah, and they wonder why they have teacher shortages. We have no say over anything. They make it impossible to do our job. The only reason that things are as good as they are is that they've exploited bright women in the past." Nancy, a business teacher, takes up the issue of gender inequality rather vociferously during numerous lunch conversations and in a later interview which I conducted with her. Below, she offers a feminist analysis of why pay for secretaries is low, for example:

I [have had] male students say to me that they do intend to be secretaries and they've asked, "How much do they [secretaries] make?" Now, that's the disappointing factor since it is basically, out there in the real world, dominated by women and [it] is a traditional woman's occupation its traditional pay is low because it is not considered equal to male work and that is a very poor perception of the males that control the corporate world because they couldn't function without those well-trained secretaries who sometimes may not have a college degree but have to take more specialized courses in their area than some people at the college level and have to prove mastery. They [secretaries] are not paid for mastery in these difficult skills. The language arts and other communication skills; the manual dexterity you need for typing and shorthand; and just the basic decision-making skills that they have to have to be able to handle the responsibility. They do not get their just deserts at all.

There is, therefore, discussion among woman faculty of gender inequality and, particularly, low pay for women. The second point of sustained criticism among female teachers is the perception that men want female servants. This is clarified in the two sets of field notes below:

September 1985[*]

In the teachers' lunchroom three women were complaining that it is the men [from the previous lunch period] who leave their dishes and napkins on the tables [the place is always a mess from the previous period].

Nancy: "They have maids at home."

All the women were complaining that the men are slobs and don't even have the "courtesy to clean up after themselves."

Susan: "They expect us to clean up after them."

. . .

May 6, 1986*

In the teachers' lunchroom, 11:00

Paul [running the in-school suspension room today] is getting lunch for three students there. He is holding one tray and drops the Tater Tots [potatoes] on the floor. He proceeds to walk out.

Nancy: "Did you ever notice how these guys expect someone to clean up after them?"

Susan: "Yeah, they really do. They leave the tables in here a mess."

Jan: "I feel sorry for the girls here who get married young. They don't know what they're getting into."

Nancy: "They have this knight-on-a-white-charger crap. They think they'll get a knight on a white charger, and they get a horse's ass."

Susan and Jan get up and clean up the Tater Tots from the floor.

It is noteworthy that the separatist spheres are maintained, and, at the same time, that the female sphere contains emerging elements critical of men within it. Some of the women constantly criticize both the fact that women earn less than men, and that men expect to be picked up after. However, it is important to note that the woman do, in fact, pick up after the men. Thus, when Paul spills the Tater Tots, Susan and Jan, although critical of male behavior, proceed to clean up. They do, in some sense then, see that as their role.

Men also invade women's space, whereas the reverse is not true, as I noted earlier. This extends to the classroom itself where, as I noted on many occasions throughout the year, male teachers walk in and out of female classrooms to check equipment, grade papers, and so forth. It is seen as perfectly appropriate to invade women's space in this way. Conversely, I never saw a female teacher invade male space, either public in the sense of teaching space, or private in the sense of the faculty lounge.

Separatist racial spheres are also maintained at Freeway High. It is noteworthy, for instance, that the two black female faculty members always sit with the monitors and aides at lunch, some of whom are black, rather than with the white female teachers. Teachers also referred to the racially segregated nature of Freeway on many occasions, as the following makes clear:

April 30, 1985[*] (entry notes)

The meeting with social studies faculty was interesting. I simply introduced myself and then let them make comments. Ms. Heyman said the students would react differently [to school] depending on the part of the city they were from. They all agreed that there were "two worlds" in Freeway. The one part has "green lawns, people who became foremen in the plant; they made it, and either moved to a certain part of Freeway or _____ [a nearby suburb]."

. . .

October 23, Social Studies class[*]

Before the test announcement Mr. Simon was talking about integration. He said, "Is there a bridge in Freeway?"

James:	"Yeah."
Mr. Simon:	"Do blacks live on one side of the bridge?"
Rick:	"Yeah."
Mr. Simon:	"Yeah, you just don't see blacks on this side of the bridge."
Clifton [a black male]:	"You can move if you have the money."
Mr. Simon:	"Yeah, legally you can. But your neighbors might not talk to you. Your children may not be allowed to play with the other children on the block. It's different if you are making a hundred thousand dollars a year.
	Blacks and whites live together in those neighborhoods. Do you think anyone cares if O.J. Simpson [a well-known former football player] moves in next door? Hey, O.J.! He's famous! Oh, yeah, he's black, but

who cares? That's where you see the
change, in the rich areas."

· · ·

April 20, 1986*

A school-board member walks into the teachers' lunchroom.
She is very tan, having obviously just returned from Florida or
the Caribbean. She walks up to a black aide: "I'm as dark as
you; let's compare tans. I'll go and buy a home on _____" [in
the "black" part of town, across the bridge].

No one would dispute the fact that there are largely racially segregated
neighborhoods in Freeway. The large housing project "across the tracks"
is virtually all black and Hispanic , and the area surrounding the school—
the area of "green lawns"—is entirely white. This community-based
segregation is played out at the faculty level, too. There are only three
minority teachers, despite the fact that the school is approximately 15
percent minority: one black female teaches special education, and two
minority women are in secretarial science. The school thus encourages
separatist racial spheres and white dominance. This is reflected in lunchroom seating patterns and teacher discussion of neighborhoods, even in
classrooms. Until recently, Freeway was segregated in terms of schools;
blacks attended one set of schools and whites another. This has, with
legal action, broken down within the past ten years, but the segregated
nature of the community is still almost totally intact. Under these circumstances, it is not surprising to find overtly racist comments such as those
below.

March 5*

I went to see Johnnie Aaron [the football coach] to see if the
Nautilus room could be used for interviewing.

He said, "It's always in use; there's always someone in there."

William, a black male student, was in Johnnie's room, as well
as John, a white male.

Johnnie: What happened to your hair, "boy"?

William: It fell out. I was nervous before the game. [He
shaved his head.]

Johnnie has, on other occasions, referred to black males as "boy."

. . .

April 21*

Johnnie: [Talking to a black male, pointing to another black male] Get that little pygmy over there and tell him he owes me twenty-eight dollars.

. . .

Study Hall*

Anthony [a black male]: Hi, girls [to two white girls].

Mr. Antonucci: Stop talking to white girls.

Anthony: Got any colored ones?

Mr. Antonucci: You don't seem to understand why I moved you up here [to the front]. [He kicks him out of the classroom.]

. . .

April 21* [in the women's lounge].

Johnnie: [to a black teacher aide] Be nice to me.

Edna: Kiss my ass.

Johnnie: Hey, some black lady in there is being mean to me [to others in the hall].

Edna: I repeat, kiss my ass.

Although directly racist comments such as those above were relatively infrequent on the part of faculty, comments such as those below were not, suggesting a deep racism that lies within the teacher and school culture generally.

February 26, Lunchroom*

Jean, a business teacher, had left her lunch on top of the fridge. She threw it away, with the comment, "We all know what's in there."

LW: What?

Susan: Cockroaches.

LW: I never saw a cockroach here.

Susan: You're lucky.

Marsha: You know, I have a friend that just got a job
teaching in [the nearby large city], on _____
and _____, or something like that [right in the
black ghetto]. She's straight from suburbia and is
teaching middle-class values. She was using a big
chart, she's teaching kindergarten, to teach the "M"
sound. The kids were saying "M" and all of a
sudden a cockroach walked across the paper. She
stiffened; the kids did not seem to even notice,
they're used to it. She just took off her shoe and
killed it. Then she had the kids say, "Mommy" to
practice words with a "M" sound. One little boy
burst out crying and said, "Mommy got drunk and
left." She said to herself, "What am I doing here?"

Barbara: Oh yeah, and they [black kids] love to come up and
feel your hair [she makes a face as if this is
extremely distasteful to her].

. . .

September 5, 1985*

Talk with Mr. Weaver, the assistant principal.

I ran into Mr. Weaver in the hall. He was telling me what a
"good system this is here. The kids are good. The [college
preparation] courses are as good as the [college preparation]
courses anywhere."

"This is a realistic situation here, about fifteen percent black or
minority." He thinks that if a school gets "too black," it is no
longer "serious." "Too many of their homes are giddy places,
not serious enough. If you get too many blacks in the school, it
is not serious. Fifteen percent is fine. They can't act that way
['giddy'] in school if they are only fifteen percent."

The point is that not only are separatist cultures maintained in the
school but also that these cultures and the distributed notion of white-
male dominance encourage the virulent sexism and racism noted in
chapter 2, in particular. This is not conscious, of course, and faculty
no doubt would deny the argument presented here. However, there *is*
separatism within the school itself and this separatism tends to reinforce

racism and, in the case of white males, the setting up of black as "other" in their constructed identity. It also encourages the setting up of a female "other" and assumed male dominance which lies within the identity of working-class white males.

For females, separatism encourages the setting up of a male "other," in the sense that their own identity becomes formed in relation to that of a constructed notion of men. Whatever progressive elements exist within the identity structures tend to be only minimally encouraged, in comparison, by the school. This is somewhat less the case for gender than race. In the case of gender, there are some glimmerings of gender challenge among the faculty themselves, reflective of the same social movement and economic changes that are encouraging the beginnings of gender challenge among young females in the high school. Women, although existing within a separate sphere, partially defined and certainly invaded by men, do, in fact, render problematic certain elements of female existence, and there are some active attempts on the part of the school to encourage challenges to traditional gender identity. In the guidance office, for example, an article entitled "Message to Daughters—Learn to Go It On Your Own" is prominently displayed. The article suggests that women should carve an economic niche for themselves and not simply be a wife and mother. These glimmerings must be seen as related to the tendencies within female identity noted in chapter 3, a topic that I will pursue at some length in chapter 7. By and large, however, the school tends to encourage separatism and the inequality that, in a concrete setting, accompanies such separatism. It must also be remembered that many of these progressive messages are eroded at the level of classroom practice as noted in an earlier chapter.

I have argued here that administrators engage in a ritual of control over teacher labor which serves to encourage an emphasis on form rather than substance, and that this emphasis on form has its analogue in the way in which classroom knowledge is packaged and distributed by teachers. This emphasis on form, in turn, fuels the contradictory attitudes toward education and knowledge in evidence among working-class youth. The school also encourages separatist race and gender spheres, emphasizing white-male dominance. I will, in the next chapter, explore more carefully the way in which teachers themselves, and the cultures they consciously or unconsciously create, play into these processes.

5
Freeway Teachers

What I dislike. I dislike this aggravation where I feel as if my abilities aren't being used. Okay. Where they are being completely circumvented because that's like coming up and spitting in my face. That's what I don't like about it. What I like about the place is that as of tomorrow I'm going to be off for two weeks [at Easter break]. Then when we come back the kids aren't going to do any more work because it just shuts off. Before, they did very little [work]; now they're going to do none, and then the days are going to keep getting warmer, and warmer and warmer, and we are going to go through the graduation ceremony where a couple of us are going to stand back there and whistle the theme for the Laurel and Hardy movies as they are marching up to the stage. Because that's bullshit, too. And the kids are going to go up there with their paper caps and gowns; somebody's going to open up his gown as he gets his diploma and flash the whole audience wearing a bikini or cotton cock or something like that, you know, and at the end they're going to throw their little hats up in the air, somebody is going to get hit in the eye with one and that's it. That's what they think of education. It's a big fucking joke.— Mr. Poletti, a computer teacher

The Freeway teaching force encourages identity formation as discussed in chapters 2, 3, and 4 in some rather important ways. Aspects of youth identity are shaped *in relation* to schools and teachers and it is, therefore, critical that school processes and, as I suggest in this chapter, teachers themselves embody certain characteristics in working-class communities. I will examine who the teachers are in terms of their background; what they see as the positives and negatives of their job;

and the ways in which these factors may contribute to a teacher culture which encourages emerging social identities. My intent here is not to criticize, rather to understand the way in which spheres of social identity may interact and intersect in a working-class community so as to encourage the creation of high levels of alienation and the identities emerging in post-industrial society.

It is no accident that this chapter is male dominated, especially the section on steelworkers and teacher comments relating to wages and fringe benefits. Although 35 percent of the Freeway teachers are female, and I spoke with the female teachers, they were relatively silent. The issues that emerge as categories are, in the final analysis, male oriented, and male teachers had more to say about them. It is significant that in this working-class community the female teachers were silent, suggesting a silence in the public sphere of paid work. This is in line with some of the data on separatist spheres presented in the last chapter, where, as I suggested, male teachers feel comfortable invading female space but female teachers never invade male space, paralleling the traditional use of space in the private and public spheres generally. That male voices dominate the discourse is significant in and of itself, of course, for the argument presented in this book. White male teachers dominate space *and* teacher discourse in schools, reinforcing, once again, the ethos of white-male superiority. Female teachers are relatively silent, and their silence can be related to the way in which the school both promotes separatism and the superiority of white men. Future research needs to focus more directly on women teachers and industrial workers in working-class communities in order to probe the words behind the silences noted here.[1] I turn now to a description of the Freeway teachers.

Who are the teachers?

Eighty secondary-school teachers are listed for the academic year 1984–85. Of these, data on high school attended and so forth were available for seventy-five, and the analysis that follows is based on these seventy-five teachers. The faculty is overwhelmingly white. Three black faculty members comprise 4 percent of the teaching population in a community that is approximately 20 percent minority. Of these, all are female; one teaches secretarial science and two teach special education. This is significant in and of itself. There are no minority male teachers at

117

Freeway High; the three females teach in nonacademic areas. Two are in special education, where nationally a disproportionate number of black youth is concentrated, and one is in the relatively low paid female vocational area of secretarial studies.[2] In terms of a gender breakdown, fifty-two teachers, or 65 percent, are male, with some tendency toward female ghettoization in secretarial studies, home economics, and cosmetology. All the "hard" vocational areas (which have increasingly little presence in the schools) such as automotive technology, woodworking, construction technology, machine shop; and the like, are taught by males. Females tend to be spread rather evenly through the remaining subject areas. Thus, there are two female math teachers, three female English teachers, two female science teachers, two female social studies teachers, and two female foreign language teachers. The pattern of female ghettoization exists primarily in nonacademic areas rather than in the core academic subjects. This is unlike the case nationally, where there has been greater tendency toward academic subject matter ghettoization by gender.[3]

Data regarding high school attendance are particularly revealing, suggesting the highly localized nature of the teaching force. *Forty-four percent of both male and female teachers themselves attended and graduated from Freeway High.* Freeway is an overwhelmingly Catholic area, and a relatively high proportion of remaining teachers attended diocesan high schools in the immediate area. Seventy-four percent of males either graduated from Freeway High, or a local diocesan school, and 68 percent of females graduated from these schools. In point of fact, only eleven males and seven females attended a public school other than Freeway High, and only two males and one female attended private schools other than diocesan Catholic institutions. There is, therefore, likely to be relative congruence of home and school influences in this community given the fact that so many teachers are from the community to begin with. As I will suggest later in the chapter, teacher social class background is also not terribly unlike that of the students.

This is a far more locally drawn teaching population than is the case for the region as a whole.[4] Data gathered in 1983–84 in a five-county area that comprises a judicial district in the state in which Freeway is located suggest that only 25 percent of all teachers (certified nursery— 12) graduated from a secondary school in the same system in which they were teaching presently. The measure of localism used in the regional study, however, is not the same as that in the Freeway study. In Freeway, *a full 44 percent of secondary-school teachers graduated from Freeway*

High itself, not simply a "school in the *district* (my emphasis) in which they [teachers] were currently teaching." Also, elementary-school teachers tend to be more locally recruited than in secondary school, and the larger regional study concentrates on N–12. Thus, the Freeway teachers are strikingly more locally drawn than teachers in the larger judicial district.[5]

Sixty-five percent of males and 68 percent of females received their bachelor's degrees from one of three institutions in the immediate Freeway area. Seventy-four percent of teachers have master's degrees; ninety-four percent and 100 percent of males and females, respectively, received their master's from one of these same local institutions. This, again, suggests a much more localized teaching population than in the larger judicial district. About 70 percent of teachers in the region received their undergraduate degrees from colleges or universities in the region, and this is more pronounced for K-6 certified teachers. Over 40 percent of 7–12 certified teachers attended universities or colleges outside the region—the region, again, being a much larger unit than the local area noted for the Freeway teachers. Eight-five percent of teachers (N–12) in the region possess master's degrees, and the vast majority did their graduate work at regional colleges and universities.

These data suggest a very localized teaching force. The majority of Freeway teachers attended the one public high school in Freeway. They did not venture far away to college, either, with the vast majority attending college at one of three local institutions. The majority of Freeway teachers have, in fact, always been Freeway citizens. Several of the teachers comment on this below:

*February 12, Lunchroom**

LW: [to the computer teacher] Do the kids like the computer?

Mark Poletti: Well, they have no value for it. They have no reason to use it. I ask the kids to enter their names, address, and the address of three other people. They can't do it—they don't have the address of three other people. And the faculty is the same—they have the same value. Have you noticed how inbred the system is? Everyone here is the same. The teachers are the same as the kids. So the kids aren't challenged.

Our kids come in as smart as anyone else. But
in high school they don't learn to think. Their
values aren't challenged. The faculty are mostly
from here [Freeway]: they went to school here,
or they went to Catholic school. It's all this
role memorization shit. Especially in Catholic
school. How many scientists come from
Catholic school?

(. . .) You know, when my father was a
kid, the teachers were all these do-good white
Anglo-Saxon Protestants. They wanted to
Americanize the immigrants right off the boat.
Like my father. He was right off the boat. My
teachers were the children of these immigrants.
It became inbred. No one from the outside
came in. The values are the same; the teachers
are no different from the kids.[6]

. . .

*March 17** [in the teachers' lunchroom]

Richard Simon was talking about the inbreeding in the system.

Richard: Almost all the teachers in Freeway are from
Freeway. Everybody knew somebody in order
to get the job [he is also from Freeway].

Sam Mouton: Yeah, my first day here everyone was asking
me who I knew. I live in _____ [the larger
city]. I had to *know* [emphasis his] somebody
to get the job.

Richard: Oh yeah. It's all political. Freeway is a political
town; the school system is political, too.

LW: Was it accidental that so many teachers were
from Freeway? Were they the only ones who applied?

Richard: No, the board *wanted* [my emphasis] to hire
people from Freeway. You really had to know
someone to get hired. Half this school is related
to the other half. That's why nobody talks
about anybody else—you're not sure who is related to whom.

Dave Zabel:	One time they hired outsiders because there was a shortage of teachers. A bunch of those people were laid off, though.
LW:	Why hire people from Freeway?
Richard:	You hire friends and relatives. To give a job to the son of a board member who is graduating from college this year. There was a story about two guys [who were related to board members] who were going to graduate and needed jobs that fall. There was only one job so they denied tenure to someone else so that they could have two jobs.
Dave Zabel:	You can control people better [if you hire "your own"]. No one rocks the boat if they're all related or thankful to certain people for their job.
Sam Mouton:	Oh, yeah, that happened at my tenure time. _____ [a central administrator] called me into the office in March and said he might not write a letter for my tenure file if I didn't do something for him. I slammed it down and said, "Take your fucking letter—I was hired mid-year." He thought he'd get me but I already had tenure.

The political nature of hiring is quite apparent. Although Alan Peshkin finds a similar localized hiring pattern in Mansfield, a small rural community in the midwest, the reasons for such hiring appear to be different. Peshkin suggests that the school board *deliberately* hires people who have a certain "country" orientation in order to preserve "community" in its ideal sense. In the case of the hiring of a superintendent, for example, Peshkin notes the following:

I wouldn't do nothing different and I wouldn't go anywhere else, says board president George Robinson. His colleague Rex Borden observes, I've never been anywhere but Mansfield. Small-town life is something you feel; you can't always express it. And Bert Holcomb agrees, I've seen lots of places but I never thought of staying there. These are the underlying sentiments that selected Mansfield's new superintendent (these are the school-board members, responsible for all hiring). To be sure, board members did not seek out their alter ego. Nonetheless, after hearing the deliberations, who could doubt that they sought a person who would administer the school system in their spirit, true to the prevailing outlook? He's country, they agreed and thereby reassured themselves. Neither in questions to the candidate nor in their deliberations afterward did they focus on a candidate's capacity to lead Mansfield to academic grandeur. They inquired, instead, about a candidate's fit with their orthodoxy and then eliminated one man after another until they discovered they felt most right about Reynolds.[7]

In Freeway, however, the inbred nature of hiring is not so much to preserve "community" as Peshkin suggests, rather that teaching jobs, like many jobs in the city, function as patronage positions. While such hiring may function to "preserve the community" in the final analysis, it does not constitute the real reason for this hiring. Many teachers talked to me privately about the hiring process in Freeway and many noted that overt payoffs used to take place in order to secure positions. It is, therefore, no accident that such a high proportion of teachers are from Freeway. The following excerpts clarify this.

*February 13, In a car touring the community**

Mark Poletti: You know how I got a job in Freeway? I got outa school and had an interview in front of five board members. One is totally behind me, but the others wanted a little "backsheesh"; I had to pay them, twelve hundred dollars—one-third of my salary. That's how all these guys got their jobs [he names administrators]. They all gave a little "backsheesh." They're principals with nine credit hours. How can you have a good school district when that goes on? The only way to fix it is to run them all out and start over again. (a computer teacher)

. . .

Peter Frank: [on being hired at Freeway] I'd just graduated. I'd finished school in September 1970 and I

	lived on _____ [in Freeway] and I was driving over to Freeway Steel to look for a job in their pollution abatement program and on the way I stopped at the junior high school, saw _____, the principal there, an old family friend who told me I was a damn fool for going to Freeway Steel because it was cold and I'd get hurt and he had a job for me teaching biology.
LW:	Did you have a teaching certificate?
Peter:	No, I had a B.S. in biology from _____.
LW:	So, then what happened?
Peter:	More or less a lark, really. I hadn't seen him for a couple of years. In any case, since this is a core area here, they could hire a noncertified teacher if no one else is available, and through my friendship with _____ and [the fact that my] family was in the school system for years [his father used to be principal of the high school], my association with the superintendent and a couple members of the school board, it went through. I was hired. They simply had to file a statement with the state, I guess, that no other qualified teacher was available.[8] (A science teacher)

The deeply political nature of Freeway is well known, and the hiring process in the school reflects this. It is important to point out, however, that politics infuses a number of areas of schooling, not just hiring. This is particularly important given that the school is ostensibly a meritocratic institution in which, at least on an ideological level, anyone can succeed if only he/she is bright enough and applies him/herself. A number of practices within the school contradict this meritocratic ideology, however, as the teachers below note.

The first three teachers discuss the generally political environment in which they work, alluding to the way in which administrative posts and equipment are obtained:

Don Seneca:	I know faculty members who have told me that they know so-and-so [in the school system] paid

for his job [an administrative post] because they were one of the people who bid on the job and they apparently bid too low. People have told me that! And I look at them and say, "I can't believe you have enough balls to tell me that you were bidding on a job. That stinks!" "I'm just telling you, man, so you don't let this guy give you any heat because he *bought* that job. I really don't care, but I'm just saying that's the way." (a foreign language teacher)

. . .

Sam Mouton: When I first came to Freeway—I'm an outsider—I had no ties, no political influence or family ties. I found that the everyday life was consumed by politics. It's a way of life in Freeway. I also found that the mentality of the politics was the old Chicago kind—the Daley era—and that its attitude was reflected in a strong sense of unionism. As in most cases, the union philosophy is all for me and nothing for you and shaft the company and get me as much as you can for as little work as I have to do. That reflected the attitude that the administration and the board had for the teachers as if we had that same philosophy, and, eventually they forced us into that. (a social studies teacher)

. . .

[about the underfunded vocational education]

LW: Are you saying that if you had played politics you would have gotten more equipment?

Paul Pelly: Yes.

LW: Do other teachers play politics?

Paul: Yes. Our athletic department has the biggest budget. Did you go downstairs and see the athletic room? There isn't a junior college around here that has that type of equipment! [He is referring to the Nautilus Room.] You never see this in any high school. I shouldn't say never, but you probably find one percent

throughout the United States, a high school that
has that type of equipment.

(. . .) You won't believe the way they
acquired those. Normally they have a fifteen-
hundred-dollar limit (. . .) They bought about
a hundred thousand worth of equipment (. . .)
They keep getting it; they replace this stuff all
the time.[9] (a vocational education teacher)

Politics infuses scheduling in the school in much the same way as it
affects hiring in the system. Something as apparently neutral as course
scheduling is highly contested in Freeway. Whether one teaches "first
shift" or "second shift" (the high school operates on a split schedule),
or whether one teaches classes sequentially, thereby having more blocks
of free time, is subject to negotiation and has nothing to do with rules
of seniority. Since the younger grades attend the second shift, and the
eleventh and twelfth graders the first, the assignation of teachers to
particular grade levels is accomplished irrespective of academic considerations. *In other words, as in the case of hiring, there is no academic
justification; it is simply political.* By this I mean, it is simply a matter
of who knows whom and whether one can manipulate the system, as the
teachers below point out:

. . .

LW:	What do you mean you are teaching sophomores because of politics? How does politics determine what it is you teach?
Paul:	One of the board members ran for school board elections last year [and] comes out and says that I didn't support her. So then, in turn, it goes down to [the superintendent and the director of secondary curriculum]. They are going to tell me what to teach. You have no choice; you are here to work.
LW:	But how does the board member influence what you teach? I mean, the board doesn't determine teacher schedules, does it?
Paul:	The board tells the superintendent. The

125

superintendent, in turn, tells [the director of secondary curriculum]. Now we go to guidance. Guidance determines the schedule. So, when I went to see Mr. _____ [the guidance counselor], the first day, I says to him, "Dick, this is not fair. _____ doesn't know how to run a cutter grinder" [he was assigned to teach the class instead of Paul]. I said, "The kids are going to lose." He says, "Paul, you know the game." I said, "Yeah, it's pathetic."

(. . .) Okay. Now I am backing a candidate for school board. I told her I've never been involved in politics in one way or another (. . .) If I'm going to back their candidate, I said I want [her] commitment that [she] will help the area [vocational education]. So if she fails, kiss me good-bye. That's politics you are dealing with in Freeway.

Maybe these other people [teachers] aren't as open.[10] I really don't care. My son is a mechanical engineer at Kodak and my daughter works for U.S. Air. They are doing well; I'm doing well. (a vocational education teacher)

. . .

LW: What is the advantage of having periods five, six and seven free? Why would somebody want to do that?

Don Seneca: To do nothing. To have time to prepare classes, to correct papers and not have to take them home. Some people go to city hall when they have two or three classes free. They can get out and roam around the city.

(. . .) I mean, some of these guys will hustle all week, all year, that's all they do is push political people just so they can keep their few free periods.

(. . .) I never felt that people deliberately
shafted me because of me [he had a "bad"
schedule]. What happens is this. Joe Blow,
somebody's nephew, is going to get a certain
deal this year because somebody's uncle made
sure he was going to get this set. So they set
him up with whatever schedule he wanted,
whatever courses he wanted, or whatever. This
goes on right down the line. All right, what's
left? Somebody like me who doesn't know
anybody gets what's left. For years, I had no
free period. There's a state law that says every
secondary teacher in a state school gets one
free unassigned period. It's the law. Well, in
order to get somebody's friend two or three
extra unassigned duties, I had to pick up an
extra study hall. Where do I turn? Especially
when you don't have tenure yet? So, it wasn't
like they were trying to stiff me; it's just that
they had to take care of other people.

(. . .) Look around. We are overstaffed
(. . .) We could lose ten people in the senior
high with no problem. 'Cause they are hiding
people with small classes; people with really
light schedules (. . .) That wasn't easy; some
people had to take up to forty kids [to cover
them].

(. . .) Politics. That's how they get set up.
That's the schedule. The schedule comes out;
you've got three classes. Lots of people. It
comes out of guidance but the guidance counselor sits there and picks up the phone and the
guy says, "This is Joe Blow, board member,
make sure you do not assign so-and-so any
assignment on fifty, sixty, seventh and eighth"
[period]. What do you say, 'No'? Especially
when you remember that this guy is the head
of guidance [in central office] or the head
principal. [Then] the principal calls and says,
"Make sure he's free this period." You got all

these deals going. It's not just in the school system. It's the people in city politics, they call the board members and they got deals and they are calling in markers or something. It's crazy. (a foreign language teacher)

. . .

LW: How much scheduling do you actually control [as department head]?

John Teichler: Okay. I make recommendations but they make the final decisions. The principal, the guidance counselor, the assistant superintendent, and the superintendent. I put out feelers. I canvas the department. I'll say, "Okay, where will you feel comfortable, what's your expertise, and what would you really like to do?" They'll come back and say this and that.

LW: What relationship does your schedule have with the final schedule? If you recommend that "X" should be teaching ninth and "Y" should be teaching twelfth, does that look pretty much like the final schedule?

JT: No, again, you see we have a couple of people transferred. The person I recommend from ninth and tenth to eleventh and twelfth, he's still in eighth grade. A person [normally] in seventh is in ninth grade. There were about five changes last year. Last year it was politics with principals. (a social studies teacher)

. . .

Jack Simon: It is not unusual for someone from the board of education to come down and say, "I want you to change this teacher to that school and this teacher to that subject." That kind of interference has always gone on in this district as I am sure it goes on in other districts, too.

LW: Why would that go on? Why would somebody want to have period seven and eight free and, therefore, a person has to teach tenth grade

	instead of twelfth grade and that bumps the person who normally teaches that subject. Why would they want that?
Jack Simon:	Well, in our sort of situation where you have staggered shifts, if you can get out at two o'clock and you have a second job, you can make this job. If you don't get out at two o'clock but have to work 'til four o'clock, you have to give up your second job. On other shifts, it is just a case of "Well, I like to teach all my classes in the morning." (a social studies teacher)

Freeway is a highly political town, and it is no accident that so many faculty are from Freeway or married to persons from Freeway. The comments of faculty regarding the political nature of the city suggest that politics intrudes *directly* into the educational process at the level of scheduling; who teaches at what school; how many free periods one has; and so forth. Because of the union step system, differential pay is not the issue here. The issue becomes one of working conditions—working with the "better kids," and, more importantly perhaps, having free periods or teaching a particular shift so outside interests, including second jobs as Jack Simon suggests, can be pursued. Ultimately, then, this is a highly inbred teaching force whereby most of the faculty are Freeway citizens attempting to curry favor with other Freeway citizens. Teachers are largely from the same environment as the students. Although I do not have data to prove this, I suspect that similar processes operate in working-class communities throughout the country.[11]

Teachers as steelworkers

A very high proportion of male teachers worked at the steel plant at one point in their lives, whether as college students during the summer, or, alternatively, wage laborers who decided to leave the plant and pursue teaching. Many teachers, then, have direct experience in industry. For the most part, teachers are themselves from the working class, not unlike their students. Application materials for all teachers indicate that many of them, at one time or another, worked in the plant. Interviews with teachers confirm this, and teachers elaborate reasons why they left. Below, I first present information from application materials. It is significant that many faculty took care, on the application form, to point out that they worked for Freeway Steel, thus alerting hiring committees to the candidates' ongoing connection with Freeway.[12] This is, of course, important, in light of the discussion above on hiring.

Industrial Arts Teacher, Application 1961

Prior to my preparation for a teaching career, I was employed by the Freeway Steel Company from 1951 to 1958. During this time, I completed an apprenticeship in the machinist trade and worked as a journeyman machinist until I attained my position as industrial arts instructor at _____ [a high school in the larger city.]

Industrial Arts Teacher, Application 1960

I have had several years of industrial experience at Freeway steel that will help me in trying to teach the students the different processes of industry [sic].

Industrial Arts Teacher, Application 1966

I was entered into the apprenticeship machinist program at Freeway steel in December 1949 but when I had completed only three years of this course, I had enlisted in the Navy where I qualified for Machinery Repairman School (. . .) I returned to my former place of employment upon completing my enlistment, and subsequently successfully completed my apprenticeship course which entitled me to a classification of "A machinist."

Industrial Arts Teacher, Application 1968

I have lived in this city all my life and attended Freeway schools. I know how many things are done within the system. I have some industrial background, having worked five summers and the last eight months for Freeway Steel.

Social Studies Teacher, Application 1960

I have lived all my life in Freeway and for the past seven years I have been employed by the Freeway Steel corporation.

Because I have shared many of the same experiences as other Freeway parents I feel I know what they want for their children. Also, because of my experiences, I feel I can better understand the attitudes and the problems of the children.

Math Teacher, Application 1962 (on Résumé)

7/66–9/66 Steelworker, Freeway Steel. Worked in billet yards as a laborer and loader.

Business Teacher, 1971 (on Résumé)

General Laborer, Freeway Steel, Full-time Summer Employment, 1968 and 1969.
Main duties: Piled and banded steel, hooker; straightener machine operator; roller operator.

In fact, a high proportion of male teachers worked in the plant at one time or another, as interviews and informal interactions throughout the year made clear. At my initial meeting with the social studies department, for example, I was struck by the fact that every male there had some experience in the plant, and the women had fathers, brothers, uncles, or husbands who had worked there. It is not, therefore, only the industrial arts teachers who were former plant workers, although potential industrial arts teachers, not surprisingly, tend to highlight this more frequently in their applications. Many of the academic area teachers also worked in the plant on a full-time basis, or during summers when they were in college. These are not the sons of professionals earning summer money, however. These are sons of factory workers, earning money by working in the plant so they can attend school, thereby escaping having to work there forever like their fathers, uncles, and grandfathers. As a number of men point out below, working in the plant during the summer was one way of convincing themselves that they wanted to go back to college so as not to have to spend their entire lives there. Data below are more revealing in this regard.

Paul Pelly: I've lived here all my life. When I got out of high school, I had an opportunity to go to college and I took machine shop in high school and I said, "Oh, I'll go to Freeway Steel and get hired as a machinist for apprentice; so I went to the apprenticeship

program and I started there in '49. In
March of 1951 I went into the Navy for
four years (. . .), came back to finish my
apprenticeship and I kept working at
Freeway Steel (. . .) And then I had some
radical surgery done on my hip, and then
the whole socket had to be rebuilt—and I
saw where I wasn't going anywhere.
Looked at the people coming in with the
buckets over the years that I was there and
looking at myself at the age of sixty, "I'm
going to be doing this?" You had to get a
lot of seniority to get a summer vacation. I
always had to get odd days. You couldn't
get holidays. You couldn't get Christmas;
you couldn't get Easter; you couldn't get
something.
(. . .) So, at the age of thirty-seven, I
decided to go back to school (. . .) So,
anyway, I came here [Freeway High]
around Thanksgiving of '66 and I didn't
know if I was going to like teaching, and I
didn't want to give up my job at Freeway
steel. I had eighteen years. But eventually it
was getting hectic. I was teaching during
the day and working nights at the plant, and
going to school. There was a time when I
had two days of three hours of sleep. Really
a drag on my wife (. . .) So I decided I'm
either going to do one or the other so I quit
the plant. (a vocational education teacher)

. . .

Sam Lunetta: When I was in college, my first three years,
four years, I worked in the plant. They
hired thousands and thousands. In the
summer we made big money. At that time,
we'd make fifteen hundred dollars in the
summer, which was a fortune in 1972.
That's good money (. . .) We were all
working. We all went in there. I sat in a

room with three hundred guys and they hired every college kid. Some were good; some weren't. Do goofy little things—cleaning things up—they'd give you an area this big [indicates a small area with his hands] and say, "Sweep it all day." Some days you worked with the men.

(. . .) I worked four summers. And it was great as far as college because you'd catch overtime, and at time and a half you were making a hundred dollars a week. The next year we got smart. I took the mechanical test, and then you got to be somebody's helper which meant you walked around with the guy carrying his tools. (a social studies teacher)

. . .

Bob Eckles: At Freeway Steel, I had eleven years and I did many things—laborer, shovel gravel, or whatever. But in my final years, the last five years, there was a job like that, I was a hooker. What they call the bar roll. I went back to school when I came out of the service. When I started teaching here, I could not work during the daytime at Freeway Steel, so they created the "supervisor in charge of the roll shop"; they actually created a job and it was at the bar mill roll shop, and that's where I worked for about three years. (guidance counselor; former teacher in the system)

. . .

Jim Cleaver: I worked at the steel plant during the summers when I was going to school, and I worked with my father, who was a contractor.

LW: Did you think about staying in the steel plant or did you always know you were going to come out?

JC:	My father's feelings were that, if I were to go to the steel plant, I would have an incentive to go to school and he did not appreciate the steel plant—the noise, just that particular group's life-style.
LW:	Did he ever work there?
JC:	Yes, he did. In the thirties. He was right. I didn't like the noise of the cranes overhead and the general dirt that was always associated with the plant at the time. It was a good incentive [to stay in school]. (a vocational education teacher)

. . .

John Teichler:	I'm a native-born Freewayian (. . .) How I got the job [teaching] is just a fluke. I was working at the steel plant at the time and I put my application in at various businesses and schools and I just happened to be called for an interview (. . .) (a social studies teacher)

. . .

LW:	Were there points when you thought you would stay in the steel plant instead of coming to Freeway [high school]?
Tim Constantine:	No, that never entered my mind. My father worked at the steel plant all his life and I had brothers that worked in the steel mills. I was of the idea that I didn't want to work seven to three or swing shift or nights. It didn't appeal to me. (. . .) Like I said, my father worked there all his life and he worked like a dog and I just didn't feel like I wanted to do that the rest of my life. (administrator; formerly a teacher in the system)

. . .

Bob Pritcher:	I was a machinist at Freeway Steel and machine repair at Chevy. Just to give you a

little background, I made twelve thousand eight hundred dollars at Chevrolet and went down to about four thousand four hundred dollars teaching here. I was a disaster. For the first three years of my life [here], I didn't think I was going to make it.

LW: Why did you do it [switch jobs]?

BP: For numerous reasons. Number one, I wasn't very happy with the steel plant because I was working the night shift; and, number two, I was at Chevrolet, I was working and it didn't seem like I had any time off at all. I was working thirteen out of fourteen days, and I was working twelve hours a day or ten hours a day. I had four children.

LW: So you never saw them?

BP: I never saw daylight to be honest with you. I used to go to work at five in the morning and I would get home at seven-thirty–eight o'clock in the evening. By the time I had supper, it was nine o'clock—back to bed. The first one on the streets to cut tracks in the snow. (a vocational education teacher)

. . .

Tony Torcivia: My father worked at the steel plant here (. . .) And I appreciated what I saw when he came home from work. How hard he worked, how tired he was, grimy and what have you. Working on a heavy industry job like that. The money that he made was pretty good. But he encouraged me to go to college (. . .) He kind of encouraged me to say, "Look, you see what I'm doing. I don't want you to do that."

(. . .) Let me be very honest with you. What happened to me is that I went to _____ [a university out of state]. I

really did kind of mediocre the first year—a
C average right on the button. I was kind of
disillusioned with the whole thing (. . .)
Then I decided I wanted to work. So my
father says, "They are hiring at the steel
plant, why don't you look for a job there?"
So I did, and I don't know if he called
anybody or what have you, [and he]
specifically bugged me to work in the coke
ovens.

(. . .) [I worked in the coke ovens] for
the first summer of my freshman year and I
couldn't believe what people did to earn a
living in that place (. . .) This grimy old
character that was the foreman (. . .) had
a bunch of us college kids up there, "All
right," he said, "tomorrow you are going to
report to this place to work," "I want you to
wear heavy dungarees, long underwear, a
heavy shirt, like a flannel shirt." And, of
course, we all figured he was setting us up.
So I went in with very light summer clothes
working in the coke ovens. And it was an
extremely, extremely hot day, and you get
on top of the coke ovens where we were
working, it was additionally 185 degrees
because of the heat coming up from the
coke ovens and, of course, the summer
weather. And it was brutal. Five out of the
six of us didn't wear what he prescribed.
And we had a rough day.

So he said, "All right, you guys,
tomorrow you'll understand." And he went
on to explain that all this heavy clothing
trapped all our sweat, and, by the
evaporation of our sweat, allowed us slowly
to keep cooler. But after four weeks there—
this dirty, filthy environment—and I used to
shower there, come home, and shower
again. That's how dirty it was. Soot and

grime in my mouth and nose and eyes. It
was a continuous thing. The clothes that I
wore for work, then, were just black.
(. . .) So, after working at it four
weeks, probably not even that long, my
father was driving me to work one day on
his way to work and I said, "I think I'll
work about one more week." He says, "No,
you won't. You are going to stick it out—
finish the week before you're supposed to
go back to school." He said, "You made a
commitment and you're going to live with
it. I don't care if you like it or not." Okay,
so I did, and, by the time it was over, I
was ready to go back to college. I couldn't
wait to go back to college and I did a lot
better. I took a piece of coke with me and
put it in my desk so that if I found any
distractions I knew what I had facing me. (a
science teacher)

The teachers at Freeway knew, then, that the alternative to school
was a life of heavy industry and they "chose," either early or late in life,
to opt for schooling. Schooling was seen, by the male teachers at least,
as a way out of the coke ovens, blast furnace, bar roll, and so on.
Education represented a way out of the plant, and teachers chose to take
it. Many of their relatives worked in the plant, and they envisioned that
as a distinct possibility for themselves. Some chose the plant and escaped
back to teaching. Others chose teaching from the very start. The bottom
line, however, is that Freeway teachers are, by and large, local people
whose own lived experience is infused with that of the working proletariat, the children of whom they now teach.

When teachers entered the system, they met a highly political environment which numerous teachers comment upon. Instructional imperatives
do not guide the system. It is, rather, whom you know; how much you
pay; and whether you are from the area or married to someone from the
area that shapes your entry into the profession and the "perks" you
ultimately receive within it. Thus schooling, although seen as an escape,
is *also* for these teachers only a "ticket." It is the *form* of schooling (the
"ticket" or credential), not the substance, that enabled teachers to move

through the system once they escaped heavy industry. The fact that it is the form rather than the substance of schooling that facilitated escape from manual-laboring jobs helps shape teacher identity, and ultimately, student identity. Teachers perceive that although you need a credential, the way you *really* move through the system is by whom you know and so forth. It is not knowledge per se that can be exchanged for valued goods—what is exchanged is something that has nothing to do with education, although schooling is a necessary "ticket" to getting into the game.

The positives of teaching

The fact that so many teachers see themselves as escaping industry is related to the way in which teachers view their job. While it is fashionable among academics to view teaching as an increasingly proletarianized position, teachers do not necessarily see it this way, especially if they are from the traditional proletariat.[13]

Freeway teachers articulate the positives of teaching mainly in terms of the conditions of work as compared with those in heavy industry. This does not mean that faculty are satisfied with everything at Freeway High. As pointed out in chapter 4, there are a number of issues revolving around control over teacher labor that remain points of contention for faculty. Nevertheless, on balance, faculty tend to compare teaching with heavy industry and decidedly favor teaching. In addition, Freeway teachers state that they like working with children, often because they identify with them or their parents. The following reflect the "positives" of teaching as teachers see them. It is noteworthy that teachers state that they choose teaching not only because they "like children," but also because teaching compares *very* favorably with envisioned alternative ways of earning a living.

> *Joan Snapple:* I like it [teaching] very much. I just felt that in having your own [beauty] salon [which she had previously and still operates part-time], you really had a lot of responsibility and had to work very long hours. It was excellent money or I would have come into teaching sooner. I only

came into teaching because I liked it. I certainly didn't come into it for the money. I had, by this time, been doing hair [for] close to twenty years.

LW: When you say long hours, what do you mean?

JS: Fourteen hours a day, and this would be five days a week because I just wouldn't work the sixth day—I could have, but wouldn't. And this was when I had the salon here at home and I worked. Fourteen hours were common.

    (. . .) [As my son grew] I did my traveling to [State College] to get my degree and then I just decided that I really didn't think I would want to go back into hairdressing full-time because of how strenuous it was and that you had to pay for your own Blue Cross, Blue Shield [insurance]. I was responsible for that and responsible for the unemployment insurance [for my employees]. (. . .) I felt, too, I could also do hair (. . .) I taught and did the hair, then I realized this was perfectly easy. Of course, now, as I've gotten older, eight hours is enough of it. But when I first started teaching, I would do twenty-five, thirty hours [a week] of hair along with the hours I was in school. (a cosmetology teacher)

. . .

Avis Trottier: I enjoy the kids. They are really nice kids and I enjoy working with them and I enjoy the faculty. (a math teacher)

. . .

Dwayne Patrick: As far as teaching itself, I really like it. I like the kids. Most of the kids are really nice. I enjoy it. (a business teacher)

· · ·

Sam Mouton: I like the kids. I like the faculty and since I've been here I have had probably more positive situations and things happen to me with faculty and with the students. I enjoy working with the age groups; I enjoy working in the courses I'm teaching— criminal justice and consumer economics— two fabulous courses. (a social studies teacher)

· · ·

Tony Torcivia: I like working with people. I really enjoy that. I enjoy working with kids. (a science teacher)

· · ·

Bob Pritcher: Well, from the positive standpoint, teaching, you have Saturdays and Sundays off plus the fact that you've got ten weeks out of the year for golf. At that particular time [when I left the steel plant], I played baseball and a lot of golf and that was very appealing to me.

BP: I [also] can walk the streets, as I do live in the town, I walk the streets and the kids are on the streets—former students of mine with kids—with their wives, and when I get a good introduction or I don't get ignored, or I [don't] get snubbed or something, I know I'm doing a good job.
(. . .) When I was in industry, I remember going to work and I'd think out of a six-day week which was always a six-day week, I think I would dread going to work four or five out of the six. Probably the only time I wouldn't was payday. Get paid; that was a gut feeling I always had. But in teaching, I still like coming to school nine out of ten days. Not ten out of ten, but nine out of ten (. . .) My wife always

says, "I don't see how you can be that
cheerful in the morning." (. . .) Basically,
I would say 95 percent of the time I enjoy
getting up in the morning. (a vocational education teacher)

. . .

Tim Constantine: I have a lot of fun with the kids. Let's say
80 percent of them. I get along good [sic]
with the majority of the students in the
school. I have for the last ten years (. . .)
They still come and see me. Like the first
graduating class I had in '77. It was funny
because one of these students was a senior
at that time
(. . .), I knew her. [I was] very close with
the mother and father and see, as a very
young child, she used to call me Uncle
Tim. So when I got transferred here [from
the junior high school] she saw me, and she
called me Uncle Tim and all the students in
the senior class starting [calling] me Uncle
Tim and this went on all year. And still
continues. I can walk in a tavern or a local
restaurant. People who graduated in '77
who are now twenty-six and twenty-seven
years old, I walk in and they say, "Hi,
Uncle Tim." They come and see me; they
invite me to their picnics. (an administrator,
former teacher)

. . .

Johnnie Aaron: The idea of my being single allows me
more time [with the kids]. The idea of
coaching gives me a double level with the
students in and out of the classroom, and
being an only child without the brothers and
sisters I can just—this is also part of my
recreation. So I don't have to go sit in a
bar. I get some fun out of this, too. Besides
being a job, I enjoy it. (an English teacher)

. . .

Dwayne Patrick:	The positives of teaching [are] the hours. I prefer to be in a routine; it's endless the hours there [he sold furniture prior to teaching business subjects at Freeway High].
LW:	Can you give me an example?
DP:	You can work sixty hours, seventy hours a week at the job selling (. . .) The hours are shorter coming here. Job security would be better [in teaching], the benefits, a pension. [In retailing], you have nothing. You can be let go at any time. (. . .) You notice people coming and going almost every week over there [in retailing].
LW:	Why do they get fired?
DP:	Not selling. There's a lot of pressure on you (. . .) In fact, one of these stores just went out of business, _____. They have, like, fifteen salespeople there. And every month they fire somebody. If you're at the bottom, you're out (. . .) These guys [the successful ones] make really good money (. . .) forty or fifty thousand maybe. The top salesman. But if they don't [sell] and they get down on the bottom, I think, like, two months on low, they are out. They get rid of them (. . .) So I didn't want to do that all my life. (a business teacher)

The positives of teaching revolve around working with students as well as the perception that the conditions of work are far more favorable than in industry or the type of businesses in which these people could participate. Numerous teachers cite the benefits of teaching as being able to work in the daylight, have holidays off, better vacations, and so forth. *The conditions of work are seen as far superior to those in alternative jobs they had or could envision for themselves.* Industry, for example, is grimy and one has to put in long hours, as is the case for retail business and self-employment such as hairdressing. In the case of hairdressing, Ms. Snapple states that she also had to provide for her own health insurance at considerable expense. Teaching is simply seen as *easier* work and also less alienating given that teachers express an attachment to the product of their labor, that is, students.

Negatives of teaching

In chapter 4, I suggested that teachers feel that administrators encroach on too many of what they consider to be *their* professional rights and responsibilities (plan books, what to photocopy, and so forth) and that these issues are discussed publicly by teachers as constituting the battleground between the two groups. The biggest private complaint (to me) of teachers is the pay, however, given that many compare their pay with what they used to earn or could have earned in heavy industry, construction, and so forth. Wages, however, are seen as the *only* positive point of work outside of teaching, and teachers are well aware that the industrial economy no longer exists for them or their students.

John Teichler: Another reason why I would think of leaving teaching after twenty-five years here, I'm making probably two-thirds of what I would be making had I chose [sic] to go into another profession. You still have the people in the factories making more than the teacher does. I told you, my first year of teaching here. I had a kid sleeping in the back of the room, I woke him up a couple of times, "Hey, you with us?" [He said] "I worked last night at the steel plant. I worked the eleven-to-seven shift. Sorry." At the end of that week he came to me and showed me his check. He was making more than I was, and I had been teaching three years and he'd just gotten a job a month or two months before that! (a social studies teacher)

. . .

Bob Pritcher: From the negative standpoint, the money situation was by far number one. I remember coming in here [Freeway High], this is the honest-to-God truth, I remember coming in here and I used to clear for the first year (. . .), one week I was bringing home a hundred eighteen dollars clear and [two weeks later] a hundred twenty-two dollars clear. And my mortgage payment was a hundred twenty dollars a month. So two weeks of my pay went towards my mortgage.

(. . .) I was in the hole (. . .) So in the summertime, I sold beer; I did all kinds of things. I worked as a machinist, a tool and die maker—those kinds of things. (a vocational education teacher)

. . .

Sam Lunetta: Money is the biggest problem. There is going to be a terrible teacher shortage, already in math and science. Can you honestly say if you were a chemistry major and a junior and you looked at the situation and alternatives [that you would teach]? Are you going to go through all this and then start at fifteen thousand dollars, or, are you going to go with a company and start at twenty-two thousand dollars?

. . .

Bill Sykes: I tell [the students] in class, "I'm going to tell you something; the plant's gone, Republic's gone, Ford's gone. When I started teaching, I made ten thousand dollars and I knew guys who didn't get out of ninth grade working at Chevy tearing down thirty thousand dollars." (a social studies teacher)

. . .

Dwayne Patrick: The only negative [about teaching] is that you don't make enough money. That's the

	big thing, or you have to work a part-time job.
LW:	You really believe that's the case? That you must work a part-time job?
DP:	Oh, definitely. Depends on what you want. If you want a little something extra, you want to go to Florida [during Easter break, for example, which is common among Freeway teachers]. (a business teacher)

. . .

Paul Pelly:	[When I left industry] I took a six-thousand-dollar cut in pay (. . .) Actually the starting salary was less, but they had previous teachers in vocations. For experience in industry, they gave them two additional steps. So the superintendent told me, he said, "Hell, I have to recommend you for the first step, but I think the board would give you two additional steps like they did the other people." And here I am. (a vocational education teacher)

. . .

Tom LaPorte:	At one time, with a master's degree, I was the lowest paid on the street. It was nothing for guys on my street to be making forty, fifty thousand dollars at the steel mill. That's good money plus all your benefits and everything else. The big thing was then they took pride in the fact that they made more money than the educated people.
LW:	Did they say that to you?
TP:	Oh, sure. They were making the bucks. (school social worker)

. . .

Bob Pritcher:	I was a machinist at Freeway and machine repair at Chevrolet. Just to give you a little background, I made twelve thousand eight hundred dollars at Chevrolet and went down

to about four thousand four hundred dollars a year teaching here. It was a disaster for the first three years of my [teaching] life and I didn't think I was going to make it. (a vocational education teacher)

. . .

Tony Torcivia: I made good money [in the steel plant.].

LW: Like how much were you making?

TT: Going back down to 1968–69, I was probably making a couple of hundred dollars or more a week, depending [on] whether I worked holidays; of course, we got the bottom of the barrel, so we got double time and a quarter on holidays, so you made lots of money. But the thing is, socially, I did nothing. I was exhausted from the shift. Most of the time I worked from three to eleven, which is a horrendous shift to work. What do you do after you get home at eleven o'clock, and what do you do early in the morning?

(. . .) I came into teaching and pretty much took a pay cut. My first paycheck here was, turned out to be something like ninety dollars a week in 1967. I would have been better off working in the steel plant. A lot of the faculty members here have that attitude. "You know, we could be making more; why are we treated like this professionally when we could be making more in the steel plant?" (. . .) A lot of the kids went on right to Freeway [steel] and made a good living.

LW: Did faculty at the time talk about that?

TT: Oh, yeah. Definitely. The benefits. You are always comparing benefits and salary with people who are working in the Ford plant, for example, and the steel plant. (a science teacher)

Teachers, then, center complaints on pay, the ritual of administrative control (although not seen as a ritual), and politics which result in a scheduling process that looks distinctly political rather than educationally based. Basically, however, they like students, for the most part, and the conditions of teaching compare favorably with those in other work which they feel they would be doing if not teaching. These are not people who compare their own conditions of work with those of lawyers, doctors, or university professors. They are comparing themselves with their fathers or uncles who worked in the industrial sector, and/or with what they themselves used to do in industry or business. Teaching, in that sense, compares favorably, except for the pay.

Teachers and youth identity

Freeway teachers are, in many ways, like their students. They are, by and large, from the same industrial background and face the same structural changes in the economy as students and their parents. The teachers, however, successfully used schooling to obtain stable employment as the industrial economy declined. For them, schooling "worked" in that it offered them stable jobs that compare favorably to those in industry. It is noteworthy that the most common complain of teachers revolves around pay and that they compare this pay with what they could have made in the plants. Thus, Tony Torcivia says, "My first paycheck here was, turned out to be something like ninety dollars a week in 1967. I would have been better off working in the steel plant." Tom LaPorte states, "At one time, with a master's degree, I was the lowest paid on the street." The teachers are embedded within the same original class location as the students, but schooling has enabled them to obtain stable employment in the face of economic change.

Teachers do not, however, adhere totally to the meritocratic ideology normally associated with schooling. Upon entering the system, teachers meet a set of noneducational decision-making processes in the educational realm. Schedules, for example, are drawn up unrelated to teacher expertise or even desire to teach certain courses, but to, politics. This results in teachers being assigned to teach new courses and new grade levels, often at the last minute. They teach "first" or "second" shift (this is, significantly, teacher language), not because they are better able to teach ninth or twelfth graders, but because they know someone on the board and wish to teach at a certain time, "thus freeing the rest of their day for a second job, and so forth . . ." It is widely perceived that if you "curry favor" with someone on the board, you can obtain a better schedule. These are seen by teachers as a set of political decisions rather than decisions made in the best interest of students.

In addition, teachers perceive that there is too much administrative (read management) control over what has come to be defined as the instructional/educational area. This ultimately serves to alienate teachers from their labor, to some extent, and undermines the notion that education acts to move individuals into true professional positions (the idea that a window covering is not really a professional decision gets lost here, however, as noted before). The political climate undermines the notion of a meritocracy; the perceived heavy-handedness of management erodes the idea that they have moved into a profession. It is only the fact that teachers "like children," (it is important also, that these children are like themselves), and that they perceive this work as more satisfying than that in other available jobs, specifically industry, that prevents their total alienation from the product (students) of their labor.

It is in the above two senses that teacher stress on the *form* of education rather than its substance can be understood. It is, in fact, the *form* of education that enables them to live their current lives. Schooling has acted as a "ticket" out of the brutal and increasingly nonexistent industrial sector, in particular. This, in addition to the ritual of control enacted by administrators, contributes to an emphasis upon form rather than substance in the classroom. This is not conscious, of course, but is— given the political climate, the ritual of control, and their own lived background in which is embedded a contradictory code of respect toward schooling to begin with—in fact, what occurs. It is not inconsequential, then, that Freeway teachers are themselves from the working class. This is not to say that teachers originally from the middle class or teachers who do not teach working-class children would not also elaborate an identity that centers on the form of schooling. They may very well do so, and numerous studies point out a generally alienated teacher force and student population. In the case at hand, however, this has to be seen in light of class movement. As the working class moves through into post-industrial society, the role of the school must be analyzed. Here the school encourages the dominant male separatist form and also an emphasis on the form of education rather than its substance. The school is *actively* (although not necessarily consciously) encouraging both aspects of youth identity. In this sense, then, the school acts to encourage, as I will argue later, a potential relationship between working-class white males, in particular, and the New Right. The school does not, however, encourage a link between females and the feminist movement in the same way. I will explore these points when I return to a social-action perspective in chapters 7 and 8. In the next chapter, I will examine the role of parents in emerging youth identities.

6
Freeway Parents

It has been alleged in the literature that working-class parents perpetuate their own class status through what they expose their children to in terms of books, culture, and so forth. In other words, one of the reasons why working-class students remain working class rather than climb the class structure is because their parents do not encourage them not to remain working class. This argument can, of course, take the form of a highly class-reductionist position most carefully articulated by Samuel Bowles and Herbert Gintis.[1] As they argue:

> [The] reproduction of consciousness is facilitated by a rough correspondence between the social relations of production and the social relations of family life, a correspondence that is greatly affected by the experiences of parents in the social division of labor. There is a tendency for families to reproduce in their offspring not only a consciousness tailored to the objective nature of the work world, but to prepare them for economic positions roughly comparable to their own. Although these tendencies can be countered by other forces (schooling, media, shifts in aggregate occupational structure), they continue to account for a significant part of the observed intergenerational status-transmission process.[2]

The point here is that it is often suggested from a number of perspectives that working-class parents prepare their children for positions in the economy comparable to their own current positions. In the case of Bowles and Gintis, this is accomplished through a reproduction of consciousness which is necessary to operate within a particular sector of the economy. Thus, working-class children are taught the norms of obedience and rule following suitable for positions that require submission to authority. The middle class, on the other hand, teaches its children "internalized norms." They are, as Melvin Kohn argues, taught "to internalize authority and act without direct and continuous supervision to implement goals and objectives relatively alienated from their own personal needs."[3] Kohn, for example, finds that "parents of lower-status children value obedience, neatness, and honesty in their children, while higher-status parents emphasize curiosity, self-control, consideration, and happiness."[4]

Questions can be raised about the reproduction paradigm which is elaborated by Bowles and Gintis, and I have raised some of these questions in chapter 1.[5] It is not my intention to pursue these issues here, however, but to point out that a number of scholars have discussed, from a variety of perspectives, the role of family in the future status of children.[6]

It is for this reason that I dwell briefly on parents in this volume. I did not gather data on parents to nearly the same extent that data on students and school processes were gathered. I did, however, interview 50 percent of parents of interviewed students. While numerous questions remain regarding the role of parents in identity formation of youth, the data presented here are suggestive of some trends. Future studies must probe these issues more directly than I do here. A profile of parental input into youth identity formation as the working class moves into post-industrial society can, however, be offered here, as data are suggestive in this regard.

It is certainly not as simple as to argue from the data that working-class parents promote a form of consciousness suitable for manual-laboring positions. As I argued in chapter 1, such positions are being phased out since the industrial economy is itself in a state of change. What is most apparent from interviews with parents is that they *desperately* want their children to attend college, and many state that there is nothing for their children if they do not do so. Parents understand clearly that the jobs in which they participated upon leaving high school are no longer available. They have lived through de-industrialization and stress to their children that education is the only way to obtain stable employment.

Given their background, however, parents do not know how to encourage their children to take appropriate steps to obtain entrance to college. They have not themselves taken the PSAT, SAT, or achievement tests, and do not understand the college admittance process. There are a number of points that middle-class parents simply know because they have been through it themselves, whereas working-class parents do not. Parents thus expect the school to take a more active role than they feel it does in ensuring their children's future.

There is, in fact, a tension between parents and school personnel, precipitated to some extent because they are all largely from the same background. Parents simply do not feel that the school does enough to compensate for their own deficiencies in helping children go to college and obtain what they see as stable employment. Given data presented in chapters 4 and 5 of this volume, they are, of course, correct. School, as these students experience it, will not facilitate the kind of mobility parents desire for them. School personnel, on the other hand, as I will suggest later, are critical of parents for not being involved enough in their children's education. Each (parents and school personnel), in a sense, blame the other for not taking responsibility for the children of the working class.

Parents also encourage their children to defer marriage and family. This is equally the case for parents of males and females. Thus, in some key ways, parents encourage certain aspects of the identity of youth. They value education highly and hope their children will put off marriage. In many ways, they hope their children will live lives unlike their own. I did not hear from parents, however, the emphasis on male-dominant families articulated by male youth. This may, of course, be because it is so taken for granted among parents that it need not be articulated. On the other hand, parents may understand that such relations cannot, in many ways, be sustained under the current economy. While parents may not have abandoned these notions entirely, they may no longer be elaborated on in the same way as they are by youth. In fact, the sentiment expressed by parents that children should delay families and finish schooling first can be seen as a partial encouragement of girls' emerging identity.

It is significant that there is no sentiment among parents that the working class is a positive social form that ought to be preserved. There is no sense of class community, in other words. Parents want their children to have social mobility and express this in highly individualistic terms. Most parents are from Freeway or have spouses from Freeway. They did not, in other words, stray far from home. As will be seen later, this is not something they wish to preserve at all cost, and this represents a radical shift in the nature of working-class family and community. Many express strongly that their children ought to leave the area, and often the state. I will, in this chapter, explore three themes as expressed by parents: 1) desire for children to attend college; 2) marriage and family; and 3) attitudes toward the school itself.[7]

Desire for college

For the most part parents want their children to go to college. They talk specifically about the fact that there is "nothing" without college and they have every hope that their children, whether female or male, will succeed. This means breaking out of the working-class community in which they are embedded. Parents respond as follows:

LW:	What do you think Penny will do when she leaves high school?
Ms. Southworth:	She's planning on going to college. She doesn't know which one yet. She wants to go into a science field—biology, chemistry, probably.
LW:	And what kind of career is she looking for?
Ms. Southworth:	Maybe research or something. She likes biology and chemistry so she hasn't really . . .
LW:	What would you like her to do?
Ms. Southworth:	Anything that she's happy with, I've told her. She's got to pick something that she may be working at for about forty or fifty years; you never know, down the line.
LW:	You'd like her to go to college?
Ms. Southworth:	I think she deserves to go. She's a smart girl, and she deserves to get ahead a little bit.

. . .

LW:	What do you think your daughter Carla will be doing when she leaves high school? Has she ever discussed her plans with you?
Ms. Dedinsky:	She's going to college.

153

LW:	(. . .) What is she looking at? What type of major or degree program?
Ms. Dedinsky:	From what she said so far, she wants to get into something in psychology. I think she's going into liberal arts to start out with to build her foundation and possibly to diversify from there.
LW:	Is that more or less what you would like her to do? Would you like her to be in a more professional type of position?
Ms. Dedinsky:	In all honesty, whatever the two daughters, whatever they choose to do as long as they do it to the best of their ability [is fine with me]. I've always said, since they were very little, it was never *if* you go to college, it was always *when* you go to college. And whatever they choose, whatever field they want to go into is fine with me.
	. . .
Mr. Janke:	Well, [Vern's] not ready to go to college [in response to a question regarding what will your son do after high school]. At least this way he can get some sort of job skill in the Navy [he is entering the Navy].
LW:	Would you like to see him go on to college?
Mr. Janke:	Yes, definitely.
LW:	Does he have a job now?
Mr. Janke:	He works for the summer youth program. So that's it. (. . .) I hope he is [going to college]. I know he is aware of the fact, from what I keep telling him, that he's going to have [to have] some kind of specialized educational background if he wants to have a better job. So he's aware of it now. I guess he has to experience a few hard knocks before he knows and then just get a little

bit more mature to make up his mind what he wants to do. I'm not too frustrated with it because I think it's a natural response.

. . .

LW: Has [Beth] talked about what she might want to do after she leaves high school?

Ms. Poley: Yes. She's considering going in to be a doctor. This has been one of her goals since she was a very young girl. When I speak of doctor, I'm not speaking in terms of Fifth Avenue, Park Avenue doctor. I'm talking about horse-and-buggy doctor. Country doctor. Little black bag. Midwife, the whole shot.

LW: So she wants to go on to college?

Ms. Poley: Yes, definitely.

LW: Is that something you'd like her to do?

Ms. Poley: Oh, definitely. I encourage my children. We, I have many children [they have a combined family—she has one child from a previous marriage], but somehow, their education has been such that they have graduated from high school but then to go on to more difficult fields or endeavors, they haven't wanted to, but Beth seems to be a different sort. She's career goal minded and this is the way it is. I'm very pleased for her because I'm the same type of person.

. . .

LW: Has your daughter, Judy, expressed any interest in anything she might like to do after she leaves high school?

Ms. Pizillo: Well, she's definitely going to college.

LW: (. . .) What do you think she might want to major in?

Ms. Pizillo: She's talking about engineering. She's got

a good background in math and science, really. She had an excellent math teacher for two years. She was afraid of him but she got beautiful marks. The school's at a loss now because they made him a principal, so he doesn't teach anymore. I really think the kids lost out, really.

LW: What would you like her to do when she leaves high school? Do you want to see her go on to college or . . .

Ms. Pizillo: Yeah, I do. You need a college education, especially now in Freeway.

. . .

LW: Has your son, Jim, discussed anything about what kind of future he might have?

Ms. Blassingame: Well, he'd like to go on to art (. . .) Well, I don't see if there is a lot of opportunity in it [art], but if that's what he wants to do. A lot of times when you get into college or something like that you find something that you like along the way that's not what you planned to be. So I figure something, if the Lord leads him, he'll get into something that's good for him.

LW: So you are encouraging him to go to college?

Ms. Blassingame: Yes, I am, because it's good. Because there isn't going to be any opportunity if he just goes to work. I mean, he's not going to better himself there.

. . .

LW: Has your daughter, Gloria, expressed any interest in what she might do after she leaves high school?

Ms. Sobel: (. . .) She expects, she's very good with children so I think she's going to go into something with children, pediatrics,

	physical therapy, something like that. Because she's very good with younger children, as far as she has a lot of patience and understanding for them.
LW:	Is that what you would like for her to be doing?
Ms. Sobel:	I don't express any feeling towards the children's career goals, mainly because it is that they are going to have to work so I'm not going to tell them to go into any kind of certain field, except that they need an education. High school is no longer enough, and if they want to be able to support themselves in a reasonable style they will have to get some sort of educational background.
LW:	So you strongly urge them to go to college.
Ms. Sobel:	Oh, absolutely, absolutely. They are not allowed to quit high school either. Or else they move out of the house.
	. . .
Ms. Woczak [Susan's mother]:	You know, I'm really interested in education. I want my kids to do better than me and education is the only way they'll do it. The steel plant isn't there as a cushion anymore. Either they go to college and be somebody, or they'll have nothing. J. T. [her son] could have gone into the plant before.
Mr. Woczak [stepfather]:	He's too smart for that. He should have done something else, anyway.
Ms. Woczak:	I know, but if the plant were there, he'd always have a cushion.
Mr. Woczak:	It's good in that way that it's gone.

There is obviously strong sentiment on the part of parents that their children should attend college, and their language is noteworthy. Ms. Dedinsky, for example, states, "It was never *if* you go to college; it was always *when* you go to college." Ms. Pizillo says, "You need a college education, especially now in Freeway," and Ms. Blassingame states, "Because there isn't going to be any opportunity if he just goes to work. I mean, he's not going to better himself there." Schooling is seen as the *only* way to obtain stable employment. As Ms. Woczak notes, "Either they go to college and be somebody, or they'll have nothing."

When parents do not encourage their children to go to college directly from high school, or at least express to them the importance of college attendance in a de-industrializing economy, they often suggest entering one or another branch of the armed services, particularly for their sons. This, again, however, is not a denial of the importance of college but is envisioned as a point of departure from which one can *later* go to college. Parents tend to see the service as a way of having later college training paid for, or gaining a college education while in the service. The following parents articulate this.

LW: What do you think Ray will be doing when he leaves high school? Has he talked to you at all about his future plans?

Ms. Smith: Well, he hasn't said anything. If he doesn't go to school, he's not going to find himself a decent job, so maybe he'll follow his brother's footsteps and go into one of the services.

LW: You would like him to go to school, though?

Ms. Smith: It doesn't matter to me. If he wants to go to school, that's fine. If he wants to go into one of the services, that's fine because they offer training there, too.

. . .

Ms. Janke: He won't be doing anything about college until after the Navy. He's ready to move on. He's not ready for any more schooling. He's ready to do something different and this is the best way he figured he would be able to do it.

It's a good opportunity. My husband did that. He went into the Navy for three years and he really had no idea what he wanted to be doing after high school. When he left the Navy, they paid for his entire college.

[Stepfather joins interview here].

LW: [To stepfather] Has Vern discussed any plans with you as to what he might want to do?

Mr. Janke: Well, as far as the Navy, he was going to take a look at the Navy after he took about a month off.

LW: What would you like to see him do? Do you feel the Navy is a good way to go?

Mr. Janke: Well, I don't know. For around here, work, I know what it is, and there isn't really nothing for children unless you work at Burger King or work the [gas] pumps or something like that. So I would like to see him get a start there [the service], because that's what I did when I was young.

LW: Oh, you went into the Navy, too?

Mr. Janke: Well, I was in the Air Force. As soon as I got out of high school, I was seventeen, and went right in and spent four years there and basically got myself together and I came back out and went from there.

LW: So you think the Navy is a pretty good way for him to go?

Mr. Janke: Any kind of service right now. Sure. It gives these kids a nice break into life, or whatever. They've got somebody to look after them but still they are going to be on their own and away from Mom and Dad. That's the greatest thing.

LW: See the world a little bit?

Mr. Janke: Right, and get it all paid for. I envy him, really. As far as I'm concerned, that's the way to go.

. . .

LW: He hasn't discussed at all, talked at all about what he might do after he leaves high school?

Ms. Smith: Nope. None of my kids seem like they actually wanted to go any further. They were just so tired of going to school that they didn't want to enter

right into college and just be in that same
restricted element. I don't blame them.

. . . My oldest son, he graduated a year ago
June, and he just went into the Air Force in May.
So he took a year off . . . In the meantime, he
picked up a job at Deltasonic and that supplied
him with spending money and money to buy
clothes and stuff that we couldn't give him.

. . .

LW: He hasn't really decided yet about college [in re-
             sponse to his point to this effect].

Mr. Rose: No, not definitely. He knows that he has to do
             something. I'm talking to him right now about
             going into the reserves. He can get all the benefits
             of a veteran, the college tuition being paid and I
             guess loans or whatever they offer them, for
             housing or if he wants to go into his own
             business. And also the reserves is another source
             of income for him . . . They are not thinking so
             much about their future unless I sit down and
             have a conversation with them about it. They are
             typical teenagers. When I was their age, I always
             did think sort of the way I'm thinking now. Most
             kids don't. They really don't know what they
             want to do. I'm not really that disgusted with
             them. Not when I look at it from their point of
             view. They do change; hopefully they [my sons]
             will.

. . .

Parents tend to want their children to go on to school, preferably to
college, immediately. If not, the service, in the case of males, is viewed
as an acceptable alternative. It is noteworthy that parents are pushing
their children in the direction of individual social mobility. There is no
sense of struggle for the working class as a whole such as might have
been the case in the previous generation. Plants are closing, and parents
feel strongly that children must obtain further education so they can
establish themselves in the future. In a sense, then, there is, for parents,
no envisioned class to fight for any longer. It is only a question of their

children's individual survival, and schooling is seen as the only way to survive.

This is a far cry from life before plant closings, nicely described in *Rusted Dreams,* a study of a steel community in the Southside of Chicago. As Bensman and Lynch note,

> Steelworkers may complain about the dirt and hours, but they take pride in their work. Sometimes directly, sometimes merely by example, their attitude is passed on. Ken Wychocki [an informant in the study] expresses the contradictory emotions of a steelworker family, as he wryly notes that, "I can always remember my grandfather didn't want my father to work in the mill. And my father didn't want me to work in the mill. And I *know* I don't want my son to work in the mill. But, it was just taken for granted if your father was in the mill, you were in the mill. It was never thought of that you'd go anywhere else. Your father didn't want you to, but when you were of age and ready to go to work, he was the guy that got you the job, for crying out loud."[8]

Things have changed considerably in such communities, given deindustrialization. Parents such as those in Freeway are not able to "get their sons jobs" as was the case before. Now all they can do is stress the importance of schooling. Beyond stressing its importance, however, there is little of a concrete nature that parents can offer their children.

Marriage and family

Parents do not want their children to marry directly out of high school and advise them to marry only much later in life. This encourages the identity of females, in particular, as outlined in chapter 3. The following are comments by parents:

LW:	Would you like to see her [Penny] married eventually?
Ms. Southworth:	Yes, I think so.
LW:	And having a family? Before or after college? What if she met somebody now?

Ms. Southworth: Well, that would kind of mess up plans. That's what happened to me. I went back to school twenty years later. If she could finish school [college] first, it would be better. Because then it's hard to get back and finish up.

. . .

LW: Has she ever talked about getting married and raising a family?

Ms. Dedinsky: Oh yeah, but that's further down the line.

LW: She wants to get her degree first?

Ms. Dedinsky: She would rather get her degree first and her [sic] and I have had some long talks about it and I think she's going in the right direction.

LW: Would you like her to get married after [finishing] her degree?

Ms. Dedinsky: Oh, I would love to have sons-in-laws [sic] and grandchildren. The big family dinners.

. . .

LW: Has he [Larry] ever talked about getting married and having a family?

Ms. Hunt: No. I don't think he wants that.

LW: Do you want him to?

Ms. Hunt: No, he says he's never getting married.

LW: What do you say to that?

Ms. Hunt: Fine. [I don't want him to get married] for a long time.

LW: Until he's out of college at least?

Ms. Hunt: Yes. Until about twenty-five or twenty-six, twenty-eight, maybe something like that.

. . .

LW: Has she [Lisa] ever talked about getting married and having a family?

Ms. Goodall: Yes, but after college.

LW:	After college? She's pretty definite about that?
Ms. Goodall:	I hope.
LW:	Do you want to see her get married?
Ms. Goodall:	Yes, but after she's done with school [college]. Then I don't care.

. . .

LW:	What about marriage and a family?
Ms. Antes:	I don't know. No comments about that.
LW:	Would you like to see her [Jennifer] married?
Ms. Antes:	No, not necessarily. Well, we have two other children and one is married. Again, everyone has to make up their own mind. Natural progression, she'll probably end up getting married. When she completes her education. Hopefully, she'll finish her education and do both. Everybody has to do what they feel. You can't tell them what to do. Especially in marriage.
LW:	Has she expressed an interest in marriage?
Ms. Antes:	She is only sixteen years old.
LW:	Some girls, you know, that's their goal. To get married right out of high school.
Ms. Anges:	We have a daughter, twenty-six who hasn't shown an interest in marriage. She's an accountant. At this point in life, she hasn't. This isn't to say she won't.

. . .

LW:	Would you like to see him [Vern] get married eventually and have a family?
Ms. Janke:	Eventually, ten or twelve years down the road.

. . .

LW:	Has she [Beth] ever talked about wanting to get married and have a family?

Ms. Poley:	Eventually. This is not her priority at this time. She likes to get into the swing of things with the other teenagers. But top priority is her career.
LW:	What about you? Would you like her to get married and have a family?
Ms. Poley:	Eventually. I would like to see her finish her education, become established in some area, and I hope it isn't Alaska or somewhere forsaken, and then down the road find someone to share her life with, because we all need that.

. . .

LW:	Has she [Judy] ever talked about getting married?
Ms. Pizillo:	No, and she does have a steady boyfriend.
LW:	Would you like to see her get married?
Ms. Pizillo:	Eventually. Not now. After she's done with college—and work a couple of years.

. . .

LW:	Does he [Larry] talk about getting married and having a family?
Ms. Hunt:	That's not the big priority. I think he really wants to make it materially for a while and a family would cut into that a little bit.

Parents (of both males and females) and female students sound quite similar on the topic of marriage and family. Both groups stress the importance of completing education and becoming settled in a job before entering into marriage commitments. Unlike female youth, however, parents do not mention divorce as an underlying reason for this. They simply refer to the fact that it is very difficult to be married and raise a family until one has finished school and obtained employment. This must be seen in relation to their own lives. Most parents married directly out of high school and many are now trying to go back to school and obtain new employment as industrial society crumbles around them. They are, thus, responding to the conditions of their *own* lives as they advise their children. They do not have the type or level of education that would enable them to compete for well-paying stable employment in a post-industrial economy. They are themselves trying to obtain employment and often necessary education while raising families. They are, therefore, strongly encouraging their children to proceed differently. Female students are, of course, filtering these messages through the lens of possible divorce. These messages and the way in which they are partially reworked by female youth, in particular, are a direct factor in the shaping of female identity. In this sense, then, parents are encouraging the emerging identity of females with respect to notions of future family.

Leaving Freeway

For the most part, parents are either from Freeway themselves or their spouses are from Freeway and that is why they are there. This, then, is a community in the sense that many people are there to be with family. They do, however, advise their own children, in many cases, to leave the area because of the job situation. There is, in fact, a sense that children will *have* to leave and, in many cases, parents advise them to do so.

LW:	Do you see any future for her in Freeway?
Ms. Southworth:	Not really. She'll probably have to go down South or somewhere else to really find a job. (. . .) Everything here is moving out and everything is dying out.
	. . .
LW:	Do you want her to stay in Freeway?
Ms. Dedinsky:	No. I would personally, as a mother, I would like both of my girls to stay close, but I could see where just the situation here, not just Freeway all of _____ state, if they have the chance to move, I would be behind them 100 percent. Planes run all over the country.

165

. . .

Ms. Hunt: I really forsee my children having to leave the area unless something happens to turn up here. I don't like the idea. We are very family oriented and I don't like the idea of them [leaving], but what parent does?

LW: So you really feel he'll have to leave the area?

Ms. Hunt: Yes, I do. All of them will have to. Hopefully that won't turn out. [Freeway and the surrounding large city] is really a closed area right now for any type of white-collar type of workers. Whether that would change in the next ten or fifteen years, I don't know.

. . .

LW: Do you see any future for him in Freeway? Or even in the [state]?

Mr. Janke: Nope.

LW: Not at all?

Mr. Janke: Nope.

LW: Why?

Mr. Janke: Job market here is fairly tight. I just . . . even with talking with him, he's looking for broader horizons.

. . .

LW: Do you see a future for Johnnie at all in Freeway?

Mr. Rose: (. . .) There's nothing in Freeway. As a matter of fact, it's a different era. When I got out of high school in '69, all of my friends, male counterparts that graduated, went to Freeway Steel. They went to Ford and Chevy. There's no such thing now. So in that respect, no, I definitely don't see any future [here] for Johnnie or any of my kids and I have three.

. . .

Ms. Sobel:	My son has already expressed, he's in technical school and he's getting technical training at one of the area schools and he is already planning to move to Florida.
	(. . .) Gloria, the daughter you interviewed, she has hopes of getting a nursing degree and moving to Ohio. My youngest one, Sandra, has already expressed going into computers and moving out to California.
LW:	So, you don't see any future for them at all?
Ms. Sobel:	They don't wish to make their future here.
LW:	The opportunities are pretty limited?
Ms. Sobel:	Yes, they are, they really are.

. . .

LW:	Do you see a future for Ray here in Freeway?
Ms. Smith:	I don't see too much of a future in Freeway for anybody. If they happen to get into one of the smaller businesses that are really going, that's a lucky stroke, but they can't really count on that. Now my husband, he was smart enough where he didn't go into the steel plant. He went into the post office when he got out of the Army and he's got twenty-six years in now and he's counting. He's got twenty-six years now. He's got twelve more to go and then he can retire. That's the earliest he can retire.
LW:	(. . .) So you don't see a future in Freeway for any of your children?
Ms. Smith:	No, not really.

Most parents do not envision a future for their children in Freeway and accept the fact that their children will probably leave. Although parents overwhelmingly suggest that their children will leave because of the economy, a few parents stress that there is always a job if you persevere. The father below states this position most strongly:

> *Mr. Antes:*   [If she wishes to find a job in the Freeway area she can]. Her brother and sister did. There was no reason not to. They both got fine positions. They are both doing very well. One went to work immediately [after college]. I foresee her doing the same thing.
>
> The economy, particularly in the [western part of the state where Freeway is located] is not what it used to be. But the jobs that are gone are the blue-collar jobs. Those were the kids who came out of high school, I know my friends came out of high school and immediately went to the plant. Made twenty dollars an hour. You can't beat it. The rest of us went out and worked at something else and made a lot less. But now they are out of work and our careers have gone upwards. With the blue-collar jobs there gone], there are a lot of other jobs. If you want to be an attorney, you can; if you want to be a doctor, you can be a doctor. If you want to be an engineer, there are jobs for engineers. There are jobs for math teachers today. You have to persevere.
>
> (. . .) I don't know of any nurse that isn't working (. . .) Again, you have to go out and hustle. You have to go knock on the doors. If you don't knock on the doors, nobody knows you are there.

A high proportion of parents assume that their children will leave the area in order to obtain employment. This represents a radical shift in the nature of such a community and must be understood as such. As David Bensman and Roberta Lynch point out in *Rusted Dreams,*

> The extended family is the central institution of the mill communities. From cradle to grave, southeast siders [Chicago] live within a thick web of blood ties to grandparents, uncles and aunts, parents, siblings, cousins, nephews and nieces, and

children. The great waves of change in American family
patterns in the last two decades—the rebellion of the young
against parental values and the entry of women into the work
force—were experienced here as minor ripples in a placid sea.[9]

Bensman and Lynch further suggest that

For their part, children often identify with their parents and
want to follow in their footsteps. Many young people grow up,
marry someone from the community, and buy a home nearby.
Sons will ride to work with their fathers; daughters call or visit
their mothers almost daily.[10]

The fact that Freeway parents are strongly encouraging their children
to *leave* town reflects a fracturing of the collective as parents know it.
They are encouraging their children to obtain a college education, move
out of the community, and secure stable employment elsewhere, often
far from home. The degree to which these sentiments represent a major
cultural shift cannot be underestimated.

There is, in fact, no sense among parents that there is anything left
worth fighting for in Freeway. This contrasts sharply with the mayor's
statement on the occasion of the seventy-fifth anniversary of Freeway.
Although I have reprinted the statement in full at the beginning of this
book, the last paragraph is worth reprinting here:

The City of Freeway will someday be known as the city that
refused to die. In the darkest of hours, Freeway displayed the
courage, tenacity, and spirit to survive. Anyone who
underestimated Freeway, underestimated the people of
Freeway. Our spirit is rekindled, our goals redefined, our
vision is for a new Freeway that will give our children, and
their children, a great city to live in, to raise their families, to
worship, to educate their children. They will say with pride, as
we have, "We live in Freeway."[11]

The above statement stands in sharp contrast with the expressed
sentiments of parents. Parents, of course, are fighting for their own
economic survival; the mayor is not.

Parental attitudes toward the school

There is, as I noted earlier, a tension between parents and the school. This not overt in any way, but is clearly evident. Although parents talk quite positively about individual teachers and, as I pointed out earlier, extol the virtues of education generally, they complain about the fact that the school does not, in their estimation, prepare students adequately for college and a future of non-manual labor. In other words, parents think the school should prepare their children for post-industrial society in a way that they, as parents, cannot. Specific complaints center on what parents perceive to be the relative lack of attention paid to guidance toward college and jobs, reflective of the fact that parents themselves cannot do it. Parents feel that the school should move into the vacuum that they, by virtue of their own educational and job situation, cannot fill. Although they center their complaints on guidance counselors, in particular, they are reflecting more generally on the way in which the school prepares their children for a life outside the working-class community that they knew.

LW:	In choosing a career, you don't think they [school personnel] help them at all?
Ms. White [Liz's mother]:	No.
LW:	Why is that?
Ms. White:	Because I don't think they do. I don't think they give them enough alternatives and tell them what is a good field to go into. They don't do enough testing on them.
	. . .
Ms. Eller [Suzanne's mother]:	I think Freeway itself is an excellent school system. As far as their guidance, I don't think they have given much guidance to them as far as jobs, training or interests or anything. I don't think their guidance counselors are all that hot. Maybe they just don't have enough time.
	. . .
LW:	Do you think the high school adequately

	prepares her for choosing a career and helping her make a career choice?
Ms. Pizillo:	No, because even for the SATs and stuff they were supposed to have some preparation for it and they didn't.
LW:	So you don't think they even encourage the students to go on to college at all?
Ms. Pizillo:	In that way, no. Their counselors, you [students] just mark down what you want. I don't think there's a discussion there. Just feel them out to see really what they want. They did not say, she did say she wanted engineering. No encouragement whatsoever.

. . .

LW:	Do you think the high school that she is going to encourages the students in their career goals and educational goals?
Ms. Southworth:	They are not bad with like setting up the right subjects and stuff. Guidance department wise I don't know if they are too helpful in helping kids unless they really go down and bug them quite a bit.
LW:	So you feel that the students have to take the initiative?
Ms. Southworth:	I think so. They really don't tell them anything. Like what scholarships are available or anything. You just have to go constantly and bug them and stuff in order to get anywhere, really.
LW:	So you don't feel that they even encourage the kids to go on to college?
Ms. Southworth:	Well, they probably encourage them, but it's the kids' initiative in bugging them and then it is them keeping after these kids.

. . .

LW:	What about the high school? Do you

think they help the student choose a career?

Ms. Hunt: I don't. My impression with Teresa already being there and now Larry and we also have a fifteen-year-old who is a freshman this year. I don't really know that the guidance does all that much. I mean they tell them if they feel they have the abilities to go for the college preparation courses but as far as, I don't know if they really put on any career nights that really bring across anything in a way that would interest the kids, unless they [kids] themselves really aren't interested at that point yet.

. . .

Ms. Southworth: I think maybe guidance and that should be [better]. The kids say they give announcements over the loudspeaker in the morning, general announcements. If their homerooms are real noisy and stuff, they miss all these. I would think they should maybe send around bulletins or something for these kids [about colleges, careers and so forth].

LW: (. . .) Are you saying that the high school places a lot of burden on the students to find out what's available?

Ms. Southworth: I think so. I don't think they are helpful or encouraging at all. It's up to the students to take the initiative.

. . .

LW: They don't really push the students to go on to college?

Ms. Sobel: No, I don't believe they do. They tell them to go to college, but they don't really prepare for what's in college. I don't believe so.

. . .

LW:	Is there anything you would like to see changed in the high school?
Ms. White:	Besides the split sessions, which everyone wants changed, they could have preparation for SATs. I don't think they go into that enough. And probably more guidance.

Without question, parents infer that the school does not do enough to encourage and prepare students to break into well-paid stable employment in a post-industrial economy. Parents, in a sense, blame the school for what they fear will be their children's future—a future without enough education and one lacking stable employment. In other words, parents fear for their children a future very much like the one they themselves face. They suggest that they, as parents, do their job by "pushing" education to their children and that it is the school's job to see to it that this "push" is transformed into reality.

Teachers, on the other hand, view the "problem" differently. They hold *parents* responsible for what they see as lack of commitment to education. As the excerpts below suggest, teachers complain bitterly about lack of parental involvement in the school, as evidenced by parents not attending parent-teacher conference night and so forth.

Mr. Teichler:	[about parents] Just general negativeness toward education and educators. [To teachers] "You aren't doing anything for my kid. You aren't doing anything for me." Then they expect you to accept the burden of educating their children without them supporting you.
LW:	Does that happen often where the parents are not doing anything?
Mr. Teichler:	Well, it's obvious on parents' night. 'Cause I have seniors and once they're seniors no one gives a damn because they are out of here. And it's already a lost cause. Either they made it or they didn't. Even with myself teaching four classes, with the load of ninety-five to one hundred kids, you expect 25 to 30 percent of

	their parents to come in. When you are dealing with less than 10 percent, why?
LW:	(. . .) Why don't they come?
Mr. Teichler:	Low priority of education.
LW:	Why?
Mr. Teichler:	I don't know. I really don't know. Maybe they feel it's not their job. It's somebody else's job to take care of them [their children] (. . .) No, they aren't concerned. If they were concerned, we would have more people coming to [school] board meetings, more people coming to parents' night, more people coming to social functions.

. . .

Ms. Rettert:	I don't think [parents] really care 'bout the kids and even this isn't saying too much for Freeway. A lot of people, I shouldn't generalize, like when we would have, just an example, PTA meetings in junior high [where I used to teach in the district], there would be more teachers than there would be parents. And when you consider the number of students there are in the junior high.

Teachers thus think that parents do not do enough. One might speculate that this sentiment is fueled by the fact that for many years these very parents looked down upon teachers because they [parents] made substantially more money working in the plants than teachers earned in the schools. Teachers resented parents for this for many years, and these feelings do not go away easily. In addition, as noted earlier in the book, a contradictory code of respect toward education exists among working-class adults to being with, and parents never totally appreciated the mental labor which teachers represent. Now, however, things are different and teachers are quick to point out that those working in the plants used to look down upon them because they earned considerably less money, despite all their education. It is, therefore, significant that parents and teachers are largely from the same class background. The tension exhibited between the two groups reflects a set of tensions that exist within the class fraction as a whole and that center largely on the meaning of education for the collective and what it has meant historically for individuals to pursue social mobility as the Freeway teachers have done.

The tension between parents and teachers can also be seen as an attempt to place blame for what may well be the collective experience of the existing working class in post-industrial society. Parents blame teachers and school personnel; school personnel blame parents. Both, in a sense, are partially "correct," although it should not escape attention that neither group focuses on the fact that it is industry that is transporting capital and jobs outside the United States. Teachers and school personnel *do* emphasize form rather than substance as well as the superficial absorption of knowledge. In addition, it is absolutely true that the type of education Freeway youth receive is not that designed to produce top scores on the SAT and facilitate entrance to prestigious colleges and universities. Parents, on the other hand, do not monitor their children's educational program closely and do not, in fact, attend school functions. This may be, of course, because they lack the cultural capital which would enable them to feel comfortable there. In addition, as noted above, a contradictory code of respect toward schooling does exist, and teachers correctly pick up on this. Parents want their children to take school seriously because they see no options for them if they do not. On the other hand, parents themselves did not take it seriously, and, if one examines their current involvement in the school and with the education of their children, still do not take it seriously despite their stated interest in schooling.

We might understand this, of course, in light of the historic relation to wage labor for the working class which did not demand that schooling be taken seriously to begin with. In point of fact, public high schools in working-class communities served to track students directly into blue-collar jobs. Ed Sadlowski in *Rusted Dreams* recalls the following:

> When you're a kid in school, about twelve and thirteen, the questionnaire [in school] would say: What's your name? You'd say: Sadlowski. What does your dad do? You'd put down: steelworker. The counselor would put you into industrial arts. A fancy name for you know what. That's where me and my pals wound up making little holes in glass to make chimes. All the kids I knew wound up in the steel mills. The son of a gun from U.S. Steel would come at graduation time and recruit guys.[12]

Thus it is not terribly surprising, given this historic relationship to schooling and wage labor, that working-class parents exhibit this apparent paradox with respect to their children's education. There is, as noted throughout the book, a contradictory code of respect toward schooling embedded within the class fraction, stemming from concrete experience with schooling and wage labor.

It is interesting to note that data reported in this chapter parallel those provided by Connell, Ashenden, Kessler, and Dorsett in their well-known book, *Making the Difference*, a study of schools, families, and social division in Australia. Connell and his associates are among only a handful of recent investigators to probe the relationship between family practices, schooling, and subsequent academic achievement. The point here is that Connell uncovered exactly the same intense desire for education for their children among working-class parents in Australia as reported in this volume. As the authors state:

> A number of our working-class parents, looking back over their own lives, had a strong sense of having come out of poverty and deprivation into a kind of prosperity—a sense particularly sharp among those who grew up during the Depression. Some think like sociologists, that it is a move up the ladder, but most see themselves as having come out of darkness into light. And they keenly wish to protect their children from slipping back into poverty in the future. Having learned that educational qualifications were a ticket to a better kind of job—usually by not having them—this made them strongly support their kids' staying at school as long as possible. The parents, in short, saw the school as a way of putting a *floor* beneath their kids' future economic circumstances. [13]

The authors argue strongly that parents have drawn the lesson from their own lives that more schooling means better jobs, and they apply this lesson prospectively to their children. What is so striking is that Freeway parents do *exactly* the same thing as Australian parents. Having obtained jobs during the "long boom" and the structural changes in the work force that accompanied this boom, working-class parents in both countries now view schooling as the *only* way that their children will have a floor beneath them in the job market. In the Freeway case, this is apt to be even more striking to parents given the absolute demise of the industrial economy which provided them with work to begin with.

In addition to this, Australian parents point out that they feel personally diminished by a lack of schooling and do not wish their children to feel so diminished. Thus, Mr. McArthur, who left school before he was able to write or spell, states,

I want Kate to go to school longer than me, because I don't want her to be dumb like me.[14]

Mrs. Midland, also in Australia, remarks that

I feel sometimes that I am unable to communicate with people of a much higher education.[15]

Such statements are reflective of Sennett and Cobb's notion (discussed in chapter 2) that there are hidden injuries associated with growing up working class.[16] Although I did not obtain data of this sort from parents in Freeway, it may well be that in the American case, economic reasons outshine all other possible reasons for parents desiring more education for youth [at this particular moment in history.]

I have suggested in this chapter that there is a great deal of congruence between families and children in terms of desire for schooling as well as an emphasis upon the form of schooling but not necessarily its substance. Parents also share the girls' notion that marriage and family ought to be postponed. There is, then, in Freeway, a certain congruence in a number of areas: families, schools, and youth do, in fact, share certain things and families and schools impact upon the identity of youth in some exceptionally important ways. As I have indicated throughout, however, these ways themselves often embody the very contradictory tendencies in youth identity.

In the next two chapters, I return to a social-action perspective. As outlined in chapter 1, social movements both constitute society and are forged within what constitutes order at any given time. In chapters 2 through 6, I explored the identities of working-class males and females and focused on the relational aspects of identity formation. I suggested that identities are constructed in relation to ideologically constructed "others" (e.g., blacks, females, males), and that this set of ideological constructions are fueled directly by the school. I also touched briefly upon families and explored the ways in which families are contributing to youth identities (although much more work needs to be done in this area, particularly in terms of the ways in which families contribute to the ideological construction of "other," which I do not deal with at all). I now move to the meaning of these identities for what constitutes "society," and the way in which such identities may be linked to social movements. It is, then, to the women's movement, the American labor movement, and the New Right that I now turn.

7
Women and Men: A Social-Movement Perspective

Based on a survey conducted in 1956, Elizabeth Douvan and Joseph Adelson conclude that girls are less clear of their future work than boys, and that adolescent females focus on marriage and motherhood as a life plan rather than on the world of work. Education and work are conceived as providing access to these goals rather than as goals to be sought in and of themselves. More recent studies such as those by Linda Valli and Angela McRobbie reach largely similar conclusions.[1]

It is, therefore, striking that adolescent girls in Freeway differ so markedly in terms of gender consciousness. Female youth in Freeway are not emphasizing the private sphere of home and family as in previous studies. Rather, they are stressing their participation in the public sphere and state that they will consider the private only after they are established in a job/career.

I will discuss in this chapter the meaning of this change in gender consciousness and argue that females exhibit some potential for feminist critique—that their identity suggests *a moment of critique* that could, at some point, be linked to a feminist position of collectivity and struggle. At the moment, however, these girls do not coalesce as a collectivity. They, individually, wish to avoid exploitive relationships with men and their solutions are private. They do not, therefore, see their identity as shared or collective, much less as feminist.

The school, as I noted in chapters 4 and 5, does not provide a context in which young women can explore their positions *as women*. In fact, the school serves to promote the assumed dominance of white men rather directly. It thus fractures in many ways (although contradictory elements regarding gender operate within the school, as I noted in chapter 4) the very beginnings of what may be a feminist consciousness in the white working class. Here I will discuss female consciousness in relationship to feminism as well as changes in the economy that may impact upon female identity.

I will also, in this chapter, discuss the American labor movement and speculate as to its possible relationship to emerging male identity. Given the demise of this movement I raise the possibility that working-class males may, in the future, articulate with a competing social movement, that being the New Right. I will explore the possible articulation of working-class females with the New Right in chapter 8. The present chapter must be seen as highly speculative since I do not know how these social movements will play themselves out in the real world. The point is that the identities outlined in this book are, at the moment, experienced as individual rather than collective. The question is, under what conditions will identities be seen as shared or collective, and how will these identities be articulated in relation to social movements?

Females

Dorothy Smith and others have argued that the working-class family is characterized by a marked subordination of women to men. Working-class women live out a discipline that almost totally subordinates their lives to the needs and desires of males. There is, in fact, an implicit contract between husband and wife according to which she provides household and personal services demanded by him in return to which he provides for her and her children whatever he deems appropriate. Thus, according to Smith,

> The household is organized in relation to his needs and wishes; mealtimes are when he wants his meals; he eats with the children or alone; as he chooses; sex is when he wants it; the children are to be kept quiet when he does not want to hear them. The wife knows at the back of her mind that he could take his wage-earning capacity and make a similar "contract" with another woman. As wages have increased, the breadwinner's spending money has enlarged to include leisure activities which are his, rather than hers—a larger car, a motorcycle, a boat. Even a camper often proves more for him than for her, since for her it is simply a transfer from

convenience to less convenient conditions of the same domestic labor she performs at home.[2]

Numerous scholars attest to the conditions of working-class women's lives and focus on the notion of the "family wage" as being a contributing factor. Martha May suggests on the basis of a study of the Ford Motor Company that the family wage as ideology became and remained important because it appeared advantageous to all participants.[3] For the working class, for instance, it held out the possibility of an adequate income. A family wage meant that an adult worker could support his family and enable his children to attend school. To achieve this goal, however, the family wage ideology both employed and maintained existing gender distinctions in work roles. For employers, the family wage ideology held out the possibility of lowered wages for some workers (mainly women) and a stable work force whereby industry could amass long-term profits.

The family wage, however, did not benefit women. By linking gender roles and subsistence for the working class, the family waged ideology successfully reinforced the notion that women should receive lower wages than men and/or stay at home. In the final analysis, the consequences for women of the family wage ideology are that it severely limited their work force participation because women could not earn enough money to make it worth their while. The demand for subsistence among the working class thus became articulated in the form of a request for a family wage—a wage that reinforced a particular role for women and children, thus reinforcing patriarchy in the home. As May states, however,

> Ironically, that family wage was not widespread or long-lived enough to benefit more than a small segment of the working class, and it dovetailed neatly with the concerns of employers for profits. In this sense, the family wage, as ideology, served to divide the working class for a temporary gain, at the great expense of its female members.[4]

The fact that women could earn relatively little in the work force thrust wage-earning women back on families as a primary means of emotional and physical support. Thus, although many working-class women historically were in the wage labor force before marriage, their wage work experiences failed to alter their dependence on the family since nearly all jobs available to women offered less security and status than did the role of wife and mother.

Leslie Woodcock Tentler, on the basis of an extensive investigation of working-class family life from 1900 to 1930 concludes as follows:

> For the working class women, then, life outside the family was apt to be economically precarious and very lonely. It was not a life of freedom and autonomy. This was so because the great majority of unskilled women earned less than subsistence wages. They needed the economic protection of family, and without it they lacked the resources to experiment with new styles of life. Yet the price of family economic protection was, as we have seen, a surrender of considerable personal autonomy. Life outside the family, moreover, was difficult for women because extrafamiliar institutions did not offer them the emotional security, the social status, the easy personal identity of family membership. Ultimately the family provided the only world in which working class women were secure and fully acceptable.[5]

It is in the context of the above arguments that the Freeway youth responses become so interesting. Given the demise of the industrial economy which enabled the family wage to be at least an envisioned possibility (not necessarily a reality, of course) for some segements of working-class America, and the very real fact that male industrial workers are unable to locate jobs that pay anywhere near what industrial jobs paid, the family wage as even a *possible* reality for the working class is undermined. In addition, as Smith reminds us, the economy has changed such that the demand for *certain* types of women's labor increased as corporate capitalism required clerical, service, and sales workers at low cost. The implicit "contract" that restricted the employment of married women and reinforced their role in the domestic economy controlled by their husbands has been weakened because women are being called upon to participate more and more in the paid labor force.[6] In addition, inflation and the demise of the industrial economy mean that more and more women *must* enter the paid work force in order to fulfill their traditional home-based responsibilities.[7] Thus, the demand for female labor, coupled with the decline of the industrial economy, has eroded the particular form that patriarchy has taken historically in the working-class family.

There has, in addition, been a change in the consciousness of women generally, and the notion of what it means to be female in the society. Both female teachers and students in Freeway reflect in differing degrees this altered consciousness. While it is not my intention to unpack the "causes" for this change (all the above-mentioned factors are certainly contributors), the very fact of such change is important.

Zillah Eisenstein argues persuasively that women constitute a *class* by definition of the fact that patriarchal society defines a particular place for the female as a woman and that this also points to the potential of women becoming a class in political struggle. This does not mean, however, that women are a class like the Traditional Proletariat, defined by their relationship to the means of production. They are, rather, as Eisenstein argues, a "sexual class in that they constitute the basic and necessary activities of society: reproduction, childbearing, nurturing, consuming, domestic laboring, and wage earning. Women are a sexual class because of what they do as women, that is, as nurturers, mothers, secondary wage-earners and so on."[8] This does not mean, however, that economic class differences do not exist within the sexual class of women, nor is it meant to ignore that racial differences exist within secondary class status as well as within economic class differences.

The politics of sexual class, argues Eisenstein, has two aspects. To begin with, descriptively the sexual class of women refers to the fact "that it is a construction of patriarchal relations: the biological female is transformed through a series of political relations into a woman differentiated from man. The only natural thing about the sexual class of women is that they are biologically female, but nature in this instance remains an 'unknown thing.' "[9] *Women, in this sense, are a class in themselves.* In the second sense, *a sexual class for itself,* Eisenstein points to the development of being women *in the sense that they are aware that they are set apart and denied equality, in relation to both racist and patriarchal structures.* There has been, since the 1960s, a resurgence of feminist consciousness which must be seen as a sexual class in political struggle. The struggle for the identity of women as a sexual class constitutes a social movement, and the glimmerings of critique among Freeway girls must be seen in relation to this movement, as well as in relation to economic changes that affect the configuration of both male and female labor. I will expand on each of these points below.

Women, the economy, and changing consciousness

One of the most striking changes to take place within the last twenty years (in addition to the demise of the capital-labor accord, of course) is the movement of women, on a non-temporary basis, into the paid labor force. It is now the case that over 50 percent of American women work outside the home in full-time jobs, and a high proportion of these women have young children in the home. As Michael Apple points out, however, it is important to look not only at numbers, but also at the shape of women's paid labor. First, women's work reflects a *vertical* division of labor whereby women as a group receive less pay than men and work under less advantageous positions. Second, women's work is differentiated from men's on a *horizontal* basis in the sense that women are concentrated in particular kinds of work. Seventy-eight percent of clerical workers, 67 percent of service workers, 67 percent of teachers and a higher proportion at the elementary level, are women in the United States. Conversely, less than 20 percent of executive, managerial, and administrative workers are women.[10] In fact, although women entered the paid labor force at a phenomenal rate recently, they are concentrated in particular kinds of jobs—those with relatively low pay, few benefits, and lacking autonomy. As noted above, corporate capitalism requires women laborers as clerical, service, and sales workers at low cost. In addition, inflation and, increasingly, the loss of well-paid male laboring jobs, means that women *must* enter paid work in order to contribute to the family income. The rise of single-parent families also means that many more women must work in the paid labor force than ever before. Thus women will, by virtue of the economy, be more concerned with the paid labor sphere than in earlier decades and Freeway girls reflect this to some extent.

At the same time, women have, historically, been responsible for the private sphere of home and family and Freeway girls will not escape these pulls in the future. Their solution now is to deny the importance of the home/family sphere and engage in the individualistic solution of gaining more schooling, getting a job in order to support themselves, avoiding exploitative relationships with men, and so forth. It is possible, however, that they may be only postponing the moment of patriarchial assault until they have children.[11] At that point, the contradictory pulls of wage labor and home/family life may become exceptionally apparent, especially given male consciousness regarding these spheres as outlined in chapter 2.

The Freeway girls, nevertheless, offer the glimmerings of critique of women's place in both the home/family sphere and that of wage labor. They challenge the notion that their primary role is to take care of their husbands' children in return for which the men's family wage will support them. They also begin to challenge the notion that they must account to men—that they must listen as men tell them what to do. In a sense, then, they are beginning to reject the ideology of separate spheres for women and men and the accompanying notion that they must occupy a subordinate role. This can be seen in relation to the economy which, as I noted above, increasingly demands both that they *must* work in the paid labor force and at the same time offers them *certain* types of jobs. Although Freeway females are too young to understand the implications of these economic dynamics, the jobs that are offered them in the future may push them back into a self-definition of wifehood/ motherhood in the sense that their own paid work is boring, demeaning, and so forth, at the same time that the very fact of being in the wage labor sphere may encourage them to struggle for more pay and better working conditions simply because the jobs are necessary for family survival. There are contradictory pulls likely in the future, then, with regard to the identity of working-class women, even though the identity of high-school girls does not, at the moment, reflect these contradictions.

The Freeway girls' identity cannot be understood only in relation to the economy. It must also be seen as reflective, at least partially, of the identity-formation process of women as a sexual class in general, even though the women's movement has been largely colonized by the middle class. Some of these middle-class struggles have filtered down to these girls, and their beginning critique of women's place must be seen as linked to the broader struggles in key ways. Eisenstein is worth quoting in full here on feminist consciousness:

Once one recognizes the importance of feminist consciousness in actualizing the potential of women as a sexual class it becomes as important to study liberal, racist and patriarchal ideology as it is to study the capitalist relations of family life, the economy and the state. These realms impact on consciousness and the development of sexual-class identity. It is the conflicts arising between the ideologies of liberalism, racism, and phallocentrism and the capitalist patriarchal relations of society that lay the bases for a consciousness that embodies a sexual class's becoming conscious 'for itself.' The question of how women become a self-conscious political sexual class and how they work through political struggle to develop themselves as a sexual class politically is the concern of feminism. Although women constitute a sexual class by virtue of the gendered status relations of their biological sexual selves, women become a class through feminist struggle. They become a class in actual struggle against patriarchal privilege. In some sense, one could argue that in the United States the struggle from 1848 to 1920 and then the struggle again from 1969 to the present demonstrates the development, the process of a sexual class coming to a consciousness for itself.[12]

The identity-formation process of Freeway females must be seen, at least partially, in light of the above statement, although there is no question that feminism has been a middle-class movement and that the working class in this country has been relatively untouched by it. The responses of the Freeway girls reflect the development of women as a sexual class to some extent, however. The entire notion of what it means to be female in this society (and others, of course) is being contested and redefined by virtue of this struggle and the Freeway girls are not completely unaffected by this, despite the class basis of the movement. A very small number of Freeway girls even begin to articulate a feminist struggle rather directly. For example, when Jennifer discusses Amy's moving into the cosmetology curriculum (see chapter 3) she states:

> The first introduction I had to divorce was my cousin. They had a wonderful happy marriage and then one day he just said, boom, "Good-bye." And I was like, "What do you mean good-bye, you can't do that." They always seemed happy to me and when he left it was like shock. As well as things may be, things may go wrong.
>
> (. . .) Maybe we [the girls in the advanced class] think it's just a waste. I mean you have the opportunity, it's like such a waste. I mean, civil rights have come so far. If it were one hundred years ago I can see saying that [going into

cosmetology] where you were being a rebellious woman if you wanted to go out and get a job. I mean, now we have that opportunity; to relinquish that and say, I mean, I'm a cautious person and thinking of the future and saying, "What if something goes wrong?" It does happen.

LW: (. . .) What you said about civil rights, where did you get that from?

Jennifer: I don't know, maybe from history, maybe social studies. We had to fight for the vote. Maybe it's just from social studies learning about laws and stuff along the way.

Most of the students do not articulate any connection with the feminist struggle at all, however. Jennifer is, in fact, somewhat conscious of her relation to the struggle of a sexual class, although this is mediated by her direct experience with divorce. Suzanne, below, also expresses a rather direct linkage between her ideas and feminism.

Suzanne: It [marriage] started so far back and it's, like, people didn't live long. Now people live to be eighty years old. You don't stay with one person for eighty years. It's, like, impossible.

LW: (. . .) What makes you say that?

Suzanne: A lot of divorce. A lot of parents who fight and stuff (. . .) Back when they [parents] were kids, like, girls grew up, got married, worked for a couple of years after graduation, had two or three kids, had a white picket fence, two cars. Things are different now.

LW: How so?

Suzanne: Girls don't grow up first to be married. They grow up to be people, too (. . .) You've got to do it [make a good life] for yourself. I don't want to be Mrs. John Smith. I want to be able to do something.

Jennifer and Suzanne not only have the glimmerings of critique but also articulate the fact that there is a broader struggle "out there" with which they are linked in some form or another. Most of the Freeway girls, however, do not see themselves as so linked, even though their notion of gendered subject is, in fact, very different from that of their parents' generation and much different from that of Freeway males. They want to support themselves, not have to depend on a man, and wish to make their own decisions instead of having their husbands make their decisions for them. They thus exhibit the very beginnings of critique of women's place although most are not conscious of it in these terms. At the moment, they also pose individualistic solutions to the expressed "problem." As they mature and attempt to live out their ideals, however, they might become more conscious of the development of a sexual class identity. Although there are serious limitations to the development of such an identity at the moment (I will pursue this point in the next chapter), it may change in the future as they attempt to create meaning in their adult lives and meet up with the tensions surrounding their desires in the real world. Eisenstein argues persuasively here and, once again, is worth quoting in full:

> There is greater potential today than ever before for women to become more fully conscious of themselves as a sexual class given the post–World War II phenomena of the married wage earner and the "working mother" alongside the subsequent struggles with the state on abortion, the ERA, etc. These struggles have begun to uncover the way patriarchy functions through the law, through ideology, and through woman's assignment to the double day of work. Out of these struggles for greater equality, the mystified form of patriarchal rule is uncovered. It is in this sense that women's identity as a sexual class reflects political and historical processes and cannot be predefined statistically as merely a biological class.[13]

The identity-formation process of Freeway girls, then, reflects the beginnings of a critique of women's place. It is possible that these beginnings could, at some point, be woven into the collective interests of women for autonomy, interdependence, and community. It is also possible, however, that these interests could be rearticulated by the New Right, especially given the kinds of paid jobs that will be available to women and the very real pulls of the domestic sphere that they are likely to face in the future. I will discuss Freeway males in relation to the New Right in this chapter since the potential alignment is far clearer for me at this point than that between females and the New Right. I will pick up themes of feminism and the New Right in relation to working-class females in the next chapter.

The role of the school, as I have suggested in chapters 4 and 5, is largely to constrain this moment of critique, although there are aspects of the school that partially promote it: for example, the inclusion in the curriculum of some history of women's struggle (although undermined and trivialized at times by teachers and male students); a feminist consciousness among some teachers (although often contradictory); and the fact that schools can no longer legally provide separate educational and programmatic experiences for males and females because of Title IX.[14] All this must be seen as a result of conflict over gender in the state and the fact that there have been some real victories for women in the state sector—victories that filter down to the level of practice. Thus the school largely blocks, but at the same time partially encourages, the development of a self-conscious political identity for women.[15] I now turn to male identity.

Males

The male labor movement, which is the obvious social movement for boys to articulate with, is in a state of decline. A potential movement with which they may ultimately articulate, however, in the New Right. There are several issues to be explored here: 1) the importance of the male wage for masculine social identity; 2) the social movement of the American working class and, in particular, the recent history of the labor movement; and 3) the rise of the New Right and the way in which the New Right may potentially give shape and form to male working-class social identity. I will explore each area in turn below. Each is related to the virulent sexism and racism expressed by Freeway boys.

Paul Willis has argued that the male wage is key to understanding the establishment of patriarchal homes in working-class culture and the male identity in general. As he argues,

> Most importantly, perhaps, the [male] wage is still the golden key (mortgage, rent, household bills) to a personal household separate from parents and separate from work, from

production. The home is the main living embodiment of the laborer's freedom and independence from capital—apart from wage labor, of course, which is the price for the independence of a separate home. But this price really does purchase something. The household is an area of privacy, security and protection from the aggression and exploitation of work, from the patriarchal dependencies of the parental home, from the vicissitudes of the work place. The separate home is still a universal working class objective and its promise of warmth and safety more than offsets the risk and coldness of work.[16]

Willis further suggests that a sense of being a man is attached to doing and being able to do physical work. "This is, in part," he states, "because of some of the direct 'sensuous' qualities of traditional work—its heaviness, difficulty and dirtiness."

The toughness and strength required to "do the job" can both obscure its economic exploitation and be the basis for some dignity and collective identity which partially reverses the conventional ordering of class and status. It allows some active and positive accommodation within the worst terms of the mental/manual split. There can be some masculine pride in manual work. It can be superior to "cissy" and "paper pushing work."[17]

Willis thus examines the sense of masculine identity attached to labor in heavy industry and suggests that a crisis in gender industry is ensuing for working-class males. While this may be true, and Willis himself offers some sympathy for the perceived plight of males, it must be pointed out that the home was *never* a refuge for working-class females. Women trade one form of patriarchal dependence (on fathers) for another (on husbands) when they marry. The "home fires," while an apparent source of "freedom" for males, have been a source of oppression and often violence for working-class females. The notion that the working-class home is a "refuge" is a distinctly male perspective; it has not necessarily operated as such for females. Men, in addition to earning the "family wage," earned the right to oppress women at home. Women, in return for leaving the patriarchal homes of their fathers, earned the right to inhabit the patriarchal homes of their husbands. In spite of his clearly sexist perspective, however, Willis does raise an interesting point about the gender crisis and the importance of social-indentity terms of the working-class male wage. It is this point that serves partially to explain the male-supremacist attitudes of Freeway students. As Willis states,

> One "creative" form of the resolution of a "gender crisis" among young men may well be in an aggressive assertion of masculinity and masculine style for its own sake. If the essential themes and personal identities of masculinity do concern power and domination, and if they are to continue without the secret guarantees [the giving of labor in a masculine confrontation], then they must be worked through a more direct domination. Male "power" may throw off its cloak of labor dignity and respectability. This may involve a physical, tough, direct display of those qualities now "automatically" guaranteed by doing productive work, of being a "breadwinner." "Dare to say I'm not a Man." This, of course, has a logic of its own and is an exposure of just how little of a full social and cultural identity our "official" society offers when a job is not available. It may also deepen some of the brutalities and oppressions experienced by working-class women.[18]

Although I am unwilling to speculate at this moment as to the possibly brutal aspects of working-class life of the future (I will return to this in chapter 8), it can be argued that the virulently sexist statements of the boys regarding their own future reflect the sentiments Willis expresses. Now that males cannot envision a future of well-paying wage labor infused with traditional working-class definitions of masculinity, what is it they do have? It is clear from the Freeway data that males are not contemplating new forms of gender identity but are rearticulating, in a highly virulent fashion, the old forms of female domination. This can be seen as an articulation of a patriarchal form of male/female relations without the underlying substance of envisioned wage labor. In other words, here I agree with Willis. It does appear as if males are affirming the direct domination of women in the absence of its cloak of the dignity and respectability of labor. The Freeway males do not talk about labor itself since they understand clearly that such labor no longer exists. It is significant that they talk about the domination of females without discussing the way in which their own involvement with productive work will enable this to occur. They are, in fact, emphasizing the domination of women in the absence of its historic cloak of respectability.[19]

It is also significant that Freeway boys are affirming, on one level, the idea of academic achievement. As R. W. Cornell and his associates point out, masculinity cannot be grasped as a simple social form. There are, in fact, different kinds of masculinity, and the dominant form of working-class masculinity achieved in and through rejection of the school may very well be breaking down given the economy. Thus, we may be witnessing a slight change in the dominant form of working-class masculinity in the sense that the overt rejection of schooling may no longer be part of it. This lack of rejection of schooling, however, should not be confused with the competitive achievement embedded centrally within the dominant middle-class notion of masculinity.[20] What Freeway boys have embraced is the *form* of schooling and a seemingly positive valuation of it, but this should not be confused with middle-class competitive achievement.

The apparent acceptance of schooling among working-class boys also needs to be seen in light of the construction of masculinity and available jobs. Given the loss of "truly" masculine positions, what is left? Jobs like "waiter" or other service-sector jobs may be seen as even *less* masculine by working-class males (read, more feminine) than those that require schooling.[21] Thus we may be seeing here a slight reworking of working-class notions of masculinity which may embody an apparent but superficial acceptance of education that was not the case before. All this means, of course, is that this generation of working-class boys may be willing to sit through school rather than take it on directly. The domination of women, however, has remained intact in this rearticulated working-class masculinity.

The identity of Freeway males and a slightly reworked masculinity in the working class also have to be understood in light of the history of the American labor movement. As David Hogan and others suggest, the history of the American working class is different from that of the English experience, for example.[22] In the American case, the white-male working class did not have to develop class-wide political institutions to achieve political democracy. Unlike in England, the American working class was more defensive, protecting the already existing Republican democracy from perceived foes, those being monopolists, Catholics, aristrocratic impulses, and socialists. In addition, the American experience is linked historically with large-scale immigration. The formation of the working class has to be seen in light of interactive pressures created by ethnic communities. It is, therefore, more divided internally along racial and ethnic lines than is the case in England. As Hogan suggests,

> Compared to English working class culture, American working class culture is not as cohesive, thickly textured, or self conscious; it is more diffuse, fractured internally, divided along regional, racial and ethnic lines; its repudiation of bourgeois ideology less deep and incisive; its institutional infrastructure— trade unions, political organizations, voluntary associations— less extensive and weaker.[23]

Thus, the working class in America has been fractured historically for a variety of reasons. Mike Davis argues similarly as follows:

> The increasing proletarization of the American social structure has not been matched by an equal tendency toward the homogenization of the working class as a cultural or political collectivity. Stratifications rooted in differential positions in the social labor process have been reinforced by deepseated ethnic, religious, racial and sexual antagonisms within the working class. In different periods these divisions have fused together definite intraclass hierarchies (for example, "native plus skilled plus Protestant" versus "immigrant plus unskilled plus Catholic") representing unequal access to employment, consumption, legal rights, and trade union organization.[24]

This already fractured American working class was that much more fractured by 1983 with the Reagan administration successfully implementing a series of concessions of wage declarations cutting through the AFL-CIO. As Davis states, in his chapter significantly entitled "The Fall of the House of Labor,"

> A veritable earthquake was crumbling the old labor "peace," with one third to one half of their membership lost to plant closings, imports or automation, the core industrial unions have surrendered bit by bit many of the strategic gains they had won over the last forty years. In industry after industry the hard-won wage "patterns" that guaranteed contractual uniformity and preserved effective solidarity between workers in different firms

are being destroyed, their place taken by a savage new wage cutting competition.[25]

Davis's analysis is extremely helpful. Facing the "worst setback for unions in a half-century," the labor movement, the only unifying aspect of the American working class in the face of its historical development, is in serious trouble. *This leaves the American male working class with no broader historically based social movement with which to articulate.* Unlike the girls, then, Freeway boys do not have a historically rooted social movement with which they might link, whether consciously or not. The movement with which they have a historical linkage is in a state of serious disrepair.

What does exist currently, however, is the New Right as a social movement with which working-class white males may potentially articulate. As Allen Hunter notes,

The New Right is part of the broad resurgence of organized conservatism. In addition to Reagan's electoral victories, conservatives have gained power within the Republican Party, promoted and benefitted from the intellectual shift to the right, as evidenced by the prominence of neo-conservative intellectuals, and created a dense organizational presence in Washington of conservative lobbying groups, think tanks, and institutes and foundations. In this mileau several characteristics distinguish the New Right. It is that part of today's conservatism which consistently stresses social traditionalism and cultural issues, strategically focuses on extra-party organizing of backlash social movements, and programmatically is least reticent to impose its versions of morality and cultural values on the polity as a whole.[26]

What is key here is that since 1977 the New Right's coherence has been realized largely in terms of pro-family rhetoric, which could be the main link to Freeway males in the future. The pro-family rhetoric draws on images that point to the common interests of traditional groups— antigay, anti-ERA, antiabortion and the religious right.[27] As Hunter points out, "Hostilities toward women's rights and sexual independence, homosexuality, and secularism have been joined in a defense of "The" family.[28] Hunter is worth quoting in full here as one of the best analysts of the New Right currently:

> For the New Right the inherent tension between cultural traditionalism and economic dynamism is metaphorically resolved within a systematically gendered view of the world encapsulated in the "traditional family." The complementarity of the economic and cultural domains is sustained in pro-family rhetoric by the complementarity of the male and female spheres. The organic unity of the family resolves male egoism and female selflessness into a smoothly functioning expression of divine intent. Since gender is divine and natural, it follows that in neither realm is there room for legitimate political conflict . . . When men or women challenge these gender roles they break with God and nature; when liberals, feminists, and secular humanists prevent them from fulfilling those roles they undermine the divine and natural supports upon which society rests.[29]

The New Right thus holds out some possibility for white-male working-class articulation in the sense that it may give shape and form to and encourage a collective identity by rearticulating the virulent sexism and racism expressed in chapter 2. The New Right offers a possible social movement for white males both in light of Hunter's statement of the centrality of traditional gender roles and the expressed racism of Freeway boys. Michael Omi and Howard Winant have argued persuasively that while the agenda of the far right in America and racial supremacist groups will not attract a mass base, the New Right very well may do so. As Omi and Winant suggest,

> The new right cannot simply defend patterns of racial inequality by demanding a return to segregation, for example, or by reviving simplistic notions of biological superiority/ inferiority. As we have previously noted, the racial upheavals of the 1960s precluded a direct return to this form of racial logic. The new right objective, however, was to dismantle the political gains of racial minorities. Since these gains could not be reversed, they had to be *rearticulated*. The key device used by the new right in its effort to limit the political gains of racial minority movements has been "code words." These are phrases

and symbols which refer indirectly to racial theories, but do not directly challenge popular democratic or egalitarian ideals (e.g., justice, equal opportunity).[30]

Omi and Winant suggest that the New Right is a powerful social movement that does not generally display overt racism. It does, however, rearticulate racial ideology by employing code words such as "maintenance of community," or the ideology of the "family" in the case of the busing debates; arguing for "traditional" life-styles and families in the case of monitoring textbooks and opposing multiculturalism; and emphasizing the well-worn notion of "reverse discrimination." On the issue of affirmative action, the New Right simply rearticulates the meaning of "fairness" and "equality" by arguing that the state has accommodated unfairly to special-interest groups such as minority groups at the expense of well-deserving white males.[31] Thus the New Right joins racist and sexist sentiments in its focus on the "traditional family" and reaffirms white-male supremacy.

The New Right agenda offers a powerful social movement with which white working-class males may articulate in the future. With the demise of the traditional labor movement in the United States, and the rise of the New Right, it is possible to argue that if white working-class males see their identity as collective and articulate with a broader movement, it *will* be that of the New Right, which has the potential to rearticulate the already existing virulent sexism and racism in the male identity. While this racism and sexism is, at the moment, expressed largely individually, the New Right may well encourage these sentiments to become shared or felt as collective. It is, therefore, arguably the case that as these males mature, the New Right will be able, as a social movement, to offer shape and form to male working-class identity, as described here, thus changing the direction of working-class male politics from union politics to that of New Right politics.[31] I will explore this further in the next chapter.

There is a sense in which the school encourages the identity formation of males and, if I am correct, the New Right agenda of the future. It encourages, as I argued in earlier chapters, separatist forms and white-male dominance and even supremacy. Again, however, this is not total since there are countervailing tendencies within the school itself, reflective of the fact that the school is a state institution and, therefore, embodies certain contradictions. The state has itself, after all, been the site of struggle and is a major point of attack for the New Right. Thus there are countervailing tendencies in the school due to the fact that it reflects the gains of the very social movements that students are embedded within and/or oppose. At the moment, however, the school appears largely to further the identity of white working-class males and constrain the moment of critique among white working-class females. I will pursue the possibilities embedded within this moment of critique in chapter 8.

8
Whither the Working Class?

The American economy is changing radically. We are, as noted in chapter 1, moving from an industrial society to a post-industrial, or programmed, society. Jobs that served to order the lives, identities, and political struggles of the Traditional Proletariat no longer exist to the extent that they did. They are being systematically phased out as de-industrialization forges ahead. Henry Levin and Russell Rumberger offer a series of exceptionally provocative points on the possible shape of post-industrial society. It must be clear here that no one really knows the shape of future society since there are simply too many unknown factors and possible interactions. I will speculate here as to potential future scenarios regarding both the economy and identities based on my ethnographic work in Freeway. Anything could, of course, happen to intervene and change drastically the course of the economy and identity formation as well as the potential meaning of such formation. One thing is clear, however: The American economy is no longer characterized by the historical conflict between capital and labor. Levin and Rumberger suggest that

> Technology appears to be having a profound impact on jobs in the United States. Computers, robots, advanced communication systems, and other technologies are creating new jobs, while other jobs are being eliminated as robots and machines take over the work performed by human labor. Even more important, a wide array of existing occupations throughout the economy are being altered as workers begin to use computers, word processors, and other sophisticated devices to perform their jobs.[1]

It is not totally clear, however, what the effect of this technology will be in terms of the number of jobs available in the future since technology eliminates jobs as well as creates them. In the past, it appears that technology created as many jobs as it displaced, but it does not look as if the same will hold for the future. A new study by the Office of Technology Assessment of the U.S. Congress found that only 60 percent of 11.5 million workers who lost jobs because of plant shutdowns or relocations from 1979 to 1984 found new employment. Of this 60 percent, 45 percent took pay cuts, and two-thirds were earning less than 80 percent of their former income.[2]

Based on the U.S. Bureau of Labor Statistics (BLS) data it can also be argued that there will be a disproportionate number of opportunities in low-level positions relative to high-level ones. Levin and Rumberger suggest, based on their calculations of BLS data, that there will be between 500,000 and 700,000 new and replacement jobs between 1982 and 1995 for the following positions: computer systems analysts, computer programmers, and electrical engineers. In contrast, these estimates suggest that *there will be between 10 and 15 million new and replacement jobs in the three traditional occupations—custodians, cashiers, and salesclerks.* This represents from 16 to 32 times the number of openings for the three technical positions noted above. Job openings due to turnover, in particular, strongly favor the lowest-paying occupations in the economy.[3]

This suggests that if Rumberger and Levin are correct in their estimates, the jobs available to Freeway students in the future are likely to be those that offer low pay with little security and virtually no benefits.

Possible contradictory aspects of new social movements

In chapter 1, I suggest that the new social movements must be seen in relation to these economic changes. As we move into the post-industrial phase—a phase that, if Rumberger and Levin are correct, will offer relatively low paying positions to many more people, the question of new class conflicts becomes paramount. What are these new conflicts likely to be? Alberto Melucci suggests the following:

> In comparison with the industrial phase of capitalism, the production characteristic of advanced society requires that control reach beyond the productive structure into the areas of consumption, services, and social relations. The mechanisms of

accumulation are no longer fed by the simple exploitation of the labor force, but rather by the manipulation of complex organization systems, by control over information and over the processes and institutions of symbol-formation, and by intervention in interpersonal relations.

Faced with these changes in the structure of production, one must try to determine the significance of the new social movements. More and more, production no longer consists solely in the transformation of the natural environment into a technical environment. It is also becoming the production of social relations and social systems; indeed, it is even becoming the production of the individual's biological and interpersonal identity.

(. . .) The new social movements are struggling, therefore, not only for the reappropriation of the material structure of production, but also for collective control over socioeconomic development, i.e. for the reappropriation of time, of space, and of relationships in the individual's daily existence.[4]

The social movements described in the last chapter can be seen as struggles to appropriate identity. However, there is not one such struggle. *There are, in fact, competing struggles*. The feminist movement is one struggle for identity; the New Right is another. They represent, in some cases, radically different notions of the appropriate identity of the same "subject"—the identity of female being one such example here.

These identity movements can potentially serve the interests of the powerful, however. Philip Wexler points out that there are two languages being spoken within the current rightward sociocultural movement. One, he suggests, is the language of the market; the other, the language of morality. As he states,

On the one side, there is a press toward total rationalization, toward the extension of the market to all social relations; a thorough triumph of the commodity form. In the other language, there is defense of the patriarchal family, fundamentalist religion, faith and incalculability. Without denying that one side may represent the interests and commitment of a particular historical class fraction, it is important to observe that this internal contradiction within the current rightist social movement is a central dynamic of the American institutional social structure. *The development of market commodity relations has taken place only with support of the surrounding social cushion of the maintenance and reproduction of the pre-market social relations of earlier social forms of sociation and solidarity* [my emphasis.][5]

Wexler suggests that assertions about the importance of connections of family and religious belief as primary constituents of society and nation may, in fact, enable the extension of commodity relations to go forward into every aspect of life. These assertions (which are embedded within New Right identity politics, in particular) may, in fact, be encouraging, in contradictory ways, other forms of control in programmed society to move forward. It is extremely important, therefore, that male youth identity in Freeway can, if I am correct, be experienced as collective under a New Right agenda. The focus on male supremacist family structure, racism, and so forth can be used as a set of identity politics to enable the further extension of a market logic (also embedded, not coincidently, within New Right politics)— a logic under which, as I suggested above, the Traditional Proletariat will suffer enormously and disproportionately in the economic realm. Fighting in identity terms for the dominance of the white-male and "normative" family structure under which separate gender spheres are maintained may be equivalent to the fight for the "family wage" at the early stages of the industrial economy (see chapter 7). The difference, however, is that the "family wage" may have brought some security for some members of the working class; the fight for an abstract white-male dominance in the post-industrial society will probably bring very little in economic terms given the trends outlined above.[6]

There is a further set of issues related to current white-male youth identity formation if I am correct in my speculations regarding the potential link with the New Right. Female youth are, in fact, moving in a totally different direction at the moment, showing some potential for articulation with feminism. Before talking about the potential clash here and fleshing out possible scenarios associated with this clash, it is important to focus more carefully on the possibilities for Freeway girls, including their potential future link with the New Right, despite current sentiments that suggest otherwise.

Female identity politics and social movements

I argued in chapter 3 that the girls examined here exhibit a challenge to male-dominant families and the separate sphere ideology associated with such dominance in the real world. They are, at least in terms of the ways in which they envision their lives, beginning to break down the Domestic Code. For them, the domestic is *not* primary; wage labor is. Significantly, they do not suggest the "part-time" work solution and/or flights into fantasy futures offered by girls in previous studies. What they do suggest, however, are individualistic/private solutions in the form of more education, getting a better job, not marrying until they are settled, "not allowing husbands to tell them what to do," and so forth. Their identity does *not* represent, at the moment, a collective challenge to male dominance in either the home or workplace. It does represent a challenge to traditional gender consciousness, however, and this should not be dismissed. It also represents a challenge to the "traditional" family as envisioned and valorized by the New Right.

This challenge is limited in some key ways, however. Many of the girls, as I suggest in chapter 3, express the desire to obtain jobs in the sex-segregated ghettos. This is not to denigrate such jobs in any way, but simply to acknowledge, along with Heidi Hartmann, that such jobs do not usually pay enough to allow women to exist outside the bounds of marriage.[7] In other words, an expressed reason why the girls want to have a job/career is the high divorce rate. They suggest that they do not want to be in a bad marriage simply because of money. In fact, as they point out, the husband might drink, have an affair, or simply leave, in which case the wife needs to have a source of her own support. Yet the jobs many of the girls envision for themselves will not give them this level of support. A secretary cannot, for the most part, support herself and her children should anything happen to her marriage.[8] In this sense, then, the "selection" of traditionally female jobs on the part of so many of the girls limits their own chance to escape male supremacist structures despite their intentions. In another sense, however, such jobs *will* be available if Levin and Rumberger are correct. This means that girls will, in all probability, be able to obtain steady employment even if not at the assumed financially rewarding level.

In point of fact, the Domestic Code in its strict sense of separate spheres has already been challenged within the society. As of 1982, 53 percent of all employed women were married, and 51 percent of married women were employed. Fifty-six percent of married mothers were in the paid labor force, rivaling the 61 percent of divorced or single mothers who were in the paid labor force.[9] Females in earlier studies tend to elaborate the Domestic Code, marginalizing wage labor, but the fact of the matter is that they will almost certainly engage in such labor. For purely economic reasons, this is even more the case for working-class females, although middle-class and upper-middle-class families increasingly must rely upon two wage earners if they wish to maintain an affluent or relatively affluent life-style. It is not the case, then, that women in previous studies actually live out the separate spheres envisioned when they are young.

Their ideas, however, set certain parameters within which later lives tend to be lived. Women who do not envision the primacy of wage labor, for example, may not prepare themselves, or argue for the right to be prepared for well-paying jobs with career ladders. If women see the domestic sphere as *their* responsibility, they may not struggle for the high-quality day-care centers that would allow them to maintain involvement in the paid labor force to the extent necessary for a career. In fact, the lines between the public and private spheres have blurred considerably in recent years and issues ostensibly "private" are now, at times, debated in the public arena. Action in the public sphere also impacts on the private increasingly, as more and more women work.

Internalized elements of the Domestic Code, combined with the reality of women working outside the home, has led to what can be called "women's double bind." Women in previous studies defined themselves primarily in terms of home and family but, in fact, worked outside the home. Rather than alter the nature of the gender interactions and division of labor within the home substantially, a "double day" was institutionalized in which labor in the home was simply added to hours spent in wage labor.[10] As Ferree notes, "Women are more and more likely to be in the paid labor force but experience little change in the division of labor at home. Employed women continue to do 4.8 hours a day of housework compared to the 1.6 hours their husbands do."[11]

It is this that the Freeway girls, may, in fact, be challenging in the long run. If they do not envision the primacy of a home/family identity, they may be unwilling to assume the "double bind" so characteristic of women in the paid labor force today. They may, then, ultimately be setting the conditions for future negotiation within the private sphere. Ferree points out that husbands in working-class families base their claims for family consideration and special treatment on the fact that they work hard at often dangerous, tiring, and certainly alienating jobs. Women will often say, "He works hard, he's earned it," in order to justify consideration of his needs for quiet, "time with the boys," and so forth.[12]

When women enter the wage labor market they also have a claim potentially to special consideration because the family needs *her* paid labor. As Ferree again notes, "When an employed woman demands consideration for her needs—quiet, escape, leisure and the like—for the family to respond to these demands will mean a shift in responsibilities greater than introduced by her simply taking a job."[13] This is more likely to be the case among girls who do not envision home/family life as their *primary* responsibility to begin with. The fact that traditionally well-paid male working-class jobs are being eliminated makes it almost certainly the case that the illusion of women working for "extras" can no longer be sustained.[14]

Although the girls do not articulate directly that they want the power to negotiate the conditions of family life, their insistence on not wanting to be "supported," on being independent, and on maintaining paid work even after marriage and children indicates that this may be in the back of their minds. Their concern for not having to "ask permission," not being told what to do, and so forth, suggests that they wish a more equitable arrangement in the home than their own lived experiences suggest is currently the case. This may, in fact, be one of the areas of struggle and potential progress for women in the future, based on my reading of working-class girls' identity. As I will suggest later, however, the male response may be less than positive.

This identity embodies its own limitations, however, and the degree to which these limitations play out in the future in terms of working-class women's lives depends to some extent on the economy. Several points need to be made here. One is that, again, many girls are still thinking in terms of jobs in the sex-segregated ghettos. These jobs, at their current relative wage schedule, are unlikely to provide girls with a high degree of choice in their personal lives. However, given that girls selecting these jobs do so in order to escape male dominance in some sense, it is possible that they will attempt to organize at some point to ensure that such jobs pay them a living wage. At least part of the reason why females in occupational ghettos have not been as organized historically as males in laboring jobs is precisely because women have envisioned and lived out a marginalized wage labor identity—thus making organization within the workplace less likely. This is not to deny sheer male power in the workplace and in the home, but to suggest that women's *own* marginalized wage labor identity has encouraged oppressive conditions to persist. The girls in Freeway do not marginalize their wage labor identity to the same degree (although again this *may* change when they confront the realities of the workplace and the home/family sphere), and it is the very centrality of this identity that may encourage greater organization and political activity in the future among female workers, most of whom are likely to be in occupational ghettos. If Hartmann is right, that it is the sex-segregated labor force that encourages male dominance in both the workplace and the home, then the sex-segregated workplace must be dismantled before patriarchy is seriously challenged. This may well be. It is also the case, however, that female workers who have a central wage labor identity may move to organize traditionally female occupational ghettos in a way not yet imagined. I tend to agree with Hartmann and, therefore, see the overwhelming selection of jobs in the ghetto as ultimately serving male power even though the girls intend otherwise. It may not, in fact, work that way, however, and the time may soon be ripe for this form of political activity given the nature of gender identity described here.[15] On another note, however, it is not clear what the fate of such organizational activity will be in the post-industrial society, even if it does occur. It is possible that *all* forms of such conflict may be eliminated if technology can displace workers to the extent suggested by some scholars.

It is also possible that, with the erosion of traditionally well-paid male working-class jobs, those jobs that Freeway males will be able to obtain may not pay more than what women in the occupational ghettos are able to earn in the future, whether they organize effectively or not. This may encourage women to live out the fact that they do not envision a primary home/family identity, thus enabling them to press for a more egalitarian family life. Since men may be as dependent on women's paid labor in the future as women are currently dependent on men's, this may signal a change of some importance, given the emerging female identity described here.

Those girls who select careers outside of the occupational ghetto have a somewhat better chance of actually controlling the conditions of their own lives, irrespective of future male wage scales, in that they may themselves earn enough money to do so. In other words, they might actually be able to determine the conditions under which they marry, stay married, and so forth because the economic constraints will not be the same for them as for the others. It should not be underestimated, however, how truly difficult this will be to accomplish. These girls will have to obtain well-paying technical and/or professional positions if they are to exert this level of autonomy. As Levin and Rumberger point out, there will be relatively fewer such positions in the future as compared with low-level occupational jobs than there are currently and the type of education they are receiving will make it difficult for them to compete with individuals from class fractions that embody a stronger competitive ethic and set of opportunities to begin with.

The solutions posed by the girls tend to be articulated in a highly individualistic manner in that each girl individually intends to obtain more education, continue working, and so on. Although their identity has been fueled to some extent by a collective social movement, they do not yet envision collective solutions to problems, whether feminist or otherwise. Only one girl stressed that she would press for good day care at work, for example. In order truly to press for change, individual problems must be seen as shared and as needing collective action. In other words, although the identity of these girls partially reflects a broader feminist struggle in the sense that gender consciousness has changed somewhat, they do not see themselves as sharing certain problems emanating from patriarchal structures—problems that, therefore, necessitate collective struggle and solution. *In other words, they are not conscious of their shared political sexual class identity even though the glimmerings of such consciousness are there.* At present each girl is trying to negotiate individually the power to lay at least some of the conditions to negotiate her own life. As these young women move into the work force and marriage, however, they will almost certainly run into the limitations of their ideals and individualistic/private solutions in the real world, and this *may* lead to the further development of a sexual class identity along feminist lines. It is possible, then, for working-class girls such as those in Freeway to be part of the broader struggle of women in the future as women become more fully conscious of themselves as a sexual class. This is one possible scenario for Freeway girls—the one in which they will be actively engaged in challenging the locations of patriarchal power and pushing forward the cause of a self-conscious political sexual class. It is also possible, however, for female identity to be experienced as shared in the future, but it may follow a New Right agenda rather than a feminist agenda. It is to this possibility that I now turn.

Women of the new right

I have suggested in chapter 7 and at the beginning of this chapter that female identity in Freeway holds out some possibility for future connection with feminism, although the moment of critique expressed in the identity of girls is still far removed from true alignment with this movement. It is also the case, however, that individual female identities could be rearticulated in a collective form under a New Right agenda. In so suggesting, I am not lending support to those who assume that working-class women are the strength of the New Right women's community or even the major base of support for Phyllis Schlafly. This is not, in fact, the case, and studies have suggested that New Right female activists are not working class at all. Indeed, on the contrary, anti-ERA activists come from middle- to upper-middle-class backgrounds.[16] There are, in fact, *no* data that suggest that New Right women are primarily of working-class origin. It is possible, however, that the pro-family coalition may appeal to working-class females in the future.

Rebecca Klatch has argued persuasively that there is a fundamental division in worldview among a diverse group of female activists on the Right. Women of the New Right are not, in fact, a single entity at all. The fundamental division can be represented by two distinct ideologies: the social-conservative and laissez-faire–conservative worldviews.[17]

The social-conservative worldview as defined by Klatch matches that outlined by Allen Hunter in chapter 7, and it is this worldview that is so likely to draw the white male working-class. The social-conservative world is rooted "in a firm conception of the proper and separate roles of men and women, which, divinely ordained, are essential to the survival of the family and the maintenance of a moral, ordered, and stable society."[18] As I have argued here; it is this view that will appeal to white working-class males and may, in the future, serve as one of the initial hooks (along with the coded racism) to draw them into the New Right.

The laissez-faire worldview, on the other hand, is antithetical to hierarchical ordering of men over women. As Klatch puts it, based on two years of intensive field work, "Faith in individual self-reliance and free will, and belief in the liberty and autonomy of every individual extends to women as well as to men."[19] They believe that both men and women can and should be capable of autonomous action. Although this may sound somewhat akin to feminist thinking, it departs from such thinking in important ways. While laissez-faire women and feminists may share some recognition of discrimination against women in the job market, they respond to it differently. Feminists stress collective action to force change in patriarchal society; laissez-faire women suggest individualistic solutions in that they argue that a woman who is discriminated against should enter the free market and obtain a new job. Ironically, although Freeway girls express the desire to negotiate individually the conditions of their own future lives vis-à-vis men and the job market, thus sounding more laissez-faire in orientation, they will probably gravitate toward social conservatism in the future, if they gravitate toward the New Right at all. It is highly unlikely that working-class females will be able to negotiate their own work force participation at the level that would be necessary to sustain a laissez-faire New Right ideology. If working-class women do gravitate to the New Right, it will undoubtedly be toward social conservatism. Given their own expressed desire to place wage labor first, how might this happen?

Working-class women will, in fact, have an extremely difficult time living out their expressed ideals in the real world. The kinds of jobs available to them will not, as noted above, enable them to lead the lives they envision unless they avoid marriage and children entirely, in which case it may at least be possible monetarily. Most of these women will marry and have children, however, and herein the difficulty may lie. At this point, working-class women may find some appeal in the New Right struggle to ensure rights and entitlements *within* marriage simply because it will be so difficult to combine the demands of wage labor and the private sphere, and because the wage labor jobs available to them will not enable them to support a family by themselves. The fear of divorce, which now leads high-school girls to state that they do not wish to get married until they are settled themselves, lead these same women to the New Right attempt to bind men to a stable family unit—thus ensuring that they are not left through divorce with nothing at all. Feminists, on the other hand, seek such security through ensuring women's economic independence from men. Although it appears now as if Freeway girls will tend toward a feminist agenda rather than the New Right, it may or may not work that way.

A recent development in the social-conservative wing of the New Right women's coalition may further encourage future working-class female participation. Given that working-class women will engage in paid labor (as will most women), the idea that women should inhabit the domestic sphere solely is unlikely to be very attractive to them. It is very significant, therefore, that Pro-family leader Connie Marshner has introduced the notion of the "New Traditional Woman" which will enable the New Right to attract women who engage in paid labor as well as unpaid labor in the home. As Marshner puts it, the "New Traditional Woman is

> (t)he mother of the citizens of the twenty-first century. It is she who will more than anyone else transmit civilization and humanity to future generations and her response to the challenges of life determine whether America will be a strong, virtuous nation. . . . She is new because she is one of the current era, with all its pressures and fast pace and rapid change. She is traditional because, in the face of unremitting cultural changes, she is oriented around the eternal truths of faith and family. Her values are timeless and true to human nature.[20]

Marshner elaborates this theme and, most importantly, discusses the difference between *conventions* and *traditional values*. Conventions are mutable; they change with the times. Examples of mere conventions include whether women are educated or not and who does the laundry and the dishes. Traditional values, however, are moral norms that *must be* followed. Certain changes in conventions regarding gender roles are merely cosmetic, she argues. It is the underlying values with respect to males and females that are important and that *must* remain constant. It is extremely significant that, in an age when most women *must* work outside the home, earning money (even more than the husband) is seen as a simple convention, but submitting to his authority is not. Marshner argues as follows:

> One traditional value is that the husband is the head of the family. A number of conventions have supported that value but one of the most widely accepted has been the general practice of the husband bringing home the paycheck, or at least the larger paycheck. Perhaps one reason for the convention is that when the husband is the economic provider, it is easier to accept his leadership. Due to extraordinary circumstances, however, the woman may become an equal or chief provider. Nevertheless the husband is still the head of the family. Accepting his authority may be more of a challenge for the

woman to accept in that circumstance, but if traditional values are to be preserved, it must be accepted. What is moral is the fact that the wife accepts her husband's authority. It is not immoral that she earn as much or more money than he does. Who earns what is accidental and not intrinsically moral or immoral.[21]

Obviously I do not have any way of knowing which social movement, if any, working-class females will align with in the future. There are competing possibilities for them. Both feminism and the New Right hold out some potential for social action in this regard and the move on the part of Marshner to recognize that women will, in fact, inhabit more than the domestic sphere may prevent large numbers of working-class women in the future from seeing themselves, by definition, as "not part of" the New Right agenda.[22] How this all plays out in the future remains to be seen, of course.

Where else might we go?

I have suggested that working-class girls hold out the possibility of articulating with the development of women as a political sexual class along feminist lines. I have also suggested the potential power of the New Right for working-class women. It is possible, in other words, that working-class women may link with a movement that is also collective, but that embodies a struggle for a different form of protection for women as a class than that desired by feminists. In order to explore future possibilities more fully, it is necessary at this point to trace more carefully a number of elements of both female and male identities as outlined here.

As I suggest in chapters 2 through 5, an important aspect of working-class identity is the changing attitude toward education and, as I argue in chapter 7, the way in which the dominant form of working-class masculinity is being reworked somewhat to accommodate this change. Unlike working-class youth in previous studies, these youth exhibit a contradictory rather than totally rejecting attitude toward schooling and school knowledge. It is important, however, that while youth are willing to acknowledge the importance of education on one level, they adhere to the form of education rather than its substance. In addition, the school, teachers, and parents reinforce this in a variety of ways. *This is not, in fact, going to enable working-class youth to use schooling in the way they envision.* Males, in particular, in reworking the dominant form of masculinity, envision that if one attends school, does not overtly reject it, and so forth, one gets ahead. This is not the case, however, particularly since they will be competing with students who have been in college tracks in high school and with those who have attended tertiary-level institutions vastly different from the ones Freeway students are even considering, much less attending. They will be competing with students (both male and female) who embody the ethic of competitive achievement—who embrace far more than the form of schooling distributed to the working class. This aspect of their identity, then, has virtually nowhere to go. There simply will not be well-paying, stable jobs that are dependent upon the type and level of education Freeway students will, for the most part, obtain. Again, if Levin and Rumberger are correct, these jobs that will be available to these students are low paying and lacking in security and benefits. Entry into the top-level professional, technical, and managerial positions is indeed dependent upon education (as is promotion within these positions, to some extent), but not on the particular form of education distributed to and embraced by these students. "Sitting" one's way through high school, the community college, or even a comprehensive four-year college will not, in all likelihood, lead to high-level employment, or even stable employment with relatively high pay and benefits. This aspect of their identity, therefore, will be blocked in the real world of work.

The virulent racism and sexism expressed by males may not be blocked, however, and it is these aspects of identity that may, as I suggest in chapter 7, ultimately be picked up by the New Right. Working-class white males may be a potential source of recruits for the New Right movement in the same way that they were for the labor movement in industrial society.[23] The language of reestablishing the male-dominant family and the coded racism of the New Right fits neatly with the identity of white working-class males and will, I suspect, encourage these males to experience their identity as collective.

There are several ways in which the initial gender clashes I envision could play themselves out. To begin with, they could play out on the individual/personal level—in which case there could be an unprecedented degree of domestic violence in this community. This picks up on a theme elaborated by Paul Willis (see chapter 7). The males are emphasizing control of women but without the legitimation of a certain form of work. This leaves bare the brutal aspects of domination and may lead to a yet unimagined level of violence toward women in the home. Second, it is possible that the two social movements—feminism and the New Right—could clash even more directly than they do presently, and that this clash will involve the working class, which is not the case presently, with males attaching themselves to the New Right and females attaching themselves to feminism. Since the reestablishment of the "traditional family" as well as white supremacy, although in a highly coded and mediated form, is a prominent set of goals of the New Right, the Right could attack feminists even more directly and with more person power than is the case now. This is not to deny the current intense attack on abortion centers and so forth on the part of the right, but to very frankly observe that things could get much worse for feminists. It is, therefore, possible for many working-class women and men to clash in a movement sense, with males and females aligning themselves with opposing movements. This could, of course, be coupled with the domestic violence noted above. Needless to say, this leaves the future of the working-class family totally uncertain.

It is also possible, as I suggest above, for Freeway females to back away from the moment of critique that seems to suggest some feminist glimmerings as they attempt to live out their ideals in the real world. The New Right could capitalize upon the distrust of men represented here and move, as it does now, to build upon this distrust by arguing that men should be *forced* to be more responsible to the "traditional family." The power of the New Right to build upon historic male dominance as we move closer to the twenty-first century should not be underestimated, however. Feminists need to be aware of the potential power of this movement and the possible role that working-class women might play in the struggle between these opposing forces.

The notion that men are irresponsible and must be forced to accept their traditional role of "breadwinner" is clearly part of New Right ideology, and women such as Phyllis Schlafly capitalized upon this in a variety of ways. Under this formulation, men are seen as "little boys" who must be enticed into assuming their proper role by a more stable female.

Indeed, one of the New Right's intellectual leaders, George Gilder, has elevated the notion that men are by nature irresponsible to scientific credibility. Men are, according to Gilder, brutes, and this stems from their "violent, impulsive and 'nearly unremitting' sexual drives." For Gilder, men's drives tilt toward rape and pillage, and it is women's responsibility to tame these drives and bring them into civilized society.[24] It is only through women pretending that they need to be taken care of, according to Gilder, that this can be done. Schlafly and other New Right leaders take up these themes directly.[25] Such themes could also give shape and form to the female identity noted in Freeway. Right now, it does not look to me as if this will happen since Freeway girls focus so strongly on obtaining entrance into the world of wage labor. It is possible, however, that as they attempt to engage both in paid work and child rearing that the pull of the New Right may be exceptionally strong. What will actually happen as working-class women attempt to live out their lives as adults is not yet clear. These identities could take on a variety of different forms. Feminists would do well to move swiftly to encourage working-class women's participation in the movement before the New Right does.

It is, of course, at least theoretically, possible that working-class men may seriously reconsider their own gender identity and move more into line with feminist thinking.[26] I am afraid, however, that I do not hold out much hope for this. Given historic white-male dominance and the existence of the New Right willing and able to capitalize upon this set of ideas for its own end, I am less than convinced that this is a possibility. The fact that there will be fewer and fewer stable jobs for this group throws into even greater relief for me the possible assertion of male dominance rather than the reverse. I take as given the fact that working-class white men will attempt to live out their dominance in one way or another. The question for me is how this plays out on an individual/ personal and collective-movement level and which way working-class females will go.

In an unanticipated way, the school serves to support aspects of the New Right agenda. The school is indeed encouraging those elements of white-male identity that suggest the greatest promise of being picked up and used by the New Right in the sense that it encourages an emphasis on the form of education that, as I suggest above, will lead nowhere for these students, as well as the separatist and dominant white-male orientation that will enable the New Right to draw its recruits from this class fraction. The school also does not provide an arena in which girls can explore their emerging identities as women, thus providing a space in which an alternative consciousness can begin to take hold. There are contradictory tendencies, to be sure, within the school, but at the moment they are too weak and unarticulated to challenge the alternative. The school, then, does not act so much as a repressive apparatus in terms of social movements as Philip Wexler suggests (see chapter 1); rather it acts to encourage one movement as opposed to another. It is true that feminism is largely repressed by the day-to-day workings of the school. Aspects of New Right identity politics, on the other hand, are not. It is important to remember that not all social movements are progressive. Contrary to Touraine, I do not see the necessary emergence of a single movement of social-identity formation. There are competing movements in the United States and they do, in fact, have opposing agendas. Whether the struggle between and among movements in the United States ultimately results in a single movement of identity politics as Touraine suggests remains to be seen. If so, it will be a bitter struggle.

It has been my task in this book to chronicle historic change—that being the move to the post-industrial or programmed society—through a look at working-class youth identity. I have captured aspects of the identity-formation process among females and males in high school. Identities, however, are always in flux, and it is important for others to follow such youth as they become adults to test carefully my notions and speculations regarding the future. This needs to be looked at both in terms of the individual/personal level as well as the movement level. I encourage others to look carefully at the identities of the working class and others as we move into post-industrial society. It is, after all, our future and that of our children that is at stake here.

Appendix
Open-ended interview questions—
students, faculty, parents

Students

1. What is your major here? How did you choose this major; do you like it?
2. If you could change anything at Freeway High School, what would you change? Why?
3. Do you work after school? Where? How many hours a week? What time do you get off at night? How do you get there?
4. If yes to question 3, is it difficult to go to work and school at the same time? Which is more important to you? Why?
5. If yes to question 3, do you plan to keep the same job after high school?
6. What do you want to do after you graduate from high school? Do you think you will be able to do it? Why or why not? What made you decide to do this?
7. Ultimately what kind of job would you like to obtain? Do you think you will be able to obtain this job? Why or why not?
8. Do you think Freeway High School prepares you for this job? Why or why not? What do you think Freeway High School prepares you for? What do you think the school (teachers, etc.) want you to be?
9. If it were possible to change your studies here to prepare you better for your future, what kind of changes would you suggest?
10. How would you like your life to look five years from now? (house living in, job, and so forth)? What do you really think it is going to look like?
11. How would you like your life to look ten years from now?

*Faculty**

1. When did you first begin to think of teaching in a high school? How did you come to teach in Freeway?
2. Were there any crucial points of decision when you could have chosen another path?
3. Would you like to move to another position in the future? To what? Why? Is there anything that prevents you from doing so?
4. Did you have any difficulty orienting yourself to Freeway High School?
5. Do you see any difference between your male and female students? Black and white? Do you find yourself responding to them differently? If so, how?
6. How do you define success in teaching at Freeway High School?
7. Is there anything that prevents you from being as successful as you would like to be?
8. Where do you see your students going from high school? Why? (Push for distinctions among student groups and individuals.) How do you try to orient them?
9. Is there anything you especially like about teaching here? Is there anything you especially dislike or would like to see changed? What? How do you deal with these problems?
10. Do you see any difference between teaching here and at other high schools? If so, what?

Parents

1. When did your family come to Freeway? Under what circumstances?
2. Do you plan to stay in Freeway?
3. What do you think your son/daughter will do when he/she leaves high school?
4. What would you like him/her to do?
5. What kind of job do you think he/she will get eventually?

*A variation of this was used to interview guidance counselors, administrators, and other school personnel.

6. What kinds of jobs would you like him/her to get?
7. Does your son/daughter talk about getting married and having a family?
8. Do you want him/her to get married and have a family?
9. Do you think the high school adequately prepares your son/daughter for his/her future? What does the high school do well and what would you like to see changed?

Notes

Series Editor's Introduction

1. See Michael W. Apple, "Redefining Equality," *Teachers College Record* 90 (Winter 1988): pp. 167–184 and Samuel Bowles and Herbert Gintis, *Democracy and Capitalism* (New York: Basic Books, 1986).
2. Allen Hunter, "The Politics of Resentment and the Construction of Middle America," unpublished paper, Havens Center for Social Structure and Social Change, University of Wisconsin, Madison, 1987, p. 9.
3. Samuel Bowles, "The Post-Keynesian Capital-Labor Stalemate," *Socialist Review* 12 (September-October 1982): 51.
4. Paul Willis, *Learning to Labor* (New York: Columbia University Press, 1981).
5. For a review of this literature, see Michael W. Apple, *Education and Power* (New York: Routledge, revised ARK Edition, 1985) and Henry Giroux, "Theories of Reproduction and Resistance in the New Sociology of Education," *Harvard Educational Review* 53 (August 1983): 257–93.
6. See, for example, Philip Wexler, *Social Analysis of Education* (New York: Routledge, 1987).
7. For further discussion of this, see Michael W. Apple, *Teachers and Texts* (New York: Routledge, 1988) and Lois Weis, ed., *Class, Race and Gender in American Education* (Albany: State University of New York Press, 1988).
8. Examples include important work such as Linda Valli, *Becoming Clerical Workers* (Boston: Routledge, 1986) and Angela McRobbie, "Working Class Girls and the Culture of Femininity," in Women's Studies Group, ed. *Women Take Issue* (London: Hutchinson, 1978), pp. 96–108.
9. Linda McNeil, *Contradictions of Control* (New York: Routledge, 1986).
10. Lois Weis, *Between Two Worlds* (New York: Routledge, 1985).
11. Apple, "Redefining Inequality" and Stuart Hall, "Popular Democratic and Authoritarian Populism: Two Ways of Taking Democracy Seriously," in Alan Hunt ed., *Marxism and Democracy* (London: Lawrence and Wishart, 1980), pp. 160–161.

1   Introduction

1. For a discussion of identity formation, see Philip Wexler, "Symbolic Economy of Identity and Denial of Labor: Studies in High School Number 1," in Lois Weis, ed., *Class, Race and Gender in American Education* (Albany: State University of New York Press, 1988); pp. 302–316.

2. My book, *Between Two Worlds: Black Students in An Urban Community College* (Boston: Routledge and Kegan Paul, 1985), lies squarely within the reproduction framework, albeit in the critical culturalist challenge to the framework.

3. Numerous scholars have worked within this tradition. Some of the most influential are Henry Giroux, Michael Apple, Samuel Bowles and Herbert Gintis, and Paul Willis. See, for example, Michael Apple, *Ideology and Curriculum* (Boston: Routledge and Kegan Paul, 1979); Michael Apple, *Education and Power* (Boston: Routledge and Kegan Paul, 1982); Henry Giroux, *Ideology, Culture and the Process of Schooling* (Philadelphia: Temple University Press, 1981); Henry Giroux, *Theory and Resistance in Education* (South Hadley, MA: Bergin and Garvey, 1983); Samuel Bowles and Herbert Gintis, *Schooling in Capitalist America* (New York: Basic Books, 1976); and Paul Willis, *Learning to Labour: How Working Class Kids Get Working Class Jobs* (Westmead, England: Saxon House Press, 1977). This is not to denigrate this work in any way; it has been exceedingly important and has challenged successfully the notion that schools serve as the great engine of democracy.

4. Allen Hunter, "The Role of Liberal Political Culture in the Construction of Middle America," *University of Miami Law Review*, vol. 42, no. 1 (September 1987): 101.

5. Samuel Bowles, "The Post-Keynesian Labor Statement," *Socialist Revolution* (September-October 1982): 45, as cited in Hunter, p. 102.

6. Both Allen Hunter and Michael Apple discuss the demise of this accord. See Michael Apple, "The Politics of Common-Sense: Schooling, Populism, and the New Right," in Henry Giroux and Peter McClaren, eds. *Schooling and the Politics of Culture* (Albany: State University of New York Press, forthcoming).

7. Philip Wexler has argued this point exceptionally well in *Social Analysis of Education: After the New Sociology* (New York: Routledge and Kegan Paul, 1987).

8. This is Alain Touraine's notion. See Alain Touraine, *The Voice and the Eye: An Analysis of Social Movements* (New York: Cambridge University Press, 1981).

9. Philip Wexler, "Movement, Class and Education," in Len Barton and Stephen Walker, eds., *Race, Class and Education* (London: Croom Helm, 1983), p. 19.

10. Although Philip Wexler offers an important critique of the "new sociology of education" and suggests directions for future work, there is of yet no full-scale ethnographic investigation that uses a social action perspective. Julia Wrigley offers a social action point of view through the use of historical

data. See Julia Wrigley, "Class Politics and School Reform in Chicago," in Maurice Zeitlin, ed., *Classes, Class Conflict and the State: Empirical Studies in Class Analysis* (Cambridge, MA: Winthrop, 1980), pp. 153–171; and Julia Wrigley, *Class Politics and Public Schools* (New Brunswick, NJ: Rutgers University Press, 1982). See Philip Wexler, *Social Analysis of Education: After the New Sociology.*

11. Some excellent examples of largely descriptive ethnographies related to schooling include Alan Peshkin, *Growing Up American* (Chicago: University of Chicago Press, 1978) and Philip Cusick's *Inside High School* (New York: Holt, Rinehart and Winston, 1973). Recent examples of excellent critical ethnographies done largely within a reproduction framework include Mark Ginsburg, *Contradictions in Teacher Education and Society* (New York: Falmer Press, 1988); Linda McNeil, *Contradictions of Control* (Boston: Routledge and Kegan Paul, 1986); and Linda Valli, *Becoming Clerical Workers* (Boston: Routledge and Kegan Paul, 1986).

12. Dick Hebdige raises this point with respect to subcultural styles. See Dick Habdige, *Subculture: The Meaning of Style* (London: Methuen, 1979).

13. Philip Wexler makes this point in "Movement, Class and Education."

14. Although this is not central to my analysis, I touch on parents briefly.

15. Barry Bluestone and Bennett Harrison, *The De-Industrialization of America* (New York: Basic Books, 1982), p. 26.

16. Katherine S. Newman, *Falling From Grace.* (New York: Free Press, 1988), p. 33. Newman is one of the only scholars who actually chronicles the effects of job loss today. She works from an individual mobility framework, however, rather than a perspective of social movement and competing classes. This limits the utility of her work for the current project. Ellen Israel Rosen discusses specifically the effects of job loss on women. See Ellen I. Rosen, *Bitter Choices* (Chicago: University of Chicago Press, 1987).

17. For an excellent example of this, see David Bensman and Roberta Lynch, *Rusted Dreams: Hard Times in a Steel Community* (Berkeley: University of California Press, 1987).

18. Katherine Newman makes this point. See Newman, p. 33.

19. Bluestone and Harrison, pp. 6–7.

20. Touraine, pp. 6–7.

21. Touraine, p. 11.

22. My thanks to Allen Hunter for helping me work through portions of the argument on social movements as constitutive of society as well as transforming the context within which such movements operate.

23. See Touraine and Alberto Melucci, "The New Social Movements: A Theoretical Approach," *Social Science Information* 19, 2 (1980): 199–226.

24. The black and women's movements in the United States are often placed within the category "new social movements". These are not *new* movements in the strict sense since they have been around quite a long time. It is only an orthodox understanding of "true" struggle as being that between capital and labor that would render these movements "new." That having been said, however, it *is* the case that these movements now seek to contest

the realm of knowledge and information and are, therefore, "new" under Melucci's definition.

25. There has truly been some outstanding work done in this area, and we have come a long way toward understanding the culture of schooling. The problem, however, is that such work often suffers, in retrospect, from the constraints of the reproduction framework in which it was generated. See Linda McNeil *Contradictions of Control*; Jean Anyon, "Workers, Labor and Economic History, and Textbook Context," in Michael Apple and Lois Weis, eds. *Ideology and Practice in Schooling* (Philadelphia: Temple University Press, 1983), pp. 37–61; Michael Apple, "Curricular Form and the Logic of Technical Control," in Apple and Weis, pp. 143–167; Robert Everhart, *Reading, Writing and Resistance* (Boston: Routledge and Kegan Paul, 1983); Charles Payne, *Getting What We Ask For: The Ambiguity of Success and Failure in Urban Education* (Westport, CN: Greenwood Press, 1984).

26. The school is itself the site of numerous contradictory tendencies. This is best laid out theoretically by Martin Carnoy and Henry Levin *Schooling and Work in the Democratic State* (Stanford, CA: Stanford University Press, 1985).

27. Technically, data collection and analysis proceeded in a manner similar to that outlined in the appendix of Lois Weis, *Between Two Worlds: Black Students in an Urban Community College* (Boston: Routledge and Kegan Paul, 1985).

28. The Preliminary Scholastic Aptitude Test (PSAT) and Scholastic Aptitude Test (SAT) are administered by the Educational Testing Service in Princeton. Most four-year colleges require the SAT for entrance.

29. The governing body of the state educational system administers a series of tests which must be taken if entrance to a four-year school is desired. Not all students take these tests, however, and track placement often determines whether the tests are taken.

30. These figures are based on the same SMSA data as above.

31. Data on female versus male employees were prepared from census data by Judith Kossey. My sincere thanks to her for making these data available to me.

32. *Freeway Evening News* magazine section, June 5, 1983.

33. *Freeway Evening News* magazine section, June 5, 1983.

34. Touraine, p. 25, 50, as cited in Philip Wexler, *Social Analysis of Education*, p. 88.

35. Touraine, p. 29, as cited in Wexler, p. 89.

2 Freeway Males

1. The contradictory set of attitudes toward education and schooling among members of the black underclass has been discussed at length by John Ogbu and me. See Lois Weis, *Between Two Worlds: Black Students in an Urban Community College* (Boston: Routledge and Kegan Paul, 1985); and John

Ogbu, "Class Stratification, Racial Stratification and Schooling," in Lois Weis, ed., *Class, Race and Gender in American Education* (Albany: State University of New York Press, 1988), pp. 163–182.

2. Paul Willis, *Learning to Labour* (Westmead, England: Saxon House Press, 1977), p. 26.

3. Willis suggests that, in rejecting the world of the school and the compliance of the "ear 'oles" (so named by the lads because they sit and listen), the lads reject mental labor, cross-valorizing patriarchy and the distinction between mental and manual labor. Thus, for the lads, manual labor is associated with the social superiority of masculinity, and mental labor with the social inferiority of femininity. Harry Braverman, Michael Burawoy, and others have argued that hierarchical capitalist social relations in industrial society demand the progressive divorce of mental from manual labor and certainly profit from (if not demand) gender-based distinctions. Thus, Willis suggests, the lads' rejection of the world of the school, and the way in which this rejection is linked to masculinity, reproduces at an even deeper level the social relations of production necessary for the maintenance of a capitalist economy. Although the lads live their rejection of the school as a form of cultural autonomy and freedom, Willis argues that they help, at the level of their own culture, to reproduce existing social structure. Harry Braverman, *Labor and Monopoly Capital* (New York: Monthly Review Press, 1974). Michael Burawoy, "Toward a Marxist Theory of the Labor Process: Braverman and Beyond," *Politics and Society*, vol. 8 (1978): 247–312.

4. See Howard London, *The Culture of a Community College* (New York: Praeger, 1978).

5. See chapter 3 of London's book.

6. Robert Everhart, *Reading, Writing and Resistance* (Boston: Routledge and Kegan Paul, 1983).

7. There is, at Freeway, a group of twenty-five juniors known as the "advanced" group who were selected for participation in an accelerated curriculum when they were in grade nine. In fact, these students are simply receiving a college preparatory course of study, not unlike that that most students in an academic city school or a relatively affluent suburban school would receive automatically. In other words, while it is "advanced" in the Freeway context, it is the college preparatory curriculum as defined by the state for testing and college entrance purposes. Students in this state get a different diploma if they go through this curriculum than students who do not go through it.

8. Willis, p. 26.

9. London suggests that absence from class is a "means of dissociating [oneself] from slavish adherence to official expectations." As such, it was defined positively. See London, *Culture*, p. 68.

10. Lois Weis, *Between Two Worlds: Black Students in an Urban Community College* (Boston: Routledge and Kegan Paul, 1985); and John Ogbu, "Class Stratification, Racial Stratification and Schooling," in L. Weis, ed., *Class,*

Race and Gender in American Education (Albany: State University of New York Press, 1988), pp. 163–182.

11. I discuss this at length in *Between Two Worlds*.

12. That dropout rates are especially high for minorities has been well documented in A Report of the Task Force on the New York State Dropout Problem, *Dropping Out of School in New York State: The Invisible People of Color*, 1986. See also Lois Weis, Eleanor Farrar, and Hugh Petrie, eds., *Dropouts from School: Issues, Dilemmas and Solutions* (Albany: State University of New York Press, 1989).

13. These figures are calculated from superintendent's reports for the months of September, October, November, February, March, and April, 1985–86. I do not have a breakdown by gender and race.

14. My thanks to Michelle Fine for making this point.

15. Cases were coded by race according to pictures on file. The 1980 files have no pictures.

16. *The Carnegie Commission on Higher Education, A Classification of Institutions of Higher Education* (Berkeley: The Carnegie Foundation, 1973).

17. Richard Sennett and Jonathan Cobb, The *Hidden Injuries of Class* (New York: Vintage Books, 1972).

18. Sennett and Cobb, p. 23.

19. Willis, p. 49.

20. Tom's mother is known by school officials to be a schizophrenic.

21. Willis discusses racism among the lads with respect to West Indians and Pakistanis. As Willis notes,

> The racism in the counter school culture is structured by reified though somewhat differentiated stereotypes. Asians come off worst and are often the target for petty intimidation, small pestering attacks, and the physical and symbolic jabbing at weak or unprotected points in which the lads specialize. Asians are seen both as alien; "smelly"; and probably "unclean," and as sharing some of the most disliked "ear ole" characteristics (49).

Racial tension between the lads and West Indians surfaces in much the same way as such tension surfaces between black and white males, at least from the white perspective, in the United States—in the sexual realm. As Willis notes,

> The lads feel direct sexual rivalry and jealousy as well as a general sense of suspicion of male West Indian sexual intentions and practices—ironic, of course, in light of their own frankly instrumental and exploitative attitudes. The lads feel, however, barely consciously and in an inarticulate way, that they are bound, at least in the serious stage of "courting," by some unwritten rules of the desexualization and monogamy which are not respected in West Indian culture (49).

22. It is interesting to note here that the teachers speak quite highly of the "Arabians." As the principal put it, "They are like whites."

3 Freeway Females

1. Angela McRobbie, "Working Class Girls and the Culture of Femininity," in *Women Take Issue*, ed., Women's Studies Group (London: Hutchinson, 1978), and Linda Valli, *Becoming Clerical Workers* (Boston: Routledge and Kegan Paul, 1986). It must be pointed out here that while this "ideology of romance" may be constructed with the hope of moving out of an oppressive home of origin and not, therefore, necessarily as "homebound" as has been seen by some investigators, it does, nevertheless, still tie women to the home of their future husband in much the same way as their mothers were tied. It is not, then, necessarily a celebration of their own home of origin but may, rather, reflect a generally ill-founded hope that their future home will be different (less oppressive) from that in which they grew up. Thus the identity uncovered by previous investigators is, indeed, homebound but may not reflect any particular attachment to the home of their father.

2. Karen Brodkin Sacks, ed., *My Troubles Are Going to Have Trouble with Me*. (New Brunswick: Rutgers University Press), pp. 17–18. See also Alice Kessler-Harris, "Where Are the Organized Women Workers?" *Feminist Studies* 3, 1–2: 92–110, as cited in Sacks, p. 18.

3. An early classic on this subject is Elizabeth Douvan and Joseph Adelson's *The Adolescent Experience*. On the basis of research conducted by means of two national interview studies in 1955 and 1956, they suggest that most boys are concerned about choosing jobs and making work decisions. The adolescent girl, on the other hand,

   > does not look at the occupational sphere as a source of a life meaning or life work. Her life plan is contained in her feminine goals of marriage and motherhood and her education and work are conceived as providing access to these goals or making her more competent and well-rounded in the roles of wife and mother. She will work for a while and then marry. She will help out with family finances, particularly in the early years before she has children. And her education and work experience before marriage will increase her efficiency in meeting the complex demands of an active family life.

   See Elizabeth Douvan and Joseph Adelson, *The Adolescent Experience* (New York: John Wiley and Sons, 1966), p. 233.

4. See, for example, Lois Weis, "Without Dependence on Welfare for Life: The Experience of Black Women in the Urban Community College," *The Urban Review* 17, 4, (1985): 233–56.

5. Jennifer is the only daughter of professional parents. As one of the central office workers put it, "He [Jennifer's father] was almost too smart in high school, you know what I mean?" (she had gone to school with him). This reflects the contradictory code of respect toward education discussed in chapter 1.

6. See Lois Weis, "Progress But No Parity," *Academe* (November/December 1985): 29–33.
7. One of the machine shop teachers also had a daughter in engineering. He was the person who initially pointed out to me that a number of students from manual-laboring families who do become professionals go into engineering.
8. Center for Education Statistics, *Digest of Education Statistics*, 1985–86 and 1986–87.
9. Jerome Karabel, "Community Colleges and Social Stratification," *Harvard Educational Review* 42, 4 (November 1974): 521–62.
10. Michael Olivas, *The Dilemma of Access* (Washington, DC: Howard University Press, 1979).
11. Katherine Newman discusses the extensive de-mobility among the well-educated middle class, for example. See Katherine Newman, *Falling From Grace* (New York: The Free Press, 1988).
12. See Valli, McRobbie, and work by Jane Gaskell. See, for example, Jane Gaskell, "Gender and Class in Clerical Training." Paper prepared for session on "Work and Unemployment as Alienating Experiences" at World Congress of Sociology in New Delhi, August 1986. Jane Gaskell "Gender and Course Choice," *Journal of Education* (March 1984) 166, 1: 89–102.
13. Ann Marie Wolpe, "Education and the Sexual Division of Labour," in *Feminism and Materialism: Women and Modes of Production*, eds. Annette Kuhn and Ann Marie Wolpe (London: Routledge and Kegan Paul, 1978), pp. 290–328, as cited in Valli, p. 77.
14. Linda Valli, "Becoming Clerical Workers: Business Education and the Culture of Femininity," in Michael Apple and Lois Weis, eds., *Ideology and Practice in Schooling* (Philadelphia: Temple University Press, 1983), pp. 232.
15. See Madeleine MacDonald, "Cultural Reproduction: The Pedagogy of Sexuality," *Screen Education* 32/33 (Autumn/Winter 1978/80): 152, as cited in Linda Valli, p. 232.
16. McRobbie, p. 104.
17. Carol's statement provides an interesting contrast with that of Amy.
18. Lillian Breslow Rubin, *Worlds of Pain* (New York: Basic Books, 1976); and Glen Elder, *Children of the Great Depression* (Chicago: University of Chicago Press, 1974).

4 Within the School

1. Jean Anyon, "Social Class and School Knowledge," *Curriculum Inquiry* 11:1 (1981): 3–42; and Linda McNeil, *Contradictions of Control* (New York: Routledge, 1986).
2. See Jean Anyon, "Social Class and School Knowledge"; Linda McNeil, *Contradictions of Control*; and Michael Apple, *Ideology and Curriculum* (London: Routledge and Kegan Paul, 1979); and Michael Apple, "Curricular Form and the Logic of Technical Control," in Michael Apple and Lois Weis,

eds, *Ideology and Practice in Schooling* (Philadelphia: Temple University Press, 1983). pp. 143–66.
3. Anyon, p. 8.
4. This section has benefited from the insightful comments of Catherine Cornbleth.
5. I have discussed this issue at length in Lois Weis, *Between Two Worlds: Black Students in an Urban Community College* (Boston: Routledge and Kegan Paul, 1985).
6. It is possible, of course, to interpret student affirmation of schooling as a ritual as well. I do not choose to do so, however, and stand by my point that there is a contradictory relationship with education emerging among white working-class youth, much as exists in the black underclass. The shape and form of this contradictory relationship will differ for the two groups, however.
7. My thanks to Allen Hunter for making this point.

5 Freeway Teachers

1. See Ellen Israel Rosen for a study of female mill workers and Dee Ann Spencer for a study of women teachers. Ellen Israel Rosen, *Bitter Choices* (Chicago: University of Chicago Press, 1987); and Dee Ann Spencer, *Contemporary Women Teachers: Balancing Home and Work* (New York: Longman, 1986).
2. I am not referring here to the salary of secretarial science teachers relative to other teachers, but to secretarial pay as opposed to the wages of others.
3. See, for example, Gail Kelly and Ann Nihlen, "Schooling and the Reproduction of Patriarchy: Unequal Workloads, Unequal Rewards," in Michael Apple, ed., *Cultural and Economic Reproduction in Education* (London: Routledge and Kegan Paul, 1982), pp. 162–80.
4. These regional data are reported in L. G. Callahan, Executive Summary, "A Status Study of Regional Teacher Supply and Recruitment Needs in [the Judicial District]," (mimeo).
5. In this same regional survey, 11.5 percent of teachers attended diocesan Catholic schools, as opposed to over 20 percent in the Freeway study.
6. Mark Poletti is also from Freeway. He obviously has a critic's eye, however.
7. See Alan Peshkin, *Growing Up American: Schooling and the Survival of Community* (Chicago: University of Chicago Press, 1978), p. 82.
8. This does not mean, of course, that no other qualified teacher was available. The implication here is that the board simply had to file a statement to that effect, whether it was the case or not. This is how, in the United States, many affirmative-action rulings have been subverted over the years as well.
9. It must be noted here that this is an accurate statement. The Nautilus room does, indeed, have over $100,000 worth of equipment. It should also be noted here that the physical education teacher responsible for obtaining this equipment became principal of the high school two years after my field work was completed.
10. In fact, however, many teachers made the same point.

11. David Bensman and Roberta Lynch's study of a steel community on the South Side of Chicago certainly suggests that the politics described here are not unique to Freeway. As they report,

    The patronage system has ruled on the streets of Southeast Chicago for decades. Its methods have become more sophisticated, but its underlying approach hasn't changed: jobs or favors are provided in return for political support. After the steel mills, city government is the region's largest employer. And estimates of the number of jobs that are controlled by the Regulars (the party machine) range as high as 3,000—many of them in the private sector (pp. 33–34).

    See Bensman and Lynch, *Rusted Dreams.*

12. This occurred in other ways as well. Applicants pointed out that they "lived in Freeway all their lives"; that they "currently own property there"; that they "worked in Freeway in summer recreation," and so forth.
13. See, for example, Michael Apple, "Curricular Form and the Logic of Technical Control," in Michael Apple and Lois Weis, eds., *Ideology and Practice in Schooling* (Philadelphia: Temple University Press, 1983), pp. 143–66; and Dennis Carlson, "Curriculum and the School Work Culture," in Philip Altbach, Gail Kelly, and Lois Weis, eds., *Excellence in Education: Perspectives on Policy and Practice* (Buffalo: Prometheus Books, 1985).

6 Freeway Parents

1. Samuel Bowles and Herbert Gintis, *Schooling in Capitalist America* (New York: Basic Books, 1976).
2. Bowles and Gintis, p. 143.
3. Melvin Kohn, *Class and Conformity: A Study of Values* (Homewood, IL.: Dorsey Press, 1969), as cited in Bowles and Gintis, p. 145.
4. Kohn as cited in Bowles and Gintis, p. 146.
5. There has been extensive critique of the Bowles and Gintis position along the lines that it is too deterministic. The points I have raised in chapter 1, however, are tied to broader issues of social movements. See Michael Apple, *Education and Power* (Boston: Routledge and Kegan Paul, 1983); Paul Willis, *Learning to Labour* (Westmead: Saxon House Press, 1977); and Philip Wexler, *Social Analysis of Education* (New York: Routledge, 1987).
6. Families are still, however, one of the least researched in institutions of society. This is undoubtedly the case because families are still considered "private." It is still much easier, for example, to gain access to a school than a family for participant-observation work.
7. Interviews with parents were conducted by a graduate assistant.
8. Bensman and Lynch, *Rusted Dreams*, p. 28.
9. Bensman and Lynch, p. 26.

10. Bensman and Lynch, p. 28.
11. Mayor's statement on the occasion of the Freeway Diamond Jubilee.
12. Bensman and Lynch, p. 27.
13. R. W. Connell, D. J. Ashenden, S. Kessler, and G. W. Dowsett, *Making the Difference: Schools, Families and Social Division.* (Boston: George Allen and Unwin, 1972), p. 141.
14. Connell et al., p. 166.
15. Connell et al., p. 166.
16. Richard Sennett and Jonathan Cobb, *The Hidden Injuries of Class* (New York: Vintage Books, 1972).

7 Women and Men: A Social Movement Perspective

1. Elizabeth Douvan and Joseph Adelson, *The Adolescent Experience* (New York: John Wiley and Sons, 1966); Linda Valli, *Becoming Clerical Workers* (Boston: Routledge and Kegan Paul, 1986); and Angela McRobbie, "Working Class Girls and the Culture of Femininity" in Women's Studies Group, ed., *Women Take Issue* (London: Hutchinson, 1978), pp. 96–108.
2. Dorothy Smith, "Women's Inequality and the Family," in Mary Fainsod Katzenstein and Carol McClurg Mueller, eds., *The Women's Movements of the United States and Europe*, (Philadelphia: Temple University Press, 1987), pp. 46–47.
3. Martha May, "The Historical Problem of the Family Wage: The Ford Motor Company and the Five Dollar Day," in Naomi Gerstel and Harriet Engel Gross, eds., *Families and Work* (Philadelphia: Temple University Press, 1987), pp. 111–31.
4. May, p. 126.
5. Leslie Woodcock Tentler, *Wage Earning Women: Industrial Work and Family Life in the United States 1900–1930* (New York: Oxford University Press, 1979), p. 135.
6. Dorothy Smith, "Women's Inequality and the Family," pp. 23–54.
7. Ellen Israel Rosen makes this point clearly when she suggests that women factory workers "choose" such jobs in order to earn more money to help fulfill their traditional responsibilities of caring for a family. See Ellen Israel Rosen, *Bitter Choices* (Chicago: University of Chicago Press, 1987).
8. Zillah R. Eisenstein, *Feminism and Sexual Equality* (New York: Monthly Review Press, 1984), p. 146.
9. Eisenstein, p. 150.
10. Michael Apple, *Teachers and Texts: A Political Economy of Class and Gender Relations in Education* (Boston: Routledge and Kegan Paul, 1986), p. 55.
11. My thanks to Michele Fine for pointing this out to me.
12. Eisenstein, p. 154.
13. Eisenstein, p. 154. This parallels the development of economic classes and can be linked conceptually to E. P. Thompson's notions of class development. As he states:

Classes do not exist as separate entities, look and find an enemy class, and then start to struggle. On the contrary, people find themselves in a society structured in predetermined ways—they identify points of antagonistic interest, they commence to struggle around these issues and in the process of struggling they discover themselves as classes, they come to know this discovery as class consciousness.

E. P. Thompson, "Eighteenth-Century English Society: Class Struggle Without Class?" *Social History* 3, no. 2 (May 1978): 149, as cited in Eisenstein, p. 155.

14. This is not to suggest that Title IX has not been subverted in some very important ways. It has been subverted, and we have a long way to go before the letter and spirit of Title IX are fulfilled. Nevertheless, the very existence of Title IX does mean that certain blatant forms of gender discrimination are lessened somewhat.

    It is also possible, however, to look at the effects of Title IX differently, in the sense that undoing sex-separate education may have undone the possibility of an emergent feminist voice among adolescent women. Under this formulation, the naive dream of coeducation may have rendered the female voice inaudible, and valorized the hegemony of adolescent male authority in the coed classroom. My thanks to Michele Fine for pointing this out to me.

15. Martin Carnoy and Henry Levin argue this point exceptionally well. See Carnoy and Levin, *Schooling and Work in the Democratic State* (Stanford, CA: Stanford University Press, 1985). It also must be pointed out here that a self-conscious political identity for women can take a New Right perspective and actively oppose the ERA and so forth. In the case of the Freeway girls, however, this is not happening at the moment. I will return to this point in the next chapter.

16. Paul Willis, "Youth Unemployment: Thinking the Unthinkable," mimeo, p. 8.

17. Willis, p. 15.

18. Willis, p. 17.

19. J. C. Walker makes the point of the importance of choices available when young people work out their sexual identities. On the basis of extensive enthographic work, he stresses the lack of available gender identity options, leaving "poofters" just that. Ultimately, the "poofters" went outside the school to the theatre in search of a group with which to articulate. See J. C. Walker, "The Way Men Act: Dominate and Subordinate Cultures in an Inner-City School," *British Journal of Sociology of Education* vol. 9, no. 1 (1988): 3–18.

20. R. W. Connell et. al., *Making the Difference* (Boston: George Allen and Unwin, 1982), p. 98.

21. My thanks to Steve Jacobson for pointing this out to me.

22. David Hogan, "Education and Class Formation: The Peculiarities of the Americans," in Michael Apple, ed., *Cultural and Economic Reproduction in Education* (London: Routledge and Kegan Paul, 1982), pp. 32–78.

23. Hogan, pp. 60–61.
24. Mike Davis, *Prisoners of the American Dream* (London: Verso Press, 1986), p. 16.
25. Davis, p. 103.
26. Allen Hunter, "Children in the Service of Conservatism: Parent–Child Relations in the New Right's Pro-Family Rhetoric," Institute for Legal Studies, University of Wisconsin-Madison, 1988, p. 6.
27. Hunter, p. 15.
28. Hunter, p. 15.
29. Hunter, pp. 15–16. Hunter further notes that:

> The New Right's family is a politicization of the 1950s suburban family in which men worked, women stayed at home and took care of their children. Men are working, married heterosexuals; indeed, the New Right Vision is consonant with the dominant early 1950 view that 'adult masculinity was indistinguishable from the breadwinner role.' (Barbara Ehrenreich, *The Hearts of Men* (Garden City, New York: Anchor Books, 1983, p. 24) The proper role for women was that critically defined by Betty Friedan in *The Feminine Mystique* (New York: Dell Publishing Company, 1963). That which Friedan attacks is what the New Right defends (p. 24).

30. Michael Omi and Howard Winant, *Racial Formation in the United States* (Boston: Routledge and Kegan Paul, 1986), p. 120.
31. See Omi and Winant's chapter 7.
32. It is noteworthy that in Buffalo, New York, two-thirds of antiabortion protestors in recent months have been male, and the leadership is entirely male. These are fundamentalist groups rather than Catholic. Although I am not certain of the class of these males, it is noteworthy that the group is so heavily male dominated. My thanks to Maxine Seller for pointing this out to me.

8 Whither the Working Class?

1. Henry M. Levin and Russell W. Rumberger, "Education Requirements for New Technologies: Visions, Possibilities, and Current Realities," *Educational Policy* vol. 1, no. 3 (1987): 333.
2. Levin and Rumberger, p. 334.
3. These are Levin and Rumberger's estimates based on BLS data.
4. Alberto Melucci, "The New Social Movements: A Theoretical Approach," *Social Science Information*, vol 19, no. 2 (1980): 218–19.
5. Philip Wexler, *Social Analysis of Education* (New York: Routledge and Kegan Paul, 1987), p. 62.
6. Unless, of course, this separateness leads women out of the paid labor force entirely, leaving more room for men. This is unlikely to happen, however,

given trends regarding women's participation in the paid labor force since World War II and the fact that capitalism needs such laborers.

7. Heidi Hartmann, "Capitalism, Patriarchy and Job Segregation by Sex," *Signs* 1, 3 (1976): 137–70.

8. Linda Valli has argued that thirty-five percent of all working women are currently employed in office education, for example. See Valli, "Gender Identity and the Technology Office of Education" in Lois Weis, ed., *Class, Race and Gender in American Education* (Albany: State University of New York Press, 1988), pp. 87–105.

9. U.S. Bureau of Labor Statistics, "Earnings of Workers and Their Families," *News* (November 1982) as cited in Myra Marx Ferree, "Sacrifice, Satisfaction, and Social Change: Employment and the Family," Karen Brodkin Sacks, ed., *My Troubles Are Going to Have Trouble with Me* (New Brunswick: Rutgers University Press, 1984), pp. 61–79.

10. See B. Berch, *The Endless Day: The Political Economy of Women's Work* (New York: Harcourt Brace Jovanovich, 1982), as cited in Ferree, p. 63.

11. Ferree, pp. 63–64.

12. Ferree, p. 69.

13. Ferree, p. 70.

14. Ellen Israel Rosen argues forcefully that this is not the case among female factory workers. See Ellen I. Rosen, *Bitter Choices* (Chicago: University of Chicago Press, 1987).

15. Linda Valli argues in *Class, Race and Gender in American Education* that the experience of office work itself encourages women to marginalize a wage labor identity since such work is repetitive and alienating. This may be the case, but the ideology of the primacy of a home/family identity for women enables this to occur, I would argue. If such an ideology is attacked to begin with, the chance of this happening on the job is lessened. In other words, the Domestic Code enables this to occur for women and not for men.

16. See David W. Brady, "Ladies in Pink: Religion and Political Ideology in the Anti-ERA Movement," *Social Sciences Quarterly* 56 (March 1976): 564–75; and Theodore S. Arrington and Patricia A. Kyle, "Equal Rights Amendment Activists in North Carolina," *Signs* 3, 3 (spring 1978): 666–80.

17. See Rebecca Klatch, "Coalition and Conflict Among Women of the New Right," *Signs* 13, 4 (1988): 671–94 and Rebecca Klatch, *Women of the New Right* (Philadelphia: Temple University Press, 1987).

18. Klatch, "Coalition and Conflict," p. 677.

19. Klatch, pp. 678–29.

20. Connie Marshner, "Who is the New Traditional Woman?" (paper presented at Family Forum II Conference, Washington, D.C., July 29, 1982), as cited in Klatch, *Women of the New Right*, p. 145. Connie Marshner is chair of the National Pro-Family Coalition and former chair of the Family Policy Advisory Board of the Reagan-Bush Campaign and Director of Education for the Heritage Foundation. (Klatch, "Conflict and Coalition," p. 677).

21. Klatch, *Women of the New Right*, p. 146.

22. The Marshner statement is brilliant from a tactical standpoint. The New

Right's rejection of the "working mother" and its determination to bring women back into the home ignores both economic realities for women and the fact that the capitalist class relies on a sex-segregated female labor force. What Marschner did was bypass the problem associated with the fact that the "old solution" of the pro-family movement (that is, getting women back into the home) is relevant for only a tiny privileged minority. This enables many more women to join potentially the ranks of the New Right. This contradiction in the old solution is nicely outlined by Rosalind Pollack Petchesky, *Abortion and Women's Choice: The State, Sexuality and Reproduction Freedom* (New York: Longmans, 1984), p. 275.

23. My thanks to Tereffe Asrat for pointing this out to me.
24. George Gilder, *Sexual Suicide* (New York: Quadrangle, 1973), p. 17, as quoted in Barbara Ehrenreich, *The Hearts of Men* (New York: Anchor Press, 1983), p. 166.
25. Barbara Enhrenreich argues persuasively that New Right women are responding mainly to the male flight from commitment in evidence since the 1950s. Feminists are taken to task for encouraging men to withdraw from the "breadwinner" role.
26. Paul Willis has suggested that white working-class males may reconsider their gender identity in light of the reconsideration of such identity among females. Unfortunately, I could not disagree more. See Paul Willis, "Youth Unemployment: Thinking the Unthinkable," mimeo, pp. 17–18.

Index